John Freeman

Lights and Shadows of Melbourne Life

John Freeman

Lights and Shadows of Melbourne Life

ISBN/EAN: 9783337252434

Printed in Europe, USA, Canada, Australia, Japan

Cover: Foto ©ninafisch / pixelio.de

More available books at **www.hansebooks.com**

LIGHTS AND SHADOWS

OF

MELBOURNE LIFE.

BY

JOHN FREEMAN.

LONDON:
SAMPSON LOW, MARSTON, SEARLE, & RIVINGTON,
LIMITED,
St. Dunstan's House,
FETTER LANE, FLEET STREET, E.C.
1888.

[*All rights reserved.*]

LONDON:
PRINTED BY WILLIAM CLOWES AND SONS, LIMITED,
STAMFORD STREET AND CHARING CROSS.

CONTENTS.

	PAGE
INTRODUCTION	vii
MELBOURNE IN '88	1
WHAT WE HAVE IN OUR MIDST	14
THE PADDING KENS	25
THE POLICE COURTS	36
PUBLICANS AND SINNERS	46
THE RACES	54
THE ZOO	62
THE THEATRES	69
THE BLOCK	78
THE ELITE	86
THE MARKETS	94
RESTAURANTS	104
BOARDING HOUSES	111
CHURCHES	117
THE MELBOURNE PERIPATETICS	120
BEGGARS	122
MATCH-SELLERS	134
COSTERMONGERS	143
NEWS-RUNNERS	150
FISH-HAWKERS	158
GATHERERS	166
OYSTERMEN	177
THE FLYING STATIONER	183
THE TRAVELLING DRAPER	191
STREET MUSICIANS	198
TINKERS	206
WATERCRESS MEN	213
THE PERIWINKLE MAN	221
CLOTHES-PROP VENDORS	230
CHIMNEY SWEEPS	237
SAVELOY-MACHINE MEN	247

INTRODUCTION.

While the Melbourne Centennial International Exhibition of '88 commemorates the foundation of our nation, and shows the world how Australia stands at the end of her first century, this book treats only of Melbourne, the capital of Victoria—of its institutions, and the manners and customs of its people.

Fifty-three years ago Melbourne was founded, and in that short space of time—for half a century is not much in the life of a nation—it has developed in a manner few cities have ever done in the same time before. From a few wattle-and-dab huts and weather-board shanties has risen the magnificent city to which we are all so proud to belong.

As the visitor passes through its broad streets, he will marvel at its stately buildings and manifold signs of prosperity. He will notice the well-to-do look of the people he meets; he will admire the grace and demeanour of the women, and the manly, independent bearing of the men.

Let him now turn down one of the arteries leading from the broad streets to the little ones at the back, and he will see that although we have so much to rejoice in, we have also something to deplore. He will find that Melbourne has its shadows as well as its bright spots, its hovels as well as palaces, low life as well as high, and abject poverty side by side with boundless wealth.

Some of these papers have already appeared in the Melbourne daily journals, for which I wrote them some time ago; but that should be no drawback to this book, for what is worth reading once may be read with profit twice, and those who have not read them will, on their perusal, be all the better for an insight into the inner life of Melbourne.

JOHN FREEMAN.

Melbourne.

LIGHTS AND SHADOWS

OF

MELBOURNE LIFE.

MELBOURNE IN '88.

If some of the old inhabitants of Melbourne who departed this life in the "forties" could leave their neglected graves in the old cemetery, and take a stroll round their former haunts, they would fancy they had made a mistake, and come to the wrong place; for they would never recognise in the Melbourne of to-day the disjointed city of that name they left behind them.

Although this book treats of Melbourne as it is at the present time, a glance at its early history may not be out of place.

It was on the 26th May, 1835, that Mr. John Batman, with three other white men and some Sydney natives, sailed up the Yarra, and, having landed just below the Falls, pitched his tent, and settled on what is now called Batman's Hill.

Batman knew perfectly well that, whenever the white man plants his foot on savage land, his black brother ceases to be the owner of it. Acting upon that knowledge, and believing in the principle of "first come first served," he obtained a nice little block of land, six hundred thousand acres, in exchange for a few blankets, clothes, knives, and other articles, among which were thirty looking-glasses. Unfortunately for Batman, an unappreciative government, thinking the bargain much too one-sided, ignored it; so the enterprising colonists had to appease their "earth hunger" in some more legitimate manner.

In August of the same year, Batman was followed by John Pascoe Fawkner; and to that gentleman is due the credit of being the actual founder of Melbourne. On the 29th September, 1836, Captain William Lonsdale selected the present site of Melbourne, which, being approved of by Sir Richard Bourke, the Governor of New South Wales, was by him named after the then prime minister of England.

In 1842, Melbourne obtained its municipal rights, and became a corporation, of which Mr. Henry Condell, a brewer, had the honour of being the first mayor. On the 26th June, 1847, it was created a city; and in the following year the Rev. Charles J. Perry, the first Anglican bishop, was installed in St. James's Cathedral.

Things went on improving, and the city grew apace, till 1850, when the district was separated from New South Wales, and called Victoria, after our gracious Queen.

At that time there were in the heart of the city numerous scrubby waste places supposed to be of so little value that purchasers were hard to find. But their value has since been discovered with a vengeance, for blocks of land that were then sold for pounds, have since fetched more than as many thousands, showing how wonderfully this fair city of the south has developed in thirty-eight years.

The city was still increasing in size and importance, when, in the next year, 1851, the discovery of gold in our soil gave a fresh current to men's thoughts, and an impetus to their energies they had never known before. They speedily became disgusted with the slow, though, perhaps, sure process of making gold in the ordinary way of business; for why should they toil at the counter, or in the workshop for years to obtain it, when there was plenty lying within a few miles inviting them to come and pick it up? A general rush from Melbourne was the consequence. The shopkeeper sold off his goods, this time in reality, at an "Alarming sacrifice," and hurried to the gold fields with a view to nuggets. The artisan dropped his tools, and shouldered a swag, and hastened off in the same direction, light-hearted, and hopeful of being at the end of a few weeks independent of work for ever. Lawyers, seized with the general epidemic, rushed to the diggings, and left their clients to settle their disputes among themselves; and if a similar stampede of the legal fraternity were to take place at the present day, society might, perhaps, in time become reconciled to it. Doctors deserted their patients, who, doubtless, on being left to nature and their own constitutions, soon recovered, and started off to the same land of promise after them; and clerks dropped the pen for the pick, and went at it like English navvies; in fact, all classes thought of, and strove after, nothing else but gold. It is true they did not all dig in the right place, but most of them did, and that was sufficient to inspire the others with the hope of being equally fortunate in the end.

On the passing away of the gold fever, these men returned to Melbourne, accompanied by some of the thousands whom the fame of the gold fields had attracted to our shores; and the city grew more rapidly than ever in size and population.

Soon the gaps in the principal streets were filled up with handsome shops of brick or stone; and now trade has developed into such proportions, that there is not an inch of space that is not required for business purposes.

A few samples of our early shop architecture are yet to be seen in some of the chief thoroughfares, wedged in between fine lofty buildings, like shabby dwarfs between well-dressed giants.

In Melbourne proper, that is, without the suburbs, there are 66,878 inhabitants, and 13,706 dwellings to shelter them.

The city is divided into seven wards, each of which sends one alderman and three councillors to represent it in the City Council. The Town Hall, where these civic fathers meet, is a noble building, and being at the angle of two of our principal streets, shows to advantage when admiring strangers come to see the sights of Melbourne.

The Parliament Houses in Spring Street are not yet completed, but when they are they will be a noble pile of buildings, and in every way fit for the collective wisdom of the colony to meet in for the despatch of business.

Lower down, going south, is the Treasury, a fine stone building, with a noble flight of steps in front, up which the jaded minister can mount without fatigue, when he goes to meet his colleagues in cabinet, or executive, council assemblies.

At the back of that are the Crown Lands and Water Works departments, two fine buildings of brick and cement.

Our Post-Office is now being completed according to the original designs, and when finished it will be something for the Melbourne people to be proud of.

We can boast of a fine Public Library, with picture and sculpture galleries, and technological museum attached. We have, also, on the University grounds, a Museum of Geology and Natural History, containing many choice specimens of the animal and mineral kingdoms, with numerous models of mines, and the various kinds of machinery used in mining operations.

We have two Universities where our future Esculapii, bishops, and judges, are trained for their high callings by professors equal in learning to any teaching staff in the world; and a Working Man's College, where the intelligent artisan, who aspires to something above the mere manual drudgery of his craft, and beer, can fit himself for any position his skill and industry may raise him to.

We have colleges and grammar schools to prepare the sons of the well-to-do for the University, private schools in abundance, and State schools wherever wanted. Attendance at the latter is compulsory till the age of fifteen, or till the pupil has reached a certain standard, and the education is free, and absolutely secular.

The number of churches and chapels in our city show that a very fair proportion of its inhabitants devote one day out of the seven to the worship of the true God, however diligently they may bow down to Mammon during the other six.

Two noble cathedrals, one Anglican and the other Roman Catholic, are in course of erection; and when completed they will add much to the beauty of our city.

We are well off for charitable institutions, where all the "ills that flesh is heir to" are properly attended to, and where ailing poverty can find relief, and a home till restored to health, or till claimed by the Inevitable. We have two Orphanages, really deserving institutions, but, like most deserving institutions, they are always in debt; and Ladies' Benevolent Societies, that do a deal of unostentatious good to women whose husbands have deserted them, or are sick, or in prison.

We have a Lying-in Hospital, where the poor married women, and the poor unfortunate are alike treated with the care and attention their condition requires. There is a Hospital for Sick Children; another for convalescents, and several for the treatment of special complaints. We have a Blind Asylum, an Asylum for the Deaf and Dumb; a Benevolent Asylum, where the aged and decayed of both sexes can find rest, and a home for the remainder of their days; and what is called the "Immigrants' Home," where the casual is housed and fed, and where the invalided vagrant and loafer can crawl into to die. The whole of these form an array of charitable institutions which speaks volumes for the benevolence of our citizens.

We have a large permanent Exhibition building, where in 1880 our handicraftsmen compared the work of their hands and heads with that of their fellow toilers in the other parts of the world, and came out of the contest with credit. When not used for exhibition purposes, the building is let for monster concerts, and other affairs that draw a large concourse of people together. Attached thereto is an Aquarium, well supplied with many kinds of the marine monster, and remarkable members of the finny tribe.

The old Supreme Court yet stands on the old spot, but Justice no longer holds the scales there, that lady having taken up her abode in the well-arranged Law Courts on the western side of the city. At the corner of the next street is the Mint, wherein the gold found in our soil is converted into sovereigns.

Perched on a high hill, south of the Yarra, may be seen a grand pile of buildings. This is Government House, the residence of his Excellency the Governor. To the east of that are our beautiful and extensive Botanical Gardens, open to the public daily, free of charge.

No city in the world is so well off for "lungs," as the open spaces have been rightly called, as Melbourne, for they are so numerous and spacious, that, speaking in metaphor, you can throw a stone from one into another. On the northern side of the city, in what is called the Royal Park, are the Zoological Gardens, large, and well-stocked with a great variety of wild animals, birds, and fishes.

The wants of the Melbourne people are supplied by eight markets—two for vegetables, one for fruit, another for fish, and one for meat; while on the northern side of the city are markets for the disposal of horses, hay, cattle, and pigs.

We have a Royal Observatory, presided over by an astronomer of world-wide renown, who, with the aid of one of the largest and best telescopes procurable, keeps us au courant with what is going on among the heavenly bodies. He has, also, a mysterious instrument for detecting earthquakes when they are not sufficiently demonstrative to make themselves felt. It is called a seismograph, and is so sensitive in its nature that, with almost human sagacity, it mistook, a few years ago, the firing of a gun in the bay for a subterranean disturbance.

The spacious blue stone barracks in the St. Kilda Road are now the headquarters of our permanent corps; they are also used as barracks for our mounted police. It was there the imperial troops were quartered at the period when it was thought we were too weak to stand alone. Things are altered now. We can not only stand alone, but are beginning to run remarkably fast. We have, besides the permanent corps, a well-trained and numerous militia; a naval reserve, and what is by no means of the least importance, a cadet corps attached to each State, and public school and college. Boys have a habit of developing into men, and, by-and-bye, these youngsters will be a body of well-trained soldiers, on whom we may rely in the hour of need; and as there will be a great annual increase in their number, we shall, in the course of time, have a powerful and efficient landwehr to fall back upon, should a foe, by any chance, land upon our shores.

We have nineteen banks and banking companies to take care of our surplus cash, or advance us some if we need it. In addition to these, we have two savings-banks for the smaller capitalists—the Post-Office and the Melbourne; while the latter has, within the last year or so, started branches in most of the suburbs, greatly to the increase of their business.

Eighty-seven insurance companies compete for the privilege of insuring our persons and property against every possible mishap that can befall us. With all their diligence, however, in search of business, much property in and around Melbourne remains uninsured, which is to be regretted, both for the sake of the owners and the companies; for, unlike most other businesses, the more "risks" the latter incur, the better it is for them.

The forty-eight building societies we have are great boons to the working-man, who can invest his savings to advantage in them, or, by their means, acquire a home of his own.

We have numerous benefit societies in which the prudent can provide for a time of sickness, and, also, for a respectable funeral when dead.

We are well off for learned societies. Every branch of art and science has a society of its own, composed of men the most famous in each particular branch. We have debating societies, mutual improvement societies, a society for the prevention of cruelty to animals, a royal humane society; and, by-and-bye, in all probability, we shall have a mendicity society.

We have four clubs—the Melbourne, for the elite of our society, and distinguished visitors; the Athenæum, for the higher professional men; the Australian, for squatters; and the Yorick, for those of Bohemian tendencies.

We have several first class hotels on the western side of the city, where our wealthy country visitors may be found when they come to Melbourne, and some rightly called coffee palaces, for they are palatial in most senses of the word.

We have a Melbourne servants' home and governesses' institute to which ladies of that ilk can retire while waiting for a situation; a sailor's home to keep Jack out of the clutches of the land-shark; and three homes, or refuges, for fallen women.

Melbourne is pretty well off for newspapers and other publications. There are four dailies—three morning, and one evening; Law, Physic, and Divinity have their organs, and trade and commerce their "Review," and "Journal." There are comic papers for the light-hearted, and fine

religious ones for the serious, though, by the way, some
of the latter journals occasionally indulge in comicalities
that must have reached their editors by mistake, the
writers having evidently intended them for our old friend
Punch. There is one in the interests of the Catholics, and
another favouring the Jews. The teetotallers have their
"News," and the licensed victuallers their "Advocate." We
have two illustrated monthly journals; a sporting paper to
keep our young athletes posted up in the latest records of
all possible sporting events; a monthly journal of light
literature, and other publications too numerous to mention.

Our prisons and madhouses prove our civilisation to be
equal to that of any of the older cities of Europe. It may
appear strange that civilisation, among its many blessings,
should have the peculiarity of increasing the necessity for
these places; but it is so, nevertheless, and the higher the
one, the more numerous the others.

There is a retreat for inebriates, to which our dipso-
maniacs can retire till they have overcome their abnormal
thirst, and a discharged prisoner's aid society to take by
the hand those who have erred and are willing to be led
back to the right path.

We have reformatories, wherein we try to nip crime in
the bud, before our juvenile criminals have time to open
out into the full blown burglar or garotter; while our
industrial schools show how anxious the State is to act *in
loco parentis* to a certain section of the rising generation—
an anxiety shared in by many of the parents of these
children, as it saves them the trouble and expense of
bringing them up themselves. Certainly, when the
magistrates send these children to the schools, they go
through the formality of ordering the parents to pay so
much per week towards the maintenance of their offspring, but that order is usually more honoured in the
breach than in the observance.

We have an intelligent body of police, veritable sons of
Anak, assisted by a shrewd and effective detective force,
to watch over the persons and property of our citizens.
Our thieves are far behind their London brethren in
intelligence and digital dexterity. We have none of
these elegantly-dressed swell-mobsmen and women who
find their way into fashionable gatherings, and ease
people of their valuables while they charm them by their

conversation. Our unrecognised conveyancers do their business in a more vulgar manner. Few of them have "forks" sufficiently deft to dive into the inmost recesses of our pockets while we are quietly walking along the street, or seated comfortably at the theatre or opera; but two or three stick their victim up at night as he is going home, or wait till he is lying dead drunk in the gutter before they attempt to remove anything he may have left after his debauch. What are called "area sneaks" at home are represented here by a class who prowl about the rights-of-way "snow dropping," or "snapping up any unconsidered trifle" they may see lying about. Our burglars and housebreakers operate less skilfully than the Londoners do; we hear of no cleverly got-up affairs here such as occasionally startle the British public; but when a "crib" is "cracked" here it is done in a rude and primitive fashion; nor are the thieves here knit together by so strong a sense of honour as they are in England, though "honour among thieves" is not always the rule there. We have no elegantly dressed lady thieves, who so successfully "work" in omnibuses, or wherever those who have anything to lose most do congregate.

We have not yet imported those interesting creatures who write on the pavement "I am starving," and then squat down by the side of it to receive the contributions of the full-bellied passers by, or till they see a policeman coming; nor have we those artistically gifted individuals who chalk on the flags with coloured chalks a dish containing half a salmon, and then sit down by the side of it in the hope that some admirer of the fine arts will appreciate their skill, and reward it with a copper.

Our solicitors (non-legal) are composed of blind men, decrepit tap-loafers, who beg about the city, and the habitués of the padding kens, who "work" the suburbs, all of whom get enough money in three days to find them in beer the whole seven; but the business of the blind ones is far too profitable to be neglected, so they all work six days a week, and many of them seven.

Like all large cities, we have a *demi-monde*, some of the members of which are of a rather high tone. As a class, they are as well conducted as the frail sisterhood in any part of the civilised world, and as numerous in proportion to the population, seeing that we have five hundred and ninety seven of the fallen angels in this noble city of ours.

The "social evil" has been a problem for mankind to solve from the earliest ages, and it will remain unsolved till the human race has been civilised into sterility, or the millennium arrives.

At the present time it appears to be looked at in two different ways, by two different kinds of people. One would sweep it off the face of the earth by a process that would be both speedy and effective. These, it may be noticed, belong to that section of mankind who have lived long enough to recognise the wisdom of Solomon's assertion that "all is vanity." The others regard it from another point of view. Whilst deploring the existence of the evil, they do not ignore the fact that "flesh is grass," and as they know there are certain contentions in man's nature in which the animal will overcome the intellectual, even in the most philosophical, they see the impossibility of suppressing it, and would therefore control it by allowing the *traviate* certain gathering grounds where they could meet without stepping upon the skirts of respectability, or outraging the feelings of those whose only objection to vice is its open display.

The social habits of the Melbourne people are British in every sense. We are fond of dinners, parties, balls, picnics, and social gatherings of all kinds; we flock to all kinds of sports and out-door exhibitions with all the abandon of school boys. Holidays are plentiful, and no opportunity is ever missed of making additional ones.

The Melbourne people are hospitable to a degree. When we are honoured by the visits of distinguished or famous personages, we unite as one man to do them honour, and sustain the credit of the colony; our only danger being, that, in our desire to play the host on a liberal scale, we rather overdo it, and somewhat mar the, in every other respect, favourable impression we may have made upon the minds of our guests. Having done our best to entertain them in a manner befitting their rank or fame, it is only reasonable we should feel gratified in knowing our endeavours have been rightly appreciated, and, it may be said, our guests usually leave us with the assurance that words can hardly express the pleasure they feel in having been entertained in so cordial a manner, though one, on taking his leave, acknowledged our hospitality by a parting recommendation to us "not to blow," while another acknowledged the proffered hospitality of his would-be entertainers by a characteristic display of "himself."

That we are fond of music and theatricals may be gathered from the fact that we have six theatres, and a whole host of minor places of amusement, each and all of which are filled nightly by appreciative audiences; whilst the number of public-houses and hotels are equally indicative of our bibulous tendencies.

Three railway termini, at present not much to look at, are the outlets and inlets for the travelling public to and from all the suburbs, and every centre in Victoria.

For urban and suburban traffic we are well supplied with conveyances. Cabs, busses, and cable tramways are the means of transit for those citizens who prefer riding to walking when going from one side of the city to the other, or to any of the surrounding suburbs.

Our water supply is second to none in the world; the pressure at the plugs being sufficient to throw the water over the highest buildings in Melbourne, if required for the repression of fire. The fire brigade in Melbourne is an organised and paid body of men, though in the suburbs the voluntary system obtains.

Melbourne is guarded seawards by the terrible Cerberus, and it would require a much stronger sop to put her to sleep than the one Sibyl administered to her namesake. Besides the Cerberus, there are a frigate, two steel gun-boats, three steel torpedo boats, and three armed dredges belonging to the Harbour Trust. To man these boats, we have a volunteer Naval Brigade and Torpedo Corps, all that we require to protect us against a sudden attack; for as long as England has command of the seas no enemy can do us more injury than might be done in a flying visit.

Gambling is carried on to a much greater extent in Melbourne than is known or suspected by the bulk of the population, who are apt to look upon the external signs of well-doing as proofs of the internal correctness of things generally.

How greatly the spirit of gambling influences the minds of a certain section of our population is from time to time brought to our knowledge through the police reports, or by hearing that some well-known character has levanted, or committed suicide; then there is a deal of virtuous, though harmless, indignation hurled at those highly respectable gentlemen who have had a hand in bringing things to such a melancholy pass. But it soon evaporates, and the select "hells" keep on preparing subjects for Pentridge, or the Yarra, as briskly as ever. The games mostly affected are loo, nap, poker, and Yankee grab. It is generally supposed the latter is only played at for drinks, but that is simply a mistake, for large sums are daily and nightly won and lost at it.

Like that of all young countries, our native youth display a considerable amount of animal spirits, which are set down by their doting parents as a manifestation of natural genius. They have been likened to the Spartan youth of old, though in what, save the imaginations of gushing writers, the similarity is to be found, is difficult to see, for the Spartan youth were remarkable for obedience to their parents, and respect for old age, and these two characteristics cannot be discovered by the keenest observer among the virtues of our colonial youth.

But however much they may suffer from undeveloped bumps of veneration, it is undeniable that they are no fools; but are the possessors of a considerable amount of smartness, or native impudence, which is just as useful in helping a man on through life. The next best thing to being clever is to get people to fancy you are. If you can do that, you avoid a deal of study and hard work, for what is the good of striving after the substance when the shadow will do as well? Thus it is with our boys, who, from constantly hearing their parents and "indiscreet" friends say how clever they are, have come to believe it themselves, and that prevents their standing intellectually as high as the same boys do at home, who, not having the same belief in their own natural abilities, strive the harder to acquire confidence by the tedious, though necessary, agency of books.

The liveliness of a certain section of our boys takes the form of what is called "larrikinism," and that, as a nuisance, stands second to none of those we are in the habit of regarding as such.

Cowardly and treacherous as wolves, that portion of

our Spartan youth, unlike their prototypes, require the confidence inspired by numbers before they can muster up sufficient courage to commence operations. Then, twenty or thirty, armed with road metal, will attack a solitary policeman; or three or four assault a decrepit old man or defenceless woman. Then they will vary their amusements by smashing windows, or looting a public-house, or get up a fight among themselves; but, unfortunately, the latter part of their programme is usually interrupted by the police before much damage is done.

Our girls are so proverbial for their precocity, that it has been said they are seven years old at their birth. Whoever it may have been who made that remarkable discovery, he must have had a very limited knowledge of the female portion of our young colonials; for, though we meet with some demoiselles with remarkably old heads on their young shoulders, they must not be taken as fair samples of the Victorian maidens, who are as pure and engaging as any girls in the world. As a rule, they may not be as pretty as their English sisters, but in all other respects they compare favourably with them, and where not, it is as much owing to parental neglect as to natural inclination induced by a southern climate.

WHAT WE HAVE IN OUR MIDST.

On the breaking out of the first French Revolution, fifty thousand human beings came forth from the various holes and corners in Paris, whose very existence had, till then, been unknown—human only in form, for every other attribute of humanity had been stamped out of them by ages of tyranny and oppression. Sunk in the lowest depths of poverty, their minds had become embittered against all who were better off than themselves, and, when the time came, they sought to wash out their wrongs in the blood of those who had oppressed them.

It is to that class that all the frightful horrors and excesses that accompanied the social disruption are due; and naturally no other result could be expected, for as we sow, so shall we reap. If we sow in wrong we shall reap the bitter fruits of it. The harvest may be long in ripening, but, in the inevitable course of events, it will ripen at last, and return us a hundred-fold the injuries we have inflicted.

We, too, have a dangerous class in our midst, lurking in holes and corners away from the public gaze, where they mature undisturbed their plans against society; and where vice in every form flourishes unchecked by aught that might have a restraining influence over it. With us, however, they are not driven to poverty and desperation by oppression, for here all are equal before the law; and none need be poor who will work. Yet, although we have not engendered a criminal class by persecution, we may have done so by leaving unperformed duties that are as obligatory upon communities as the proper care and supervision of a family are upon the head of it, and to neglect the one is as wrong and blameworthy as it is to shirk the other.

Many good and worthy people would be greatly astonished on being told that they are responsible for half the crime that darkens the page of our every-day life. Yet it is so, and as long as they allow nurseries for its culture to exist, it will thrive, and turn upon them as the Frankenstein monster did upon him who had created it.

There is another danger, pestilence, equally the offspring of man's neglect, lurking in the foul and overcrowded localities, none the less deadly because invisible, and still more terrible because, having once issued forth, no hand but the Almighty's can arrest its progress.

Running from the great to the little streets of this city are lanes crowded with human habitations. From some of these lanes there branch off at right angles " places " containing three or four houses. Those recently built are of brick, for the Corporation has long since stopped the erection of any more wooden ones. Others are old tumble-down wooden shanties, packed as closely together as space will allow; without any regard for the convenience of those who dwell in them; dirty, alive with vermin, close and fœtid, with the sharp pungent odour of decaying wood ever appealing to your nostrils; roofs not waterproof; doors without fastenings, and frequently with only one hinge; windows patched with paper, or stuffed with rags; floors rotten and full of holes, through which the rats come and devour the food they doubtless think has been left there for their use by the equally rattish and predatory dwellers above.

Conveniences that ought to be kept at the back, out of sight, are frequently placed in front, and common to two or three houses, the effluvium from which strikes you long before you can see whence it comes.

Yet these "places" are within sight of, aye, and overshadowed by, magnificent buildings devoted to the trade and commerce of the colony—squalor and poverty side by side with magnificence and wealth. Bad as these houses are, however, they bring in rents that quite justify the auctioneers, when they have any for sale, in styling them "valuable city properties." Strange as it may seem, many of these queer places belong to men ranking high in religious and "morality" circles, who receive the rents from their agents with the same complacency Vespasian did the proceeds of a certain tax, and would, no doubt, if questioned, give the same reply he gave to his son Zitus, who doubted the purity of money obtained in such a way.

Living in these dens are human beings, who, unless brought to the surface by some disturbing influence, such as a fire in their neighbourhood, or having to make an enforced visit to the police court, are never seen, save by those who visit them in their slums; women who have retained nothing that is womanly; men dead to every manly sentiment; and children in whom nothing that is innocent or child-like can be found.

Others living there are people whose besetting sin is drunkenness—working-men, who only work long enough to get the means of going on the "burst," but who are in perhaps other respects superior to their neighbours.

Some of the blind beggars, too, retire there at night to spend in riot and debauchery a portion of the money they have wrung out of the soft-hearted, and equally soft-headed, individuals who so unwisely perpetuate the nuisance by giving alms in the street to men who, in many instances, are comparatively wealthy, and all of whom make more money daily than the most skilful artisan in the colony; for, from the earliest days, a pair of sightless eyes has been an appeal to the human heart few can resist, and the "*Date obolum*" of Belisarius was not more effective as a conveyancer, in the transfer of small change, than is the "Please remember the poor blind" of to-day.

Costermongers, in a small way, likewise affect these quarters. When a man in that line, with his wife and family, only occupy one small room, it is difficult for the uninitiated to understand how and where he stows away the unsold portion of his goods from one day to another; as it would never do for him to leave them unprotected in the right-of-way at night, if he wishes to find them in the morning. But the business is simple enough. Although the room is more than half taken up by a large bedstead, there is a space underneath it available for stowing away the more delicate and perishable articles, such as grapes or fish; but whether, having regard to freshness and soundness, that is the best place for them, is a matter of opinion. The cabbages and coarser kind of produce are thrown anyhow in a corner. It's a wise old proverb which saith, "What the eye does not see, the heart never grieves about."

Some of these lanes are almost exclusively inhabited by our Celestial brethren, who there have their dens, to which they entice young girls and stupify their brains by opium as a preliminary to debauching their bodies. There, also, they carry on their national and highly intellectual game of pantan, amid a din of exultant chatter on the part of the winners and angry imprecations from the losers, that has no parallel except in the noise issuing from a crowd of angry monkeys.

A number of well-meaning gentlemen have formed themselves into a society, called the "Chinese Mission," the object of which is to bring as many of the followers of Joss into the pale of the Christian Church as possible; a matter by no means easy of accomplishment, even at the expenditure of much time and money. We do not know the value of a "heathen Chinee" when converted, but if he is worth all it costs to convert him, he is valuable indeed. The mission can give a very satisfactory annual report, no doubt, but from the little we know of "John" we are inclined to think that these reports do not harmonise with the actual results. If we might be so bold, we would suggest to the missionaries the advisability of adding a little arithmetic to their gospel teaching, for it is only right that such of their *protégés* who are connected with the vegetable hawking interest should know that each pound contains sixteen ounces—a truth their Asiatic minds appear at present unable to grasp, for when taxed with trying to palm off seven pounds of potatoes for ten, their oleaginous faces shine with a look of such conscious innocence or unconscious guilt, that it is evident our system of computation and theirs are not in accord.

Mendicants of all sorts, and both sexes, sally forth from these places as soon as they have recovered from the previous night's debauch, to levy their daily contributions from the public. The men help themselves along with sticks, for the quantity of beer they drink makes them rather dropsical about the feet, a symptom which they palm off upon the benevolent as "rheumatic gout."

The women are mostly provided with a basket, wherein they stow away whatever may be given to them in the shape of scraps of food, old clothes, or anything else that is worth carrying away. Sometimes they carry a child in their arms, or have one toddling at their sides, and, if it is very pretty, or very sickly-looking, it is a great source of income.

Some of the itinerant musicians who discourse such sweet sounds in our streets, also favour these localities with their presence when they are at home. In fact, all that is doubtful in our population seek in these lanes, and rights-of-way, a refuge they can find nowhere else, for here they can lead the lives most agreeable to themselves, without fear of scandalizing their neighbours.

Such is the state of things here in Melbourne, the chief city of the southern hemisphere, in the Nineteenth century, with all its boasted civilisation, and in spite of an efficient system of police, and of numerous religious bodies.

Let us suppose a fire, fanned by a stiff breeze, were to break out among these closely-packed shanties. Where would it end? Might it not, in spite of our magnificent water supply, lay half the city in ruins? And when we reflect how easily such a thing might be brought about by the drunken carelessness of those who dwell there, we can only wonder it has not happened before this.

The respectable inhabitants living round about there are quite alive to the danger constantly hanging over their heads, and they would gladly see the whole of the rookeries, houses, and people, cleared out by any means whatsoever, even though it were by the dangerous agency of fire itself. There is one guarantee, however, for a certain amount of care on the part of those who live in the back slums, and that is, the difficulty they would have in finding other quarters, if they were burnt out of their present ones. The localities available for such characters are always crowded to their utmost capacity, and if a whole rookery were driven to seek a fresh hiding place, it is hard to say where they could find it. It is the knowledge of that fact that causes such terror and excitement when a fire does occur in their midst.

We were passing down one of the little streets some time ago when there suddenly arose a cry of fire. It was an old wooden shanty down a narrow lane that was burning. To the right and left of it were other wooden shanties, with passages of about three feet in width between them. In an instant the lanes and rights-of-way all around pour forth their affrighted denizens, who rush to the corners to see whose place is burning, and to be prepared to save their goods if the all-devouring element should come towards their own squalid homes. Prematurely old women, made so by vice and drink, come forth like unclean animals from their holes. Their blear eyes shine with excitement, and their bloated faces, in some cases made still more unlovely by bruises, are blanched with terror at the awful cry. Birds of night slink out of their lurking places, blinking like owls suddenly thrust into the sunlight; for, late as it is, it is too early for them to be about. These, however, do not come forward like the rest, but stand in some corner where they can see, without being seen, as they do not care to come within the ken of the policeman. Young girls—young in years but old in vice—look on, and bandy obscene jests with ill-looking larrikins at their sides. Little girls, nursing babies almost as big as themselves, get mixed up with the crowd, and seem in danger of being trodden to death. Loafers, with their unsavoury looks and still more unsavoury odour of beer and tobacco, watch the fire with a quiet sort of enjoyment.

If a genuine loafer were asked for his idea of elysium, he would say it was a good position for witnessing a fire, and unlimited beer.

Respectable tradesmen, too, were there, with fierce looks of exultation in their faces, as they see the probability of the neighbourhood being relieved of, at least, some of its disreputable inhabitants.

The flames roared and the wood crackled, but the crowd did not as usual rush in to save the furniture of the threatened houses, or, more properly speaking, destroy it by hasty removal. Apathy seemed the order of the day. No expressions of sympathy were heard in the crowd, but wishes were freely uttered that the whole place might be cleared out before the fire brigade could arrive.

A woman with a child in her arms rushed out of the house next to the one in flames. Anxious to save her babe first, she gave it to a woman looking on, and hastened back to rescue what she could of her effects. She soon reappeared at the door with a small table, loaded with crockeryware, in her hands. In hurrying out, the corner of the table struck against the door-post, and a crash

ensued. That appeared to excite the pity of one of the
onlookers, a black man enveloped in a thick great coat,
as though it were the depth of winter. He flourished a
whip he held in his hand, and darted with it into the
house. He soon came forth again with the bed and
bedding in his hands, and the whip under his arm.
Depositing his load beyond the reach of the fire, he
hurried back to save something else. Soon a hurtling
noise was heard, followed by a crash; then he reappeared
with the greater part of a large wooden bedstead. This
time he held the whip between his teeth. All this time
the woman was making frantic efforts to save what she
could of her belongings, and the darkie worked like a
nigger to help her, while, from exertion in the combined
heat of the sun and fire, his face became as glossy as
polished ebony. Still he persevered, and after a few more
visits the house was emptied; then, as though he felt he
had done something to be ashamed of, he and his whip
disappeared in the crowd.

Those living in the other houses were also striving
desperately to save their goods. A brawny half-dressed
woman brought out a table loaded with all manner of
things. These she put in safety at the end of the right-
of-way, and hurried back for more. Her naked arms
showed many a bruise in various stages of recovery, and
on the biceps of the left one were tatooed a heart, and
the initials of, we suppose, her own and some one else's
name. The next house appeared to have four occupants—
two men and two women. The men might have been
honest; if so, they were sadly libelled by their looks, for
no men's faces ever showed more plainly the compound
look of the thief and bully than theirs. The vocation of
the women was unmistakable.

The first thing they tried to remove was a colonial sofa,
with a quantity of bedding piled up on it. It was too
wide for the doorway, and had to be turned on one side
before it could be got out. That, of course, caused the
bedding to fall off, which added still more to the confusion
by partially blocking up the passage. When that obstruction was removed, which was not done without the
discharge of a few score of oaths, the business of removal
went briskly on. One of the women came out with a
tray loaded with cups and saucers, a jug, and some glasses,

one of which was half full of beer, showing the fire had surprised them in the midst of a carouse. As she put the tray down, a ragged urchin of about twelve pounced upon the glass containing the beer, and swallowed its contents with a gusto that showed plainly enough he had already acquired a taste for that liquid, and that, in the future, the reputation the neighbourhood bore for drunkenness would be pretty safe in his keeping.

One of the men and a woman now brought out a large box between them, on the lid of which were placed several small pictures, a looking-glass, and some books, one of which was a Bible, that had, in all probability, been given to them by some missionary, as it is questionable if they had ever taken sufficient interest in its contents to buy it; neither would they, for the same reason, be likely to run the risk of imprisonment by stealing it. In hurrying along, the looking-glass fell to the ground with a crash. A titter ran through the crowd, which had anything but a soothing effect upon the already ruffled temper of the man, who roared out in his passion—"Do you call yourselves men, to stand there laughing while people's things are in danger? I should be—well, ashamed of myself, to stand idly by, without trying to save something." Doubtless. It is such as he who do take an active part at fires, rushing in on pretence of saving property, but in reality to steal whatever valuables they can put their hands upon. His appeal, however, received no other response than a few jeers.

By this time the houses in danger had been cleared of their contents, which were piled anyhow on the pavement at the end of the lane, where they were watched over by a policeman, otherwise, poor and dirty as most of the things were, many of the smaller articles would have disappeared with a celerity astonishing to one unacquainted with the peculiarities of the people living round about there.

The house on the right of the one in flames now began to blaze, and the shingle on the roof of the one on the left began to smoke. The destruction of all the houses in the lane seemed inevitable, and the faces of those who desired it wore a pleasant look. Jokes and doubtful witticisms were heard on all sides, some more expressive than elegant, but all showing some little sympathy was felt for those who were being burnt out of their homes.

A greasy-looking individual in his shirt-sleeves stood at the corner of the lane talking to a loafer, who was calmly watching the progress of the fire, while smoking with more than usual satisfaction an old wooden pipe, the fumes from which almost overpowered those arising from the house on fire.

"There'd be a blaze if them stables was to ketch," said the former, nodding towards some stables at the far end of the lane, which would most certainly have been in great danger had there been a strong wind from the north.

"My word!" asserted the loafer.

"There'll be a great loss of life over this job," chimed in a man standing close beside them.

At that remark the greasy one laughed, and the loafer licked his lips, for they both understood perfectly well the meaning hidden in those few words.

We looked at the last speaker, and, from his unwholesome looks and dirty condition, came to the conclusion that there would also be a great loss of life if he himself should happen to take fire.

The flames roared, and the wood crackled, as a sudden puff of wind caused two fiery tongues to lick the side of the as yet unignited house.

"Here she goes," said a butcher, who, in company with the publican whose house was at the corner, and a neighbouring baker, stood watching the fire. "There wont be much left if the reel isn't quick."

"And a good job too," said the baker.

"No fear," observed the publican, who knew if the houses were burnt down he would lose a number of his best customers.

"If you want the fire out, you'd better throw a few bottles of your whisky over it; there's water enough in that to put out any fire," said the butcher, who wanted to be funny at the publican's expense.

"Go and get two or three sides of your mutton and throw them in," observed the baker, who also wished to be funny; "it'll make it blaze all the fiercer."

"Not in the least," remarked Boniface, who wanted to be quits with the butcher. "There's not enough fat about them to make a blaze, and the lean's too tough to burn."

Before the laugh caused by this last sally was over, a loud " Hi, hi!" was heard coming down the street. Soon two firemen, dragging a hose after them, were forcing a way through the crowd; others speedily attached the end to the plug, and a stream of water was poured upon the burning mass. In two minutes the flames were mastered, in two more they were entirely subdued, and what might have been a serious conflagration was now reduced to a few smoking embers.

We looked round on the crowd, but could see no signs of satisfaction on the faces of those near us; nor did we hear any sighs of relief as the danger passed away, but looks of disappointment took the place of one, and muttered imprecations were heard instead of the other.

One man remarked—

"It's a bad job the axle didn't break while the reel was coming along, so that the whole lot might have been burned out."

The woman who had been minding the baby quickly joined issue with him by asking—

"What are poor people to do if they're burned out of their homes?"

"Let them go to ——" he replied, mentioning a place where there is not much danger of the inhabitants ever being burnt out.

All danger having now passed over, those who dwelt in the lane appeared to be in as great a hurry to get their things back into the houses, as they were before to get them out.

The woman who had occupied the destroyed house was invited by one of her neighbours to put her things in her house till she could get another place to live in—an offer that was gladly accepted.

However undesirable, as neighbours, the denizens of these localities may be, they have one redeeming trait— they are kind to one another in distress.

With many a muttered curse, the two men before alluded to began to take stock of their furniture; to see what was damaged, and if anything was lost. Much appeared to be damaged, but nothing was missing, except an old pair of trousers, which some one had taken from under the very nose of the policeman.

The crowd now began to disperse, evidently to the satisfaction of the dwellers in that lane, who did not feel comfortable under the gaze of so many strangers. The firemen, having assured themselves that there was no danger of the fire breaking out anew, packed up and went also. The two remaining policemen looked round the ruins, and giving a scrutinizing glance through the open doors of the remaining houses, resumed their journeying round their beats.

THE "PADDING KENS."

Of the many queer places that are to be found in Melbourne, not the least remarkable are the "padding kens," or sixpenny lodging-houses—the temporary shelter of the homeless, the resting-place of weary poverty, and the refuge of the outcast.

The visitor to the western side of the city may see a number of houses, on the windows of which is written "Clean Beds 6d." He will also see, especially towards the latter part of the day, a number of unsavoury looking men loafing about the doors, leaning on the window-sills, or sitting on the kerbstone with their feet in the channel. If he be of a contemplative turn, he will pause, and, judging from externals, recognise the natural fitness of things in such places having such indwellers. From the outside, his thoughts will naturally wander to the interior, and he will wonder what it is like, and how its habitués pass their time when at home. It was so with us; we knew the daily habits of the men perfectly well, and thought we should like to add to our knowledge by an insight into their nightly doings. But how was it to be done? To ask permission to go round the place was out of the question; it might have been granted, but we should not have been allowed to see all, for even an official visit, when made unexpectedly, is not always to be depended upon for getting at the right state of affairs, however sharp the visitors may be; for, while they are overhauling the place in one direction, things that might be considered objectionable are altered or removed in another. The lodgers, too, on these occasions, put on their best behaviour; the conversation, that has been carried on with more vigour than elegance is suddenly hushed; the oath, more than half uttered, is strangled before it has time to come forth, and the scowl of semi-drunken brutality is changed to a cringing look of servility; for who knows, they think, but they may get something out of the visitors to have a drink with. So, in considering the matter carefully, we came to the conclusion that there was no other way of seeing things in their true light than by going among them as one of themselves.

We went up to the manager, or "chucker-out," and told him we wanted a bed. "All right." We gave him sixpence, that was all right too; we asked him where we were to sleep. He took us to a good-sized room containing ten beds, and pointed to one in a corner. On the door was pasted a printed paper showing the number of cubic feet of air allowed to each bed. We noticed the key was on the outside of the door; what did that mean? Did they lock the lodgers in at night? or did they keep the door locked during the day? Most probably the latter. It would not be a nice thing for a nervous man to be locked in with a room full of such very undesirable companions as the usual habitués of that place were.

We asked the manager when we could go to bed. "When you like." "At what time could we leave in the morning?" "When you like."

The brevity of these answers made us look more attentively at this man than we had hitherto done. A crispness about his looks told us plainly enough that a short answer was all any lodger was likely to get from him, and when we consider the class he has to do with, it is obvious that no wiser course could be taken.

The people frequenting these places are not remarkable for keeping regular hours, either in coming or going, so they come as late at night as they like, and leave as early as they please in the morning, their "doss" always being paid for before they are allowed to get into it. There is, doubtless, some one about the place to see the early birds do not fly away with the blankets, as some of them who may be going on the "wallaby," and are unprovided with a swag, might not hesitate about supplying themselves with one "on the cheap," as getting a thing for nothing is called.

Having settled the business so far, we took a stroll round the place, and this is what we saw.

The furniture is simple, and not costly. The bedding

consists of a stretcher, flock mattress and pillow; two blankets and a rug or counterpane; sometimes sheets are supplied, but not often, nor are they often wanted. There is a sitting-room lit by gas—kerosene would be too dangerous—as in the not unlikely event of a sudden brawl taking place among the lodgers, the lamp would stand a very good chance of being knocked off the table, and, by setting fire to the house, roast some of those who are to be found there every night too helplessly drunk to do anything to save themselves. This room is supplied with a daily paper, and in winter is made cheerful by a fire. There is a sort of galley somewhere about the place where a lodger can cook whatever food he brings in. Plates and dishes are dispensed with, the chop or steak being taken out of the frying-pan, or off the gridiron, and put upon a piece of bread. Should he indulge in potatoes, they are boiled with the jackets on, and when done put into the coat pocket, from which receptacle they are taken out one by one to be eaten. The salt is usually carried in another pocket, screwed up in a piece of paper. The meal is generally eaten standing in some corner, for, as a rule, an Englishman, in whatever part of the world he may be, prefers, when he can manage it, to have his meals in solitude. When he takes tea to "wet" his dinner, it is made in a billy, and drunk out of the lid, as out of a saucer. On these occasions he sits on the floor with his back to the wall, as it is more convenient than standing.

Those of the lodgers who consider a wash necessary—though there are many who do not—can indulge in that luxury by going to a tap in the yard, if they can put up with the trifling inconvenience of having no towel to dry themselves upon, or, if they happen to possess a pocket-handkerchief; though, by the way, that is an article the use of which is not general among the patrons of the sixpenny lodging house.

The place is kept tolerably clean, that is insisted upon by the inspectors, though they do not appear to be very particular about the number that occupy one bed, for we heard one man say he could count his bed-fellows by the hundreds. The sheets when used are washed once a week, the counterpanes once a fortnight, and the blankets as often as required, which is sometimes pretty often.

Any case of sickness that may arise is quickly transferred to the hospital, for it would be very inconvenient to have any one die in the house, as he would occupy a bed he could not pay for, to say nothing of the loss that might be incurred through the absurd objection many people have to lying in the same room with a corpse.

In case of a fight or other disturbance among the lodgers, the " chucker-out " tries to impress upon the minds of the belligerents the impropriety of their conduct in a way in which elegance of speech and gentleness of manner are not altogether relied upon. When he is unable to bring matters to a happy termination, the catastrophe is brought about by a *deus ex machina* in the shape of a policeman.

On entering the sitting-room, we saw fifteen or twenty men engaged in various ways. Some were seated reading the papers; others were smoking and talking over the adventures of the day, or leaning listlessly against the walls, or lying about in various postures on the floor. The room contained only six articles of furniture—a long deal table, flanked by two forms in the centre, and three colonial sofas, as hard and lumpy as though they had been stuffed with four-inch road metal, stood close to the walls. On one of these slept a man in a heavy drunken sleep. The greater part of another was taken up by a man mending his nether garments, and three others, engaged in an animated conversation, had possession of the third.

The occupants of that room were of the class always to be found in such places—real specimens of the genus loafer. There were no two men of the same height, or any two with the same cast of feature; but the expression on the faces of all was as much alike as though they had sprung from the same father and mother. The same look about the eyes, a sameness about the mouth, and the same unwholesome complexion, thus showing plainly enough the power drink has over its victims, and how it can influence their looks, as well as bring their minds to the same dead level.

Among these men we recognised some we had frequently seen begging about the suburbs; some as working-men seeking work; others as decayed gentlemen brought to poverty by misfortune and sickness.

There, too, were men who may be seen any morning loafing about the wharf as though they were looking for work, and, no doubt, they themselves believe they are: but if any one were to offer them a job, unless it were a very light one, they would look upon it as a personal affront. Umbrella menders, who go about with a few skeleton umbrellas tied in a bundle at their backs, were seated at the table resting after their day's peregrinations. Watercress men, and some who go about with cockles and periwinkles, were dozing off the effects of the many half-pints of beer with which they had been trying to keep their throats moist during the greater part of the day. The match-selling interest was also represented; so was the travelling drapery business; and the "flying stationer" was there in all his glory.

There were some there, too, whose mode of getting a living was quite as well understood, although it was not so openly carried on. We also saw the genuine tap-loafer, who manages in some mysterious way to get sufficient money to pay for his bed, and find himself in beer. Cheek by jowl with him were men who had once held respectable positions in society, but who, yielding to the temptation of drink, had sacrificed those positions, and were now only waiting, with broken health and ruined reputations, till *delirium tremens*, or the Yarra, finished a career so mis-spent and profitless. One was relating the experiences of the day in language that, as far as diction went, was faultless. The same cannot be said, however, of the subject of his conversation. Another was relating how he had, at one time, been an officer in the army, but, becoming disgusted with the service, he left it, which means that, for some fault or other, he was cashiered, or obliged to sell out.

Four of them now sat down to have a game of cards; but, first of all, it was necessary to remove a man who lay stretched out at full length on the top of the table fast asleep, which removal was brought about by pushing him off with as little ceremony as though he had been a bundle of old rags. He fell with a great clatter, first on the form and then on to the floor, from which he looked round with a puzzled look in his face, as though he were wondering how he got there.

One of the four then produced from his pocket a pack

of cards, so besmeared with dirt and grease that only those constantly using them could distinguish one from the other. A flat piece of wood, perforated like a cribbage-board, was also brought out of the same capacious receptacle, and placed upon the table. Two matches were then cut in halves and sharpened at one end for pegs, and all was ready. They played a game of cribbage for a halfpenny a corner, which halfpence were duly staked upon the table, and covered by the cribbage-board, from which it was evident that each doubted either the honour or the solvency of the other.

They were about as rough-looking a quartette as could be seen in the colony. The eldest was a tall bony fellow, dirty, and savage-looking, who apparently could not utter three consecutive words without an oath. He wore an old grey Paget coat that had evidently been made for a much shorter man than himself, for the sleeves only reached half way between the elbow and wrist, while the skirts terminated just below the small of the back. His trousers might have been made originally of one kind of cloth, but it would have been impossible from the way in which they had been patched to decide then which it was. The others differed but little in appearance from those who may be seen at any time loafing about the threepenny taps.

We stood watching the game for some time, and if we had not been disgusted with his language, we should have been highly amused at the fierce looks the tall one threw at his partner every time their adversaries pegged a few holes. He swore at him whenever he played without making fifteen or a pair, although he may not have had the cards to do it with, but that, in the tall one's opinion, ought to be no impediment whatever. Once, however, when he did pair a card, and his opponent made a pair royal of it, it had such an effect upon him (the long one), that if he had not relieved himself by the discharge of an immense volume of oaths, he must have broken a blood-vessel.

We now turned our attention to the others. There was one whose appearance we rather liked. He was better dressed than the general run of those present, and was silent and reserved in manner, as though the company he was in was not at all to his liking. We soon found ourselves at his side, and sought to enter into conversation with him by asking if he thought it would rain before morning. He answered our question by propounding another, and that was if we were going to "shout," at the same time telling us, in very lugubrious tones, that he had only been able to save enough to pay for his "doss," and hadn't tasted a drop of beer since morning. As we observed before, we had rather liked the look of this man. We had, moreover, come to the conclusion that it was through some undeserved misfortune he had been reduced to the necessity of seeking a lodging among such uncongenial spirits; but his readiness in slang and love of beer completely dispelled that illusion, and made us confess to ourselves that our reading of the human character was not perfect.

As the man seemed sober, we thought there would be no harm in allowing him to "moisten his clay" at our expense, so we told him we had a shilling left, and if he would come along with us, we would stand a half-pint. He was thankful for the offer, and promptly accepted it.

A few yards from this house there is a tap wherein "sparkling ale" is dispensed to a thirsty public at threepence per pint. Thither we went. Most of the public-houses in Melbourne have a screen before the door, to prevent people in the street seeing those who may be drinking in the front of the bar—an arrangement intended for the comfort of those who have not yet drowned all feeling in bad spirits, or washed out all respect for public opinion with that mysterious compound called colonial ale. On passing the screen we saw eight or ten loafers in various stages of intoxication; some leaning on the counter, others standing in front of it, and one, whose legs had given way under the weight of beer they had to sustain, was lying on the floor grovelling in the wet sawdust in his vain endeavours to rise. Our business, however, was not with these.

Instead of ordering two glasses of ale, we called for two half-pints—not that we wished to save threepence, or preferred the pewter, but because the crystal would have inspired those standing around with the belief that they had one among them who had been on some successful "lay," and was well in funds, in which case he is expected to shout for "all hands," a thing we by no means intended to do. The barman drew one half-pint, and that quickly disappeared down our friend's throat, and it apparently required an effort on his part to prevent the measure going as well. Just then a dirty-looking loafer emptied his half-pint, and put it on the counter. The barman took it up, and, while it was yet reeking with the slaver and tobacco-juice from the jaws of the nasty beast who had just used it, filled it for us. That was rather too much. Thinking it would not be wise to make any objection, we mumbled something about a pain in the inside and called for brandy, leaving the beer for our friend to drink if he felt disposed, and he was very much disposed, for it disappeared as quickly as the other had done. We noticed the customers in that tap were not allowed to help themselves from the bottle, as they are in some of the others. We suppose it is because Boniface fears they might take more than would be good for them, a thing he objects to—at his expense.

It occurred to us that brandy was not often called for in that department of the hotel, as our request for it caused quite a sensation among the loafers, and the barman was careful not to part with the glass till he got the sixpence.

On returning to the sitting-room of the lodging-house, we saw we had risen wonderfully in our new friend's estimation, and he gave us a history of his colonial career, which appeared to have been on an inclined plane from the very start. He ascribed his want of success to the fact of his not being a fool; for, as he said, only fools can get on nowadays, and the bigger fool he is, the better he does.

If, as he stated, the absence of brains is a sure road to success, the converse must hold good with those possessing well-furnished brain-pans, and as this man was about as poor as he could well be, we may conclude that his intellect was something stupendous.

Having thus unburdened himself, he asked us if we could lend him the price of a pint of beer till the morrow, when he would pay us back without fail. Having calculated the probable effect of another pint of beer on the top of the two half-pints he had already had, we thought we might advance him the money without the after-reproach of having aided and abetted him in making a beast of himself, so we lent him the threepence on the strict understanding that he was to pay us back on the next afternoon, which he promised faithfully to do. Whether he would have kept his promise or not, we have no means of knowing, for we never called to ask him for it.

It was now near midnight, and many of the lodgers had left the room and gone to their beds. The card-players still continued their game, while their language had become, if possible, more blasphemous than before. The man who had been tailoring had completed his job, and retired for the night. The three who had been holding such lively converse on the sofa had talked themselves into a state of thirst, which they were trying to slake with beer one of them had been to fetch in a billy. The decayed gentleman had gone to bed; so had the unfortunate working-man; while the ex-officer was writing with a pencil, on a dirty piece of paper, what we took to be the draft of a begging-letter, as he was receiving instructions from a shabbily-dressed man at his side.

Soon that portion of the lodgers who cling to the public-houses till turned out at closing time, began to arrive, and stagger off to their beds. One or two looked into the room as they passed the door, and cast wistful glances at the billy containing the beer. One was carried along the passage, dead drunk, by two others, who were far from being sober themselves, but whose objurgations upon the senseless lump of clay they bore between them might have conveyed the impression to the minds of any one who could not see them, that drunkenness was their abomination. Another came along singing snatches of a love-song in a harsh, broken voice, with all the gravity peculiar to some men when drunk. The next that came along gave vent to his feelings in another way—by standing at the door and performing a nigger breakdown to his own whistling, till told by the manager to drop his row and get off to bed. Two men now came in quarrelling about a game of "Yankee grab" they had been playing at for drinks in the neighbouring public-house. It seems one had been playing "on the bounce"—that is, without any money in his pocket, trusting to chance to win, and to his own impudence to get out of it if he lost. In this

D

instance, however, the defaulter's "cheek" would have availed him but little, for the man who had been "sold" was so riled at his treatment that, although he had done the same thing himself scores of times, he would have made it uncommonly warm for his opponent if the manager had not gone to his assistance.

The next moment the "chucker-out" gave another proof that his berth was no sinecure, by pitching a man, who had formerly misbehaved himself in the house, out into the street, with the threat that if he didn't "take his hook" he would be very likely to want the assistance of a doctor for the readjustment of some of his ribs.

All the lodgers, with the exception of the card-players, had now left the room, when we thought we might as well go to the dormitory, to see how things were looking there.

A tallow-candle, in a battered tin candlestick, glimmered on the mantelshelf, giving just sufficient light to break the darkness, and show us that nine out of the ten beds were occupied. The one in the corner, reserved for us, was still vacant, and was likely to remain so—for this night at least—as we had not the least intention of remaining in the place one moment after we had gratified our curiosity. One man only of the nine appeared to be awake, and his eyes were fixed upon us with a staring gaze, as though he were wondering if we had come there with any sinister design. One lay with his head and shoulders uncovered; another was so covered up that he must have been half smothered by the clothes; another slept on his back, stretched out stiff and straight, as though he expected to die in the night, and wished to make things easy for the undertaker; whilst the man in the next bed was doubled up, with his knees and chin close together. Some slept calmly and quietly, but one snored so abominably that it could only be likened to the noise a lusty boy makes when blowing through a cow's horn.

On the whole, it was as disagreeable a sight as one would wish to see, and we would infinitely prefer braving the mosquitoes in the scrub to passing the night in such a room as that.

There being nothing more to see, we quietly slipped out and went home.

Summer is the "slack season" at the padding kens, as many of their patrons then go on the "Wallaby track," and do not return to Melbourne till the winter sets in. Others, whose first thought in the cold weather is to save sixpence for the bed, are not so particular in summer, for the days being hot, and the nights pleasant, they prefer spending it in beer, and sleeping *al fresco*. Nor is it difficult to find in Melbourne a resting-place suitable to all tastes. There are old boilers lying about the vacant spaces on the western side of the city, with man-holes invitingly open for those who like snugness, and are not afflicted with corpulency; and also empty malt-tanks, for those who can get into them.

Some of the homeless ones seek a secluded spot in the scrub, where they can recruit the strength wasted by the day's wanderings, or sleep off the effects of the day's potations. There are, also, many other places where the impecunious can retire at night; under verandahs, in empty houses, or in any convenient hole or corner that gives promise of a few hours' quiet possession, although that promise is not always fulfilled, for sometimes the guardians of the night rouse them from their slumbers and take them to a place where, for a time at least, they are lodged and boarded without being called upon to pay for either. Yet such is the perversity of human nature, that that tender solicitude is not always gratefully appreciated by those who are the objects of it.

THE POLICE COURTS.

For those who have the time to spare, and a desire to learn something of human nature, there are few places where a morning could be more profitably spent than in one of our police courts. Certainly, the view we get there of our social life is not altogether the brightest, nor the one most gratifying to our self-love; still, as society, as a whole, is made up of many sections, it is necessary, in order to make our knowledge complete, to be acquainted with each different part—the good, bad, and the indifferent.

It is not, however, only the unamiable portion of mankind we see there; many good and worthy people are forced to appear, much against their own inclinations, to give evidence, either as prosecutors or witnesses, a position some of them have such an intense dislike to, that nothing but the fear of the pains and penalties the contumacious are liable to ever makes them come at all. How few men, or women, are there who can stand in a witness-box and not show they are in a strange element? The faltering voice, the perspiring brow and parched lips, the nervous twitching of the fingers, and the frequent change of position, show their perturbation; and frequently, too, it is painful to notice their mental agony while undergoing cross-examination. A timid, modest woman may be seen writhing under the cruel remarks of a merciless attorney, or questioned upon subjects the most abandoned woman would feel ashamed to answer, if called upon to do so in public, all the while the "public," as represented by the greasy loafers behind the railed-off portion of the court, are chuckling with delight, as they witness her distress.

There are many cases brought into court which, from surrounding circumstances, cannot fail to awaken a feeling of compassion in the hearts of those present, such as a man who, having hitherto borne an irreproachable character, has, under some uncontrollable impulse, committed a trifling theft. It is indeed pitiable to watch him as he hangs his head while the charge is being made, he, at the same time, knowing that many of his friends are there listening to it—for friends will attend on such occasions to watch the proceedings, but whether from sympathy or curiosity is a question.

A mother, whose scamp of a son has brought himself within reach of the law, may be seen pleading for him with all the fervour of maternal love; or another parent, weeping, and almost heartbroken, comes there, and casting aside the repugnance all have to making such family griefs public, implores the magistrates to save her daughter from a life of infamy by placing her where she will be beyond the influence of her evil companions. In such cases as these, pity is mingled with sorrow. There are some, however, in which our pity is changed to anger, and sorrow gives place to a feeling of satisfaction, as we see a well-merited punishment meted out to some more than ordinarily deserving subject.

The shameless perjured one may be seen rearing his vile head as he calls God to witness his lies, to save a few paltry shillings, or, to swear away the liberty, or even the life, of some one he dislikes. A youthful criminal, proud of being, for a brief period, the cynosure of all eyes, holds up his head, and tries to put on an appearance of bravado, as he looks round to see what effect his " pluck " has upon his " pals," who constitute a considerable portion of the listening " public."

Bold rascality seems pleased, as he hears his cunning dilated upon, and joins in the laughter of the audience as the victim relates, with much hesitancy, and with provoking simplicity, how great a fool he has been ; but the laugh goes over to the other side of his mouth as he hears the fiat of a month's hard labour.

Brazen wantonness stands unabashed while a recital of her conduct is going on that ought to make one, with the least particle of the woman left, sink into the earth with shame.

Decrepit filth, sometimes respectably dressed, at other times in rags, stands there cowering before the indignant glances of those who hear how he has tried to pollute the mind of some innocent child, whose trusting nature makes her so open to the machinations of such monsters.

Fraud under every shape, and vice under every form, may be seen there daily. Recitals, painful to listen to, are followed by others intensely ludicrous. These, again, are succeeded by a lively interchange of courtesies between the attorneys and the Bench, to the great amusement of the public.

In former times, the admission of the public to the courts of law was intended as a check upon the authorities, and a guarantee of fair play to the accused. Nowadays, as we have a free and ubiquitous press, it is open to dispute whether an indiscriminate admission is an unmitigated good. Look at the audience behind the rail in one of the city police courts. Are they such as would be likely to act as a check upon the eccentricities of any magistrate who felt disposed to rule according to his own inclinations, rather than abide by the letter of the law? or, does the moral influence of their presence serve as a protection to the accused? The courts are crowded day after day by the same unsavoury people, who go there in the hope of hearing something that will gratify their prurient tastes, or to gloat over the details of some horrid murder. Boys of fourteen, to old men of sixty, linger there hour after hour, covered with filth and swarming with vermin, whilst the mal-odours arising from their bodies vitiate the atmosphere of the court, and render it scarcely endurable; the vermin at the same time crawling across the floor in search of "fresh woods and pastures new," on the cleaner and more dainty bodies of the respectable portion of the audience.

Young lads go there to get a "wrinkle" in crime. They learn what numerous loopholes there are through which one may wriggle out of a misadventure. They can learn the strong and the weak points of the enemy's (the law's) attack, and prepare to meet him where he is weakest. From what they see there, they can improve on old dodges and learn new. In fact, in every sense, the police courts are the best seminaries in which youthful criminals can receive the rudiments of an education that will, in after years, fit them for high positions in the ranks of crime. Nor are these the only ill-effects of "free admission." The loafers crowd out people who really have business there, causing them much inconvenience and annoyance.

The magistrate presiding needs a cool head and logical mind, for he has much to contend with before he can arrive at a proper decision; the stupidity of some and the obstinacy of others; the hard swearing on one side, and the equally evident perjury on the other; and the whole made still more confusing by the mystifying arguments and disputes of the lawyers. He has to settle many things that would be much better settled outside, if people would only reflect a little, instead of giving way to their tempers—such as family disputes that might be amicably arranged among themselves, but which are only embittered by an appeal to him; or, two friends, over some trifling matter, are often made irreconcilable enemies in the same way, when their disagreement might have been entrusted to some mutual acquaintance, who would have smoothed it over to the satisfaction of both parties.

A deal of dirty linen is, also, brought to court to be washed, that ought to be purified at home; and the petty squabbles of neighbours occupy much of the magistrate's time, and must be a great trial of his patience. In fact, if he were to listen to all the plaintiff, and defendant, and their witnesses, have to say, he would not be able to get through one case in a week,

Mrs. M'Tadger complains of Mrs. M'Fin, for insulting and threatening language, and slapping her little boy's face.

"Plaze, your wurship," said the plaintiff, "me little boy came running to me, and tould me that Mrs. M'Fin had slapped his face. I wint and axed her why she slapped the child's face, when she up, and tould me *she* never drank six quarts of beer in one day, and had to be taken home in a barrow, and thin she called me a drunken ould cat."

"It was hardly polite to call you that," said the magistrate, "but it is not actionable for a person to assert that she never drank six quarts of beer in one day, and had to be taken home in a wheel-barrow. What have you to say in reply, Mrs. M'Fin?"

"May it plaze yer honner," said the defendant, "I was standing at me doore, whin Mrs. M'Tadger came and axed me why I slapped her boy's face, when I hadn't seen the child all the blessed day. She called me a bad name, and said she could show her marriage lines, and, ses she, what about the leg of mutton Mrs. Jones lost out of her yard, and how about the brown-paper parcel? and——"

Here the magistrate interposed by putting the question, "Did you slap the boy's face, and call her what she says you did?"

"I did not, yer honner."

"Have you any witnesses, Mrs. M'Tadger?"

That lady had about a dozen, and the defendant about the same number, for the whole of the inhabitants of the right-of-way in which they dwelt were divided into M'Tadgerites and M'Finites.

Mrs. M'Tadger's witnesses sustain their chief's story in every particular, with addenda of their own, and describe Mrs. M'Fin as everything that's bad.

The M'Finites, on the other hand, contradict, point blank, all the others state, and make out Mrs M'Tadger to be a drunken old woman, and Mrs. M'Fin everything that's virtuous and gentle.

Cases like that usually end in dismissal, when the victorious party return to the right-of-way with what they call "flying colours," and celebrate the victory during the remainder of the day with noisy jubilation, and much beer swilling. The defeated party return, a few at a time, considerably crest-fallen, but, however much their defeat may have damped their spirits, it has in no way affected their thirst, for the jug goes as often from Mrs. M'Tadger's to the hotel, and back, as it does from Mrs. M'Fin's.

Beer is a great institution. It is associated with nearly all the affairs of life, and resorted to under every mental condition. In cases like the above, it intensifies the joy of the successful, and soothes the tempers of the losing side, and reconciles them to their defeat; at least, one would suppose that to be the reason why litigants hold it in such general estimation. Certainly, there are some inconveniences likely to arise from its unlimited use, but it's a great institution notwithstanding.

Mr. O'Rourke complains of having a brickbat sent through his window, and being called an "Irish pig." This is a cross-summons case, and Mr. O'Rourke himself has to answer a charge of assault, and damaging a lady's dress, by tearing it off her back. Each side had secured the services of a lawyer, which had no other result than to make the already tangled skein still more complicated.

"Please, your worship," said Mr. O'Rourke's attorney, "my client has been exposed to a system of persecution for the last two or three months, that would have driven any ordinary man mad. His windows have been smashed, his clothes-lines cut, and the wet clothes strewn upon the dirty ground. It was only three days ago his wife was making a pudding in the kitchen, when suddenly a brickbat came through the window, and sent the pieces of broken glass among the flour, which had to be thrown away, for it would have been dangerous to eat it. Not content with that, but adding insult to injury, the defendant called my client an 'Irish pig.' Now, your worship, I'm an Irishman myself, and I can assure you it's not pleasant to be called that, especially by one who is very sensitive, when allusion is made to any of the national peculiarities. I will now call my client to state the facts to your worship."

Mr. O Rourke made his statement, and a remarkable statement it was. It went to show what a mild, inoffensive old man he is, and in what extremely unpleasant places his lines had fallen, by his having to live in the midst of neighbours such as those he was surrounded by. In cross-examination, however, he admitted he might have told the defendant she was all the scum of Scotland rolled up together, and made into a woman; and also, that he may have insinuated that she had partly worn away the door-post by rubbing herself against it, to allay the itching so peculiar to her country people, but he couldn't tell whether it was before, or after, she had called him an Irish pig. He, also, confessed to having jammed her between the gate and the post, but that was accidental; and that he might have torn the dress off her back, but that was because she struggled. His evidence was corroborated by his witnesses; while those for the defence denied it in toto, and made him out, in every way, the aggressor.

The magistrates reserved their decision till they had heard the counter-charge, which was sustained and denied by the same witnesses who had given evidence in

the former case. The result was, that each was fined a
small sum, which was made still more gratifying to them,
by both having to pay their own costs.

Sometimes the magistrates have to hear cases in which
the ludicrous forms no part. On the contrary, a tale of
sorrow and misfortune excites the pity of all who hear it.
Lazarus had been cast down by sickness, and all manner
of misfortunes, not the least of which was owing Dives a
few pounds. The usurer, knowing that Lazarus had, as
yet, goods more than sufficient to pay him his debt,
resolved to proceed against him before they were wasted
in providing food for the family. In vain Mrs. Lazarus
went to him with tearful eyes to ask for time, telling him
if he would grant them that, they would be able to pay
him by instalments. He pooh-poohed the idea. What
had he to do with other people's sicknesses and misfortunes? All he had to do was to look after himself.
They owed him the money, and they must pay him, or,
he would sell off all they had. But, very fortunately, it
was first of all necessary to bring the magistrates to the
same way of thinking, before that extreme measure could
be brought about; and, as they saw it was a case of
genuine distress, they showed themselves little disposed
to bring utter ruin upon an unfortunate family. The
debtor was asked how much he could pay per week.
Half-a-crown. Dives was asked if that would do?
Certainly not; the money was owing, and they must pay
it. The magistrates cut the matter short, by adjudging
Lazarus to pay five shillings per month—just half what
Dives had refused to take. Costs were not mentioned.

For the courts to be seen at their best, however, is when
some great scandal, or murder, is coming on for hearing,
only you must go early to secure a place. Then there is
a full bench of magistrates, looking as dignified and
sedate as the gravity of the occasion requires, or, as their
personal appearance will allow them. The attorneys look
lively; and the barrister or two who may be engaged in
the case try to appear as though they had no doubt whatever of the result being favourable to the side on which
they are retained.

The policemen seem uncommonly "spry;" and the
detectives look mysterious, and knowing; while the
sergeant is rather more pompous than usual, as he cries

"Silence in the coort." Some of the witnesses appear nervous, as they fidget in their seats, when they are lucky enough to get any, and look as though they would rather be anywhere than where they are. That frame of mind is highly conducive to thirst, which may account for the number of public-houses always to be seen in the vicinity of the courts of law. Others have a nonchalant look, which only lasts till they get into the witness-box. Then the perspiration may be seen standing in beads on their brows, or running in streams down their faces, though that is rather an advantage than otherwise to them, as it enables them to collect their thoughts while "mopping" it up with their handkerchiefs.

After the disposal of the night charges, and order being duly established in the "coort," the case proceeds. The greasy ones look expectant, as it is being opened. Soon the look of expectancy gives place to one of pleasure, as they hear the details of some monstrous piece of depravity, or atrocious murder, laid bare. Their eyes sparkle with delight; they lean forward lest they should lose one word of the horrid tale, and, altogether, it is a sight that must be seen before one can understand the native ugliness of the loafer mind. It is out of their midst that the laughter we so frequently see mentioned in the police reports proceeds, for they laugh on every possible occasion, whether there be anything to laugh at or not.

The case having been opened, the examination of the witnesses begins. The public are now entertained by a lively exchange of courtesies between the opposing lawyers. One assures the other he hardly knows which to admire most, his legal acumen, or his gentlemanly manner. The other replies by telling his friend he esteems it a great honour to be in the same case with one who possesses more knowledge of the law than all the judges put together, and that he only regrets not being in a place where he could acknowledge his urbanity in a more decided manner, and in a way much more agreeable to his own feelings.

The presiding magistrate here mildly suggests the propriety of deferring the further exchange of compliments to some more fitting occasion, in order that the business might be gone on with. This seldom has any other effect than to bring down upon his Worship a shower of flattering observations from one of the two, who assures him that his impartiality as a magistrate is too well known to need comment from him, and that his desire to further the ends of justice in the way most agreeable to all parties, fills him with admiration, and makes him feel proud in having to conduct a case before him. So they keep on, till they have exhausted the dictionary of its polite phrases, then, and not till then, the case is allowed to proceed.

The lawyers sometimes get hold of a stupid witness, or a stubborn one, or one that combines in himself the natures of both, when it is highly amusing to watch them while he is undergoing cross-examination.

"Do you mean to swear," thunders the lawyer, "that you saw the prisoner near the spot, at the time you stated?"

"Do I mean to swear that I saw the prisoner near the spot, at the time I stated?"

"Yes."

"Well, I believe I did."

"Oh! you believe you did; now a short time ago you swore you did. What do you mean by that prevarication?"

"What do I mean by that prevarication?"

"Yes; you need not repeat my question. What do you mean by that prevarication?"

"Well, I'm sure I saw him there."

"You swear it?"

"Yes."

"Are you aware you are liable to be committed for contempt of court for prevaricating in that manner?"

The witness was not aware of it; in fact, it was showing matters to him in a new light, and, if looks are at all to be depended upon, it was one the reverse of rosy.

A strange variety of witnesses have to be dealt with by the legal gentlemen. There is the willing witness, one who is glad to attend for the sake of the money he gets as expenses, who gives his evidence in a reckless, and not always satisfactory manner; and is quite prepared, if not to swear falsely, at least so to exaggerate the truth, that it almost amounts to it. He may be known by the flippancy of his answers, and the doggedness with which he sticks to what he has once said.

There is the unwilling witness, who only attends because he cannot well keep away, who gives his evidence in a nervous, timorous manner, and while in that state can be badgered into saying anything the opposing lawyer wishes. There is the unfriendly witness, who will not speak one word till he gets his expenses, and when he does open his mouth he frequently does the side that brought him to court more harm than good. Then there is the witness of the *non mi ricordo* type, who is always unable just then to "charge his memory" with some fact he knows as well as he does which is his right hand. It requires a considerable amount of nerve to play the part of this witness. If he were at all timid he would speedily collapse, and perhaps find himself on the wrong side of the prison walls. All the browbeating of counsel, or attorney, is completely thrown away upon him. In vain does the judge or magistrate frown, and tell him to be careful of his answers. He is careful, and his care consists in not saying anything damaging to the side he appears for.

Some witnesses bellow out loud enough to be heard outside the court; others speak in such low tones that they have constantly to be told to speak up. Some kiss the book with a loud smack; others just put it to their lips; and some, whose religious scruples stand in the way of their taking oaths, have been known to compound with their consciences, by kissing their thumbs instead of the book.

PUBLICANS AND SINNERS.

This paper does not treat of publicans and sinners in the Biblical sense, but as we see them in the flesh at the present day in Melbourne.

The publican of old was hated and despised by every class of society. For why? He held the office of the modern tax-gatherer, and as such exacted his dues in a harsh, unfeeling, and often cruel manner. The publican of to-day is neither harsh nor cruel, but is quite as unfeeling as the one of old. In those times he only exacted money, and with that the troubles of those who had to pay it ended. Nowadays, paying the money is the least part of the evil, as they get that in return which frequently brings with it poverty, madness, and death.

Many of the modern publicans are good fellows enough outside their business—loving husbands, good fathers, and trustworthy friends. Moreover, they always put something into the poor-box when they get their licences renewed, and it is as well they should do so, for it is the keeping them in prosperity that, in a great measure, makes that poor-box necessary.

What a contrast there is between the publican and the sinner. Look on the rags and unmistakable poverty of the one, and on the smug look of prosperity there is about the other. Notice him, as he stands in the door-way waiting for customers, just as a spider awaits, in some corner of his web, the advent of unwary flies; his two thumbs stuck in the arm-holes of his waistcoat, displaying his thick flabby fingers encircled with rings; a massive gold watch-guard, with its pendant trinkets, hanging in front of his white vest, while his snowy shirt-front is ornamented with gold studs, with a small diamond in the centre.

A customer now comes in, with whom he enters into conversation with a considerable amount of bonhomie. The weather is the first topic, and the probability of a fine day at Flemington is the next. The customer calls for a glass of ale, which he gets and pays for. The conversation now branches off into politics, a subject the customer gets rather warm upon, which necessitates another glass of ale. When that is finished and he is preparing to leave, the publican proposes a "shake" for drinks, which means a game called "Yankee grab," played with dice. The sinner, already pinned with two glasses of ale, is not likely to refuse, and that the publican knows right well. They throw, and the latter loses. Not liking to leave off without giving the publican his revenge, the other proposes another game and other drinks. A mutual acquaintance may now drop in, when he is invited to join in the play, which he does. So they keep on playing and drinking till their brains become muddled, and they themselves rendered unfit for the proper discharge of their daily business.

The barmaid now relieves the landlord from attendance in the bar. Let us see what she is like. There is a peculiarity about barmaids which marks them distinctly as a class. It is difficult to say what it is. It is independent of form, or height, or complexion. Let them dress as they like, in whatever fashion or colour they choose, the barmaid is seen through all, whether she be doing the block or adding brilliancy to the dress-circle of the theatre. There is an exaggerated kind of head-dress in favour with some; others have the hair cropped close like a boy's, with a few frontal curls left to show the femininity of the wearers. In business time they mostly affect black lustre dresses, some worn plain and some trimmed in colours according to the taste or complexion of the wearers. As one might imagine, from the nature of their employment, some of these young ladies acquire a boldness of manner that is apt to leave an unfavourable impression upon the minds of those who believe that lovely woman's brightest jewel is modesty. Others become chatty, and a trifle slangy, but at the same time they maintain a modest demeanour, bearing in mind that it is just possible that one or other of their many admirers may one day propose, as is not unfrequently and so. They are showy in appearance, and some of them possess pretty faces and nice figures, though hardly such as a painter would choose as models for a Madonna. They are great in earrings, and usually flash a pair presented to them by some soft-hearted member of their strings. Each of these barmaids has a number of admirers called her "string," and the longer that string is, the higher she stands in her employer's estimation.

A little girl, bare-footed and bare-legged, whose only clothing, it is easy to see, consists of a shift covered by a ragged frock, now enters with a black smoked billy in her hand, and asks for sixpenny worth of beer. From the confident way in which she asks to be served, it is evidently not the first time she has been there. Let us follow her to her home. A few steps from the hotel is a right-of-way. A short distance down that a "place" branches off, on one side of which are three miserable hovels, once two-roomed cottages; now they merely look like some pieces of old quartering stuck on end and kept in position by weather-boards nailed to them. The roof consists of old shingle, zinc case-linings, and flattened out kerosene tins, the whole kept from blowing away by the weight of some large lumps of bluestone. There was once a window to each room, now the glass is replaced by paper. There is a door which answers its purpose, when you can coax it to shut, which is rather a difficult matter, but that is nothing compared with the amount of persuasion necessary to get it to open again. The inside was once canvassed and papered, now the canvas and paper hang in festoons from ceiling and walls, showing the blue sky above and the rotting weather-boards at the sides. The holes in the roof are not an unmitigated evil, however, for although they let in the rain, they let out the fetid atmosphere arising from the bodies of those who dwell within. The furniture of that house is such as one might expect to find there. A few rags strewn in a corner answer for a bed; an empty case in the middle of the room does duty as a table; while two gin-cases are equally serviceable as chairs. A few broken plates, a pie dish, with part of the rim knocked off, and two or three knives and forks, some minus the handle, lie on a dirty shelf. A tea-cup without a handle and a small jam-tin, used as drinking vessels, are placed upon the case in the middle of the room along with the before-mentioned billy. In the fire-place, which is merely an assemblage of loose bricks, a large saucepan holds itself in readiness to cook whatever may be put into it; and by the side of it lies a broken-winded pair of bellows without a nozzle, which doubtless came off in some row, for that useful article of furniture, if grasped by the iron tube, is very effective in the enforcement of arguments when words are not sufficiently convincing.

The occupants of that house harmonise in every way with the house itself. A man is lying stretched upon the floor smoking; a woman occupies each gin-case, and another squats upon the floor; as miserable and as disreputable a quartette as could be seen in the colony. The little girl is evidently the daughter of the house—the man being her father, and the woman squatting on the floor her mother. The other two are neighbours who have just dropped in to have a carouse. The little girl having placed the billy upon the case, is gone into the right-of-way to play till she is wanted to fetch more beer; and well for her it is she is not in such company, for the language uttered there is simply awful. Imprecations are called down upon the head of some one who is evidently in bad odour with, at least, three out of the four. The fourth feebly tries to take his part, but is borne down by numbers, but in a half-good-humoured manner, for they are, as yet, early on their drinking bout. By-and-bye, when the beer begins to take effect, the good humour now prevailing will be changed to fury, when bitter words will be replied to by cruel blows; and a scene that opened with every appearance of friendship and goodwill, will be closed by an exhibition of the most brutal and fiendish passion.

Let us now return to the public-house.

At the side of the house is a passage with a small sliding door opening into the bar, through which the customers can put their bottles or jugs, and get what they want without being seen by those in front of the bar. A respectable-looking woman, evidently a working-man's wife, puts a jug through the trap and asks for three pennyworth of beer, having obtained which she covers the jug with her apron and takes it home.

Asmodeus-like, we will look into her home. It is just the sort of place one would expect to see where a woman

E

who "likes her beer" is the presiding genius. The
husband having to be at work by eight, has his breakfast
a little after seven. It is now past eleven, and the breakfast things are not yet cleared away, neither is the bed-
room touched, nor any of the household work done. How
the time has been spent is clearly shown by a newspaper
lying on the table, with a red-and-yellow covered sensational novel by the side of it.

A friend has dropped in, for these women who are fond
of beer mutually visit at each other's houses to have a
quiet glass, and discuss the affairs of some mutual acquaintance. As slander requires something to wash it down,
more beer is sent for; thus the day is muddled away
with novel-reading, drinking, and gossip, till she has to
hurry on with the preparation of dinner for her husband,
who returns home shortly after five.

Back again to the hotel. It is now late in the evening,
and the barmaid looks resplendent in the gas-light. The
mountain of hair on her head has been made smooth, the
black jet earrings and brooch have been replaced by gold
ones, and an additional ring graces her fingers. The
black lustre dress, with its green trimming, is still
retained, and a piece of scarlet ribbon is intertwined in
her hair; while her complexion is as fresh and natural as
violet powder and carmine can make it.

A fast-looking young fellow, who is evidently on good
terms with the barmaid, whom he calls "Polly," now
comes in. He shakes hands with her, and asks how she
"expatiates." She assures him she is quite "salubrious,"
and hopes he is in a "perfect state" himself. He gives
her to understand that he only needed one thing to make
his happiness complete, and that was the knowledge that
she was "to rights," and having ascertained that, he has
nothing more to wish for except a drink. On being
handed the bottle and glass to help himself, he assures the
smiling barmaid that the gods themselves were never
better served, and that Hebe was not a "patch" upon her.
Having delivered himself thus, he winds up by insinuating
that, although she is in health and appearance as near
perfection as possible, a thimbleful might do her good.
She is of the same opinion herself, and pours out of a
decanter a small glass of a palish-coloured liquid which
she drinks, and for which her admirer, or, as she calls

him, her "bloke," pays sixpence. It may interest some to know that the pale-coloured liquid Polly drinks is neither more nor less than cold weak tea. If she were to drink only a sip of wine or spirits every time she is asked, she would require a head as well-seasoned as a brandy cask to stand it. And if she were to refuse to imbibe when invited to do so, her employer would tell her she was taking a "shingle off his roof," a proceeding he strongly objects to; so to keep on good terms with him, and retain her faculties till bed-time, she drinks cold tea.

Boniface himself does the same thing when any of his customers pay him to drink a little of his own stuff, or when he "shakes" them for drinks.

What can be said of the poor gull who has not sense enough to see how he is tricked and laughed at by Polly? He fancies he has the exclusive good-will of that damsel instead of being only one of a dozen. He buys her jewellery, and takes her out as often as she will let him, which means, when she cannot do better by going with some one else; for, be it understood, she is most condescending to those who are the most liberal.

He stands there chatting and consuming his nobblers till he fancies he has had enough, when, wishing Polly affectionately good-bye, he departs.

We will follow our typical sinner to the end of his career, and show how, lured on by drink and designing barmaids, he descended step by step into the abyss of misery and degradation. This is no fancy sketch, but is taken from actual life, and is only one instance of many that have happened, and are happening at this moment, in Melbourne.

He held a good position in a well-known firm, with a prospect of rising to a better. The first time his irregularities were brought under the notice of his principal, he received a kind admonition. The second time he was warned that its repetition would be followed by instant dismissal. The third time, notwithstanding a fervent promise of amendment from himself, and the intercession of friends, he was dismissed. For some time that had a steadying effect upon him, and his friends began to hope. Then Polly regained her sway over him, and he sank lower. After being out of a situation for some time, he get another billet, and he might even then have regained his former position had he kept straight. Things went on better at first, but only for a short time, and he lost that in the same way he had lost the others. Soon, a change was visible in his appearance. His clothes, in which he once took so much pride, now get shabby; his boots are burst at the sides, and down at heel; his linen, once so faultless, is now more than doubtful; and his gloves, which he still affects, are not nearly so nice looking as they once were.

Polly sees the alteration in his circumstances as soon as anyone, and draws off accordingly. The sixpenny nobbler of pale brandy is now altered to threepennyworth of rum, and the glass of English ale, or stout, to half-a-pint of beer.

After repeated attempts to reclaim him, his friends have been compelled to turn their back upon him. Lower and lower he sinks, till he becomes the companion of the most abandoned. Lower, and still lower, till even they look upon him with contempt. Lower, and yet lower, till he settles down amongst the lowest dregs, where he, the educated, and once respectable, lies festering till death terminates a life whose early promise had been so woefully unfulfilled. How he came by his end may be seen in any of the morning papers. "As some boys were fishing close to the Falls Bridge, they saw the body of a man floating in the river. It was got ashore, and removed to the morgue, where it awaits identification."

Did Polly see that paragraph? If she did, was her heart at all moved by pity for one she had so greatly helped along the road to ruin? Or did she dismiss him from her mind with the remark usual when such things happen? "What a fool he has been! How well he might have done, if he had only kept 'square'!"

It is now later in the evening, and the landlady graces the bar with her presence. No black lustre dress trimmed with green does for her; neither does she flaunt the scarlet ribbon; but silks of the dearest, and jewellery the most recherché, are called in to set off her substantial, though somewhat vulgar, charms.

She helps in the bar now, that Polly may have a little more time to attend to her "string," numbers of whom flock in as the night advances. The mistress has a repartee for one, a joke for another, and a smile for all—and such a smile! A face lit up by smiles is usually pleasant to look upon, but a smile on hers means misery elsewhere. She smiles upon the working-man while he is spending the money that should go to the sustenance of his family, and she smiles upon the poor care-worn wife who comes there with her children to try to get him home. She smiles upon these ragged and famishing children, while mentally thanking God her own are not like them ; and she smiles, aye! and sweetly too, upon the dissolute wife of a respectable man, while she is disgracing herself, and bringing certain ruin upon her husband.

Glasses of ale and spirits now circulate pretty freely, and as often as asked, Polly takes her nobbler of cold tea, which is so often that it ought to strike the poor fools, who pay sixpence every time she condescends to drink, as singular that one so young can drink so much without showing it. But the day will come when the cold tea will be put aside for something stronger, weak enough at first, but gradually increasing in strength, till she becomes a confirmed toper.

At 11.30 the publican turns the sinners into the street, and closes the door. He and his wife now sit down, and count the takings, which have to-day been good, quite up to the average, and he rejoices accordingly. The business of the day over, the smiling pair finish off with a comfortable supper of cold fowl, or oysters, washed down with bottled stout. Nothing has occurred during the day to disturb their minds or impair their appetites, so the good things before them disappear with astonishing rapidity. A sufficient amount of solids, with liquid in proportion, having been despatched, they wind up with a "nip," and retire to bed, with an inward sensation of comfort, and in good humour with the world at large.

THE RACES.

Wherever a community of the Anglo-Saxon race pitch their tents, one of the first things they think of is a racecourse. In selecting the one for Melbourne, the gentlemen appointed for the purpose knew perfectly well what they were about when they chose the ground at Flemington. It is in every way suited to the purpose—as much so, as though it had been made to order. Horsey men say it can't be "beat." It is to Melbourne what Sydney Harbour is to that city, something to "blow" about. It is spacious and level, the circular course being ample to try the powers of the contending horses, while the "straight" is of sufficient length to give the best one a "show" for the first place. It is surrounded by hills, so that the thousands who annually attend the races can see the running from start to finish.

The "Lawn," on a fine day, is something to look at. It is a living kaleidoscope of magnificent dresses, of all materials, and every possible colour. The grand stands, as they are facetiously called, are not remarkable either for architectural beauty, or as comfortable places to sit in for four or five hours at a stretch, but they give a good view of the race, and thereby answer their intended purpose. They are four in number, one for members of the Jockey Club, and three for the public; in the principal one of which are two viceregal boxes. Under this stand are the luncheon-rooms and bars, where the hungry and thirsty can satisfy their wants if they can get near enough to the tables to be served before it's time to start for home.

The luncheon hour in the open sheds erected in the carriage paddock, is the jolliest part of the business. It is then care and anxiety are left at home, or in the office; and friends crack jokes and bottles of champagne at the same time. The ladies enjoy themselves with an *abandon* they would never think of displaying at home. They talk and laugh with their pretty mouths full of turkey, and drink their champagne as though they liked it. People who at other times are very careful as to what they eat and drink, dismiss their caution on these occasions, and store up a full day's repentance for the morrow.

Some parties take their lunch in their carriages, the ladies seated and the gentlemen helping them to the various good things spread out on a table-cloth on the grass. These, too, are jolly, and their jollity springs as much from the surroundings, as it does from the champagne, for all who can afford it, and many who cannot, indulge at race time in that sparkling fluid. Others of the less wealthy, enjoy their fowl, or ham-sandwich; and they laugh, and joke, and quaff their bottled beer, and sip their whiskey, and get up their "sweeps," with the same utter disregard of everything but the enjoyment of the passing hour.

Having lunched, and laughed to their heart's content, they all return to the stand to watch the running for the "Cup," in which all are interested, either by bet or sweep. Then, a glimpse may be caught of colonial "high life below stairs," when "Jeames" and the coachman and groom, before they repack the hamper with the unconsumed good things, and remove the half-emptied bottles, seat themselves at the tables and partake of lunch with, if possible, more enjoyment than that manifested by their "betters." These after-feeds, however, do not always end happily; for, the convivialists, who have been more accustomed to colonial ale than to any other beverage, finding the champagne an agreeable change, indulge pretty freely in it, without making sufficient allowance for the difference in the strength of the two liquids; with the result that, they sometimes have to be driven home themselves, instead of performing that office for their employers.

The "Hill" at the back of the grand stand, is patronised by those who cannot afford to go to the Lawn. That, too, has its grand stand, from which a better view of the race can be obtained than from any point on the Lawn. It is a sight to see the Hill from the "Flat," or front of the

Lawn, while the "Cup" is being run for. It appears to be a solid mass of human faces piled on the top of one another, with their eyes fixed with an earnest gaze upon the crowd of rushing horses; while the roar from the many thousand throats, towards the finish of the race, is almost sufficient to shake the hill to its foundation. The small fry of the tribe of metallicians do their business on the Hill, always on strictly cash principles, in so far as being their own stakeholders; but some of them are not unfrequently absent from their posts when the backers of the winning horses go to look for them.

The frequenters of the "Hill" indulge largely in shilling and half-crown sweeps, and that gives them as much interest in the race as that felt by the sharers in the pound sweeps on the Lawn.

The "Flat" is free to all, consequently it is greatly affected by the poorer portion of the admirers of the turf, who flock thither in thousands, and invest their shillings in sweeps got up for their delectation by grotesquely-dressed men, and by individuals with blackened faces. The reason these latter thus disfigure themselves is, that they may be recognisable by the clients who have been lucky enough to draw the winning horses.

It is on the "Flat" the magsmen manipulate the three cards, and thimble, and in various other ways exploiter the bipedal flats who are foolish enough to back their luck against the spieler's wits. It is rather risky work for these nimble-fingered gentlemen nowadays, for the detectives and plain-clothes constables keep too sharp a look-out for them to give them a chance of operating in the wholesale manner they used to do.

More fun is seen on the Flat than on the Lawn, or on the Hill, for Mrs. Grundy is still a power among the frequenters of these latter places, even at race time. The flatites, however, have never heard of the good lady, or, if they have, they care very little about any opinion she might form of their doings. They go there to enjoy themselves in the way most agreeable to themselves, and by the aid of the many drinking booths there, they usually succeed in doing so.

Although racing is so popular among the English-speaking inhabitants of the world, it has its opponents, as well as its admirers. The latter say it improves the breed of horses, while the former maintain it deteriorates the breed of men, by converting those who might otherwise be honest men into blacklegs and sharpers.

Whether the equine race is improved by one horse being trained to excel another in speed, or the human race deteriorates by one man training himself to excel another in wit, we will leave the disputants to settle among themselves, and confine this paper to a description of the sort of people who go to the races, and what may be seen at these annual gatherings.

The late Lord Palmerston spoke wisely when he called the English racing festival "Our Isthmian Games," for the one is as popular with the Briton of to-day, as the national gathering on the Isthmus of Corinth was to the Greek of old, the only difference being, that while our festival is annual, the other was held once in three years. What the English folk would do if they had to wait three years for their races, is hard to say; for, as it is, they are looked forward to with impatience by many as a time of relaxation, or pleasure, or gain, or all combined. Then it is that the various games of wit versus folly are in full swing, for it is the harvest time of the sharps, and the season when pigeons yield their feathers more readily than usual.

At that time may be seen hard-headed men of business, proverbially shrewd, and the least likely ones in the world to be outwitted at any other time, infected with the excitement of the moment, and betting with all the enthusiasm of the merest greenhorn; and when they see they have lost, they smile as though it was the best joke imaginable, or wash down their chagrin in a glass of champagne. Sober, steady-going, religious men, who detest gambling as much as they can detest anything, think there is no harm, at this time, in relaxing somewhat of their usual rigidity, and pacify their consciences with the proverb that "It's not wise to keep the bow always bent."

At this time, also, are to be found fast young men, who think it quite "the cheese" to be seen in the company of the knowing ones, whose "tips" they act upon with childish simplicity, and when they find they have lost, they exercise the little intellect they possess in trying to make out how it was they didn't win. These form rather a numerous class, who think to be well posted in the names of the horses, is to have an intimate knowledge of the horses themselves, though, poor donkeys, they know as much about their equine superiors, as they do of Hindustani; nevertheless, they are to be seen in the centre of small crowds talking "horse" with all the dogmatism of old stable hands.

Men holding respectable and lucrative situations, but gamblers by instinct, anxiously look forward to the racing season, when they hope, by a stroke of fortune, to make good their losses at cards, or dice, which will enable them to replace the money they have embezzled, when they will leave off gambling altogether, and never take to it again. But if they cannot win at games of chance, when what is called "luck" might at any time throw the game into their hands, in spite of the skill and knavery opposed to them, they are not likely to do so when skill and knavery are alone pitted against them. So the inevitable crash comes; and as the gaol opens its portals to receive them, they realise the fact that seeing life, and fast living, are not always conducive to a man's happiness.

Heavy swells in the enjoyment of magnificent "screws" of thirty "bob" a week now scrape sundry half-crowns together and take all manner of odds on all manner of events. The only event they do not speculate upon is the one most likely to come off—their losing. Hobbledehoys, whose wages range from ten to fifteen shillings per week, bet in the hope that they may "pull off" some event, by which they may line their pocket with a few shillings, and have something self-laudatory to talk about among their comrades. Shop-boys, led away by the example of many of their elders, are also seized with the desire of betting, and to obtain the means of gratifying that desire, they commence a life of crime, by pilfering their master's money.

The ladies, too, partake of the general excitement, and bet largely in gloves and handkerchiefs, though, we are sorry to say, they are inveterate "welchers," for when they lose, the last thing they ever think about is paying; yet, Shylock himself was not more persistent in demanding his pound of flesh than they are in claiming their winnings. For all that, being "mashed" by such interesting tacklers is rather delightful than otherwise.

The Races.

The races are also looked forward to by a class of men of a far different stamp than the general run of those who visit them. We allude to what are called "magsmen" or "spielers," from the German verb "spielen," to play. As a rule they are not remarkable for elegance, either of manner or appearance. They dress anyhow, but always with a strict regard to untidiness. Every style of garment is patronised by them, colour being as little studied as shape, and fit thought no more of than either. Their hats and boots harmonise with the rest of their covering, and they usually wear a figured shawl-scarf round their throats, instead of a necktie. There is a fishy look about them, real as well as metaphorical, which shows they sometimes turn their hands to honest employment. In the morning they may be seen about town, engaged in some line connected with the hawking interest; in the afternoon, their favourite pastime is loafing about the different lanes and rights-of-way of the city; and at night they may be seen hanging round certain public-houses in Bourke Street.

There is a "*Je ne sais quoi*" about these men that distinguish them from the rest of mankind. What it is we cannot describe, but it is something in their looks and manner, independent of any personal trait, that ought to make the most verdant of yokels button up his pocket when in their company. They have, moreover, a quick, shifty glance, a ceaseless movement of the hands, and many other peculiarities that are sure indications of an active mind, and one that is only exercised for their own exclusive benefit. The only interest they take in the races is, that the latter are the means of bringing a number of people together, among whom they calculate there will be a certain percentage of fools, out of whom they expect to extract as much "sugar" as will keep them in clover for months to come.

It is a matter of the most perfect indifference to them which horse wins, as they never bet. They come there to back their own wits against other people's, and, as the odds on that event are so much in their favour, they let well alone. If the result of the race depended upon the strength and activity of the horse's own four legs, they might perhaps speculate; but as they are much too wide awake not to know that other "legs" besides the horse's have a deal to do with the running and the winning, they fight very shy of risking any money on such uncertain undertakings, tip or no tip.

There are in society a certain number of men who have a very comfortable belief in their own cleverness. These men are called by magsmen "fly flats," and are just the ones they like to get hold of, for they are the easiest of all to be duped. When that belief is backed up, as it frequently is, by an avaricious disposition, they cannot resist the temptation of making money by means that, to them, seem perfectly correct, though to others with minds differently constituted, they would appear the reverse of creditable. They are never above taking advantage of the want of wisdom in those they have dealings with—nay, they look upon it as laudable, and will often boast of it afterwards, as though they had done something uncommonly smart. They are so intent upon "besting" their opponents, that the idea of others being animated by the same benevolent intention towards themselves, never for a moment enters their minds, so they neglect the precautions necessary to guard against it, and thus they fall a prey to men whose principles are no worse than their own, only their wits are a great deal keener.

There is another class of men so simple and confiding in their natures, that experience has no effect upon them whatever. It matters not how often they are "done," they appear to be as powerless to keep their money as sheep are to retain their wool when shearing time comes round, though the fleecing in one case is done in a less violent manner than in the other. These men are called "mugs," and furnish a very large proportion of those who keep magsmen going.

There are also some, who cannot altogether be ranked as fools, who mix themselves up with the sports for the sake of amusement, caring but little whether they win or lose, only they prefer winning.

It is both difficult and dangerous for the spielers to ply their various callings at race gatherings now, owing to the sharp look-out kept for them by the plain-clothes police. Sharp as it may be, however, the "piping" of the gamblers is quite as keen for the police. They have their signals, and their words of warning, which are passed rapidly along by their scouts, and reach the parties they are intended for long before the police can. A magsman, in the centre of a group composed of "mugs" and "buttons," hears the word "Nit." In an instant the cards, and the small board on which they are manipulated, disappear as if by magic, and the player strolls away looking as innocent as though he hadn't touched a card for a month. With all their cunning, however, they are sometimes caught *in flagrante delicto*, and sent to crack diamonds inside the walls of Her Majesty's gaol for a month.

THE "ZOO."

From the earliest ages nations have had a fancy for gathering wild animals together. Darius must have had a menagerie, or he could not have cast Daniel into the lion's den. The Romans, too, kept wild beasts, but not merely to look at, and study in their cages—that was far too tame an amusement to satisfy their active minds; they preferred the excitement of seeing the animals fight, either with one another, or with men.

The custom of keeping wild animals is as popular in modern times as it was in the olden. Who does not remember Wombwell's Menagerie, with its great variety of wild beasts, and the docile elephants that would trumpet forth their thanks for the apples, or cakes, their juvenile admirers were so fond of giving them. There used to be "the lions in the Tower," and other animals, too, till they were removed to the Zoological Gardens, in the Regent's Park.

In Paris they have the "Jardin des Plantes," where they keep a fine assortment of wild nature. In Berlin, the "Thier-garten" is rich in the number and variety of its specimens of the animal world. We, in following such a good lead, show ourselves equally desirous of having the same means of amusement and instruction, for the two go together; though our display is not yet equal to those of the older countries of Europe, as menageries, like nations, usually have small beginnings. By-and-bye, as our country becomes more peopled, our "Zoo" will become more populous also.

The gardens are prettily situated in what is called the Royal Park. The first thing that catches the visitor's eye on entering is a group of parrots, of many colours and various sizes. They are all capital talkers, but, unlike most parrots, they have been taught by one of their own kind, a loqacious old fellow in whose company they were placed when they first arrived at the gardens.

On the right of the entrance is the place for refreshment, where the inner man can be "restored" on cakes and teetotal drinks, or, if he prefer it, new milk at twopence per tumbler. Eight cows are kept to supply the visitors with the lacteal, four of which always stand in their stalls in full milking condition.

The gardens are well arranged, and extensive enough to hold all the animals we are likely to get for generations to come.

The flower-beds are kept free from weeds, and the walks free from litter, while the general management appears to be such that the imprisoned animals would have rather a pleasant time of it, if they could only forget that they were once free, for the love of liberty is common to birds and beasts, as well as to man.

The animals that get the largest share of attention from the visitors to our "Zoo" are the lions and the monkeys—the sublime and the ridiculous of the *feræ naturæ*. The monkeys receive by far the greater notice, which shows that there, as is frequently the case in civilised life, the sublime has to play second fiddle to the ridiculous.

Lord Monboddo said that the only difference between the man and the monkey was, that the man's tail grew inwards, and the monkey's outwards. Whether his lordship was right or not, need not be argued here, but it is very evident the dissimilarity in some other respects is not so great as it is in the one he has mentioned. For instance, when a monkey sees another with anything he fancies he should like, and he is strong enough, he takes it. That has always been one of the peculiarities of man. From the earliest ages it has been a maxim that no man has a right to more than he can keep. Certainly, the law objects to that theory, unless it is first of all consulted; then it frequently acknowledges the soundness of the principle, by reducing it to practice. Another feature common to both is, when one is down, there are not wanting plenty to pitch into him; only monkeys do it with their teeth and claws, while men do it with their tongues. Monkeys also have a way of prying into things that do not concern them; a similar weakness may be discovered in some men.

It is as amusing to watch the visitors round the monkey house as it is to observe the inmates themselves. The children laugh at their antics, and recognise in them fellow beings. Their elders look amused, and smile as the mind carries them back to their own monkey days; while others have a serious look, as though they were admitting to themselves that, perhaps, after all Darwin is right.

The simia is pretty well represented in these gardens. There is an orang-outang who walks about very much like an old man, and is quite as good-looking as some old men we see in the streets. There is something particularly droll about this old gentleman. He drinks out of a bottle or pannikin like a man, and prefers beer to water. When being brought over, the sailors used to make him drunk, for the fun of the thing, and the antics he would indulge in when in that state were very similar to those of the "exhilarated" human being.

In the same cage are the "drill monkey," the most active of all the simian race, and the "whistling monkey," the latter perpetually emitting a short sharp whistle. When we saw him in his cage, and heard the laughing jackass in his close by, we thought what a pity it was some of the laughing jackasses and whistling monkeys we have in society were not here to keep them company.

There are many more monkeys to be seen in these gardens, among which are the "agile gibbon," and the "lemur," of nocturnal habits, and with a muzzle like a fox's.

A little further on may be seen many fine specimens of the feline race, notably two lions—one a magnificent brute, though now well advanced in years. The poor fellow is a widower, the late very much lamented Mrs. Leo having departed this life about two years ago.

This king of beasts has a look of mildness and dignity about him not always to be seen in the faces of the kings of men, if their portraits are to be depended upon.

While noticing his powerful limbs, one cannot help reflecting on the vast superiority of mind over matter. How many men, unaided by art, would it require to take, and keep, this lion in subjection? Of what avail would their feeble strength and puny hands be against his mighty limbs and terrible claws? Man may boast of being lord of all created things, he may glory in the possession of an intellect that enables him to control the lightning; he may feel proud in the power given by faith, which assures him that if he says to the mountain, "Be thou removed," it will forthwith disappear, and he may contemplate with pleasure the mighty animals he has brought under his dominion; but, in a state of nature, face to face with that lion, he would be as powerless as a kitten before the onslaught of a bulldog. The constant walking backwards and forwards before those iron bars must, in time, have a bad effect upon the sight; and the hard, unyielding boards must be ill-suited to feet intended by nature to walk over the springy sod.

Close by are leopards, pumas, and tigers. One of the latter, and the finest of all, took it into his head one day to kill his spouse, an act he has, doubtless, since regretted, for one in his position cannot afford to lose his only companion, and she the sharer of his joys and sorrows; for that tigers have joys to share is shown plainly enough when in their playful moods; and it is hard to believe they do not know what sorrow is, when thinking of their native jungle. There are, also, belonging to this class the Tasmanian devil, quite as vicious looking as the personage he is named after is supposed to be; the savage jungle cat, our native cat, and the chaus cat.

The canine race is represented by some hybrid wolves, the offspring of an Esquimaux dog and the common black wolf; the prairie wolf, the marsupial wolf from Tasmania, dogs like racoons, two mild-looking dingoes, and a brown English fox.

Of the ursine species there are some black Himalayan bears in cages, and two brown ones in a pit; while the porcine is represented by some wild boars of India.

Of the order reptilia there are the rock python, the terrible boa constrictor, cartet, diamond, copper-head, and tiger snakes; the blue-tongued lizard, lizards of all kinds, and one large iguana.

Of the feathered tribe there is a fine display. Song birds of various plumage are confined in a large aviary, and in the melody issuing therefrom may be heard the well-remembered notes of many English birds. They breed well, but the gentlemen do not confine their atten-

F

tion to the ladies of their own kind, with the result that the progeny is rather a mixed one.

Eagles and vultures confined in large compartments covered with wire netting eye the visitors in no friendly manner. One magnificent specimen of the condor would measure thirteen or fourteen feet from tip to tip of wings, and, when standing, he must be four feet in height. There are the wedge-tailed eagle, the white-billed sea-eagle, and a whistling eagle.

There are Java pea-fowls, and pea-fowls from everywhere else. Geese from Bass's Straits, the demoiselle crane, and the long slender-legged flamingo.

Grave-looking owls sit blinking on their perches, with the solemn look of a judge about to pass a sentence of death.

Native companions and emus, the ostrich and the cassowarry, wander about in their large enclosures in an aimless sort of manner.

In another enclosure, with a pond in the centre, are four fine pelicans constantly on the look-out for fish. Macaws and parrots, from those of the most gorgeous plumage to the pure white; peacocks, pheasants, partridges, ducks of every kind, the crowned pigeon, the lyre bird, and every other specimen of the feathered tribe may be seen in our "Zoo."

A specimen of almost every known variety of the horned animal has found its way to these gardens. The curved-horned mouflla, the Burrtel wild sheep, the ibex, llama, and the yak. In their paddock are the tame and gentle deer, pushing their moist noses through the fence to receive anything in the shape of fruit the visitors choose to give them.

Here too are the water buffaloes, indulging in a bath, with only their noses out of the water; and buffaloes of every other description disport themselves in a manner most to their own liking.

Truly a strange and varied assortment of living creatures have been gathered together in this place. A land tortoise, almost as large as a full-grown turtle, swims about in a tank; there are wombats, fawn-coloured field-mice, as large as small rats; white rats, bred for feeding the boas, and other large snakes; and the black Angora guinea-pig, also cultivated for the delectation of the snakes.

There are beavers, and beaver rats—the latter just like the common rat, only ten times its size. Guinea-pigs of the ordinary kind dwell together in harmony in a miniature cottage called " Guinea-pig Cottage," and another kind of guinea-pigs live in a small red-brick castle, built for their special use. Some white rabbits inhabit a log hut, similar to those the old backwoodsmen of America delighted in. There may also be seen there a hybrid between a hare and a rabbit.

The porcupines display their fretfulness by trying to keep out of sight as much as possible; and the ant-eating porcupines have plenty of occupation in searching for ants in their cage, the bottom of which is built of brick and covered with about two feet of mould.

The duck-billed platypus is there too, along with opossums, and kangaroo rats.

Kangaroos of all ages and sizes, one of which is perfectly white, hop about in their not very graceful manner. The white one has a son, also white, with the exception of a dark patch on the breast; wallabies, like stunted kangaroos, skip about merrily in the space allotted to them, and are apparently free from all care and anxiety. Two zebras are grazing in their paddock.

They have only one elephant, and that supports itself by carrying children round an enclosure on its back; the saddle will hold six at a time, and was made at a cost of sixty pounds.

There is a double fence round the enclosure devoted to the elephant, the outer one about three feet from the inner. At first there was only a single fence, but a gentleman was one day leaning with his back against it, without thinking of what was behind him, when suddenly he felt the elephant's trunk pressing against his chest. He was not hurt, for the animal is not a savage one, but he might have been; and to guard against the possibility of its recurrence, the outer fence was put up, and notices posted all round that visitors are not to climb over.

There is a camel in the same enclosure, which is also self-supporting in the same way as the elephant. The camel's saddle holds four juveniles at a time, and on fine days it is pretty well patronised, for the young colonials, as a rule, are fond of getting into high places.

There is a stand, the top of which is reached by steps

for the children to get on and off the two patient and willing animals.

On Saturday afternoon music is added to the other attractions of the gardens. There is a fine stand erected for the players, with sounding-boards over their heads and at their backs, so that the sound can be thrown well forward on to the lawn in front of it, on which are placed chairs for the accommodation of the listeners, and tables for those who need refreshments.

THE THEATRES.

FROM the time of Thespis, mankind has been fond of theatrical displays; even before then a rude kind of representation accompanied the solemnisation of the rites of Bacchus, when the shepherds and peasants, having sacrificed a goat, would complete the ceremony by dances, and play all manner of antics, and, to give grotesqueness to the proceedings, would stain their faces with the lees of wine.

When Thespis came, he soon saw the inconvenience of the performers running about among the audience, and converted a cart into a stage for them to act upon.

Æschylus afterwards improved upon that by building a theatre, first wood, then of stone, and that still further increased the comfort of the spectators, by converting a disorderly mob of on-lookers into a quiet respectable audience. He introduced the mask as an improvement upon the face-staining disguise, and gave his characters dresses; and, to give them greater stature, he added the *coturnus* or buskin.

The drama attained to still greater perfection under Sophocles and Euripides, who were themselves actors as well as authors. It may be mentioned, to show how much the Athenians had improved upon the cart of Thespis, that they expended a hundred thousand pounds to put one of Sophocles' tragedies worthily upon the stage.

The theatre was built in the form of a horse-shoe, with the stage at the two ends. The seats rose one above another all round it, leaving the space in the centre, corresponding with our pit, to be occupied by the chorus when not on the stage. The heavens were the roof, and that would free the managerial mind from all anxiety on the score of ventilation—a painful subject with managers at the present day, for, since ventilation has been reduced

to a science, it has only succeeded in giving satisfaction to
no one, as the audiences complain that they are either
stifled by the heated atmosphere of the house, or laid up
with a week's neuralgia through being obliged to sit in
the cold draughts.

The chorus, in the days of Thespis, acted as the
orchestra. Æschylus remodelled it, and gave it far more
important functions. It was to the chorus, the performers
addressed themselves, and these, led on by their leader,
the corypheus, communicated to the audience the emotions
proper for the occasion.

The Romans transferred the drama to Rome, where, with
the exception of a species of theatricals performed by the
Roman youth called "Fabulæ Atellanæ," it had been unknown. It speedily took root in the new soil, and
attained to great favour with the patrician and plebeian
alike.

Actors were highly esteemed by their fellow-citizens
in Greece. In Rome, on the other hand, all who appeared
on the stage were stigmatised as infamous by an edict of
the Proctor. That decree could only have applied to the
small fry of the histrionic fraternity, for two actors,
Roscius and Paris, became famous, and were looked upon
with great favour by eminent Romans.

As the empire declined, so did the drama; and, when
the one fell, the other apparently died also; but it
budded forth again in the Middle Ages, under the name
of "Mysteries and Moralities."

At Dunstable, in England, the first theatre was opened
by the pious Geoffrey; but he was quite as unfortunate
as many who have embarked in the same line in more
modern times, for, shortly after, it was burnt down, as
some said, in Divine anger at the desecration. This had
such an effect upon poor Geoffrey that he went and hid
his chagrin in a cell at St. Albans.

In those days the performer combined the functions
of the ecclesiastic with those of the actor, and even at the
present day the ecclesiastic has not altogether dropped the
actor, for a little of the "hanky-panky" may be seen in
some of the preachers yet.

The strolling glee-men were welcomed everywhere, and
nowhere more so than within the walls of the monastery,
where the monks were ever ready to compose " patter " for

them, in return for the relief they afforded them from the monotony of their monastic life.

That gave great offence in certain quarters; and a decree was issued from the Council of Claverstoe, bearing the king's signature, "that *histriones*, or actors, and other vagabonds mentioned therein, should be no longer allowed access to the monasteries; and that no priest should turn glee-man himself, or turn ale-poet by writing verses for such disreputable characters."

The Melbourne folks are as fond of amusement as most people, and in the theatre are as well behaved as an audience can be; certainly there is a deal of unceremonious scrambling to secure a good seat when the doors are first opened; but that is only natural, for most people prefer sitting to standing when they go the theatre, even though it be on a hard, cushionless, and backless seat. Scrambling for a seat in the theatre is much the same as scrambling for a position in the world; the strong, pushing ones get to the front, while the timid and unassuming have to content themselves with what they can get.

There are six theatres in Melbourne, besides a host of other places of amusement, all of which are now conducted with the strictest regard to decorum.

The vestibules of some of them are the nightly resort of a motley crowd of loungers, who meet their acquaintances there by appointment, or come to watch the human kaleidoscope in its ever-changing aspects. Youths, from sixteen to twenty, hang about the bar doors trying to get a glimpse at the nobbler-dispensing beauties behind the counter. Youths, too, of a more mature age, old boys who were youths forty years ago, may be seen doing the same. Vapid swells saunter into the bar, and throw killing glances at the barmaids, which are thrown back with interest by the smiling Hebes, much to the delight of their empty-headed admirers, and much inward chuckling to themselves.

Chevaliers d'industrie are there, also, on the look out for any flat who may happen to be present with more money than brains. Spongers, in want of a drink, hang about in the hope of meeting some one they are on speaking terms with, who may be willing to shout. Loafers, rather better dressed than the ordinary run of the tribe, come there without any particular object in view, but at the

same time they are ready for whatever may come in their
way. Ragged boys of all ages hang about just inside the
gateway, begging the checks of those who come out
between the acts, or playing with one another till someone
connected with the place drives them away. A policeman
wanders up and down in a seemingly abstracted manner;
but he is doubtless fully alive to all that is going on
around him. When in want of a change, he strolls into
the pit to see what is going on there, while a detective or
two may be seen on the look-out for some stray lamb they
are in search of.

On "off-nights" the dress-circle has a somewhat
mournful look, quite as lugubrious as the looks of the
management when they see nothing but dead-heads in it.
It is no very difficult matter to distinguish a dead-head
from one who has paid for admission; there is a look of
independence about the latter that is sadly wanting in
the former, as there must necessarily be, for the good
folks who are there by virtue of payment must feel
themselves on a higher plane than those who go "on
the cheap."

On "full nights," however, it is different; then all is
joy and animation. The gentlemen chat, and the ladies
smile as they gracefully work their fans, or look through
the lorgnette at some one in a distant part of the house.
It is pleasant to contemplate the ladies' dresses when they
harmonise, which is not always the case; nor do the ladies
always select the colours best suited to their complexions,
which is a pity.

The style and variety of head-dresses one may see
there would make a rare display in a hair-dressers'
window. There is the lofty "pile," and the "plait"
coiled flat down upon the crown of the head, the "water-
fall" and the ringlets"; the "frontal curls," and the
"fringe"; the "bandeau," the "rouleau," the "straight,"
and the "frizzy."

The complexions, too, how clear and bright they look
in the gaslight, though some of them seem far too fresh
to be natural. The secret of making themselves "beautiful for ever" has not been imparted to all ladies; some
do it well enough, and, if not looked too closely into, it
passes. Others are extremely careless in putting on the
violet powder; they leave it in dabs, which detracts sadly

from the sweet face it covers, especially when seen by daylight. Nor is the rouge or carmine always properly blended with it; it is not nicely softened at the edges, consequently it has an unnatural look.

The pleasure and excitement of the situation give a look of happiness to all, and make the eyes sparkle like the paste diamonds that may sometimes be seen there doing duty for real ones.

The "family circle" has been rightly named, for it is there paterfamilias takes his brood of little ones, when they go to see the pantomime, or whenever he so far relaxes as to give them a treat to the theatre.

It is a pretty sight to see a father, and mother, and five or six children sitting in the front row of seats, all as happy as mortals can be, except perhaps the mother, who is in constant fear that some of the youngsters, in their anxiety to see what is going on in the pit, will fall over the parapet on to the heads of the people below. The father is at the head of the commissariat, and is kept fully employed in serving out lollies and apples as long as they last, and he doubtless feels relieved when they are all gone.

Respectable well-to-do tradesmen and their families also affect the family-circle part of the house. Young men who are not quite so fast as the general run of the Melbourne youth prefer being there to anywhere else, especially when they take their sisters or sweethearts with them. Family parties from the country go there, because their visit being only temporary they do not care about going to the trouble and expense of providing dresses fit for the dress-circle. Spinsters who cannot be exactly called young go there in company with one or two friends. Young women who are not fortunate enough to possess beaux go in couples for mutual protection, and, perhaps, with the latent hope that they may meet with some of the opposite sex with sufficient good taste to fall in love with them.

People who regularly attend church, and who also think they can go to the theatre without playing into the hands of the devil, affect that part because it is less rowdy than the pit, and less expensive than the stalls; and, lastly, elderly people of limited means always patronise the family-circle whenever they go to the theatre.

The stalls, too, have their regular frequenters, and the influences which cause them to gravitate to that part are as inexorable as those which attract others to the dress-circle or pit.

People who are rather deaf go there the better to hear the dialogue, and some prefer it to the dress-circle because they do not like to be "stared at," but these are mostly ladies of nervous temperament. Fast young fellows go there to be jolly; and Cyprians, with an eye to business. Inexperienced young men take their mothers, and sisters, or sweethearts there, because they think it select, and for the reason that they get a good view of the stage; and many who pay the extra price to go there would just as soon be in the pit if they could only get a good seat.

There is less lolly sucking and apple munching in the stalls than there is in the pit, though a little of both is indulged in, but in a more quiet and subdued manner; and bottles are seldom seen, except an occasional bottle of lemonade.

There is a great clearing out for the inevitable nobbler among the male occupants of the stalls as soon as the drop scene falls, and the ladies are left to take care of themselves in the best way they can during their absence.

There is as much amusement to be derived from watching the acting going on among the audience as there is in witnessing that which takes place upon the stage.

Watch the youth and maiden who have just entered, and see if it would be possible to mistake them for anything else than lovers. Notice the look of happiness in his face as, with her shawl over his arm, he leads her to a seat he thinks will give her the best view of the stage. And with what anxiety he looks after her comfort when she is seated. How different his manner is to that of the married man who has just come in with his wife. His anxiety appears to be all on his own account now, though once he was as solicitous for the comfort of his darling as our young friend is for that of the dear creature at his side. The good dame, however, appears to be quite able to take care of herself, as may be seen from the decision with which she plumps down into her seat, and settles herself comfortably to watch the performance to the end.

During the whole of the evening, the young fellow

takes but little notice of what is taking place on the stage. All his thoughts are centred in the dear object at his side. His emotions are but the reflection of hers. If she be pleased, and laugh, he laughs as well, and if she does not "think much" of the piece, he votes it scarcely worth listening to. Occasionally, as the evening creeps on, she is persuaded to dip the tips of her dainty fingers into a bag of biscuits he has brought for her delectation, and when the man comes round with the lemonade, he whisperingly suggests a bottle, but she cannot muster up sufficient courage to drink lemonade out of a bottle in such a public place. No hen, whose incubatory labours have only been blessed with one chick, could be half as anxious for its welfare as he appears to be for the comfort and happiness of his sweetheart. When the curtain falls, he wraps her in her shawl, as carefully as though he dreaded some dire results from the night air coming in contact with her ethereal body. By-and-bye, when the twain are made one flesh, he will, perhaps, think that, after all, women are only made of clay.

The patrons of the pit are found among tradesmen, shopkeepers, and labouring men of all kinds. There is another class who always go there when they go to the theatre, for the very simple reason that their means will not permit of their going to any other part—such as junior clerks, storemen, and the like, and these form small knots of three or four under the dress circle at the sides, to gossip over the news of the day, or discuss the affairs of their friends, or criticise the actresses, or talk over things theatrical. We have had many an inward snigger while we have been listening to these young fellows, when their talk has been histrionics. They appear to have the names of past and present celebrities at their fingers' ends, and discuss the subject with all the dogmatism of old stage veterans. Certainly they are seldom correct as to dates or parts; but that is of no consequence, as those they are talking to know as little about it as they do themselves.

A party of five may now be seen bustling along to get a good seat. A glance will show you that these five are composed of a man and his wife—with the baby, of course—a lady friend and her daughter, and the daughter's young man. They have evidently come with the intention of having a night's enjoyment, for the man carries a black bag, filled to repletion with all manner of good things, among which is a bottle, for the cork may be seen protruding through the clasps. There is an inconvenience attending these small parties, and that is, they all want to sit together, and they can only do that, at times, by crowding into a space where there is only room for about two, which they do without the least regard for the feelings or convenience of those already seated, which sometimes begets a little plain speaking.

The lady friend has been there before during the run of the same piece, and she takes upon herself the duty of expounding the plot, and, at the most exciting part, everyone around her has the interest destroyed by hearing her relate what is going to happen next. She has also a disagreeable habit of keeping time to the music by beating her feet upon the floor, a proceeding which is speedily taken up by the others, till it becomes pretty general, much to the disgust of those who prefer their music without such accompaniment. The baby, who has been watching the performance with great attention till the part arrives where the interest of the audience is at its highest, now calls attention to itself by crying with all the power of its vigorous lungs. The audience all over the house get indignant, and frequent cries are heard of "take it out," while one recommends its mother to sit upon it; and another, still more inhuman, suggests the advisability of throttling it. A woman, sitting close by, whose children, if she ever had any, must be all grown-up, is heard to wonder "whatever women can be thinking of to bring their babies to such places." At length the child, after its mother has exhausted all the known maternal dodges to keep it quiet, has to be taken out, and its cries are still heard from time to time in some distant part of the house.

Some of the frequenters of the pit have a disagreeable habit of munching apples all the evening, accompanied by a noise that is very trying to the nerves of those seated near them, for it is similar to that made by a pig when eating a raw turnip. Others go in for oranges, and keep sucking and talking all the night. Some take sandwiches, others biscuits, while some keep constantly crunching lollies, and perfume the air all around with the odour of peppermint. Some go provided with a small flask, from which they take a sip, and pass it round to a friend. Others take a square gin bottle filled with beer, which is poured into a teacup without a handle, and passed round to those of the party who want a drink. In fact people go to the pit to enjoy themselves, and they do so physically as well as intellectually.

The gallery is the region belonging exclusively to the larrikin class. Certainly some few working-men go there, but not many. Now the price is the same as it is in the pit. Sometimes, however, when the latter place is too crowded to be comfortable, many leave it and take their seats among the gods, where, with the exception of Saturday night, when the Olympians muster in great force, they usually find plenty of room.

Bright specimens of our colonial youth, male and female, may be seen in that part of the house. The neglected child, after running about the streets all day, finds his way there at night, the money with which he pays for admittance being probably the proceeds of some petty theft. The full-blown larrikin, hang-dog in look and careless in attire, comes there with no other apparent object than to air his filthy language, and create as much uproar as possible. Young girls, children almost, but who have, nevertheless, been on the streets for years, prefer it to the pit, because they can indulge in greater freedom of speech, and be less guarded in their actions.

The galleries are not so crowded now as they used to be when the price for admittance was only sixpence. Then it was filled nightly with some of the choicest specimens of the juvenile ruffianism hailing from the back slums, and disturbances were so frequent that the management, to keep as many of these interesting creatures out as possible, raised the price to a shilling. That had, in a great measure, the desired effect; for many who could raise a sixpence were unable to scrape together a shilling, and the houses are much quieter in consequence.

THE "BLOCK."

All large cities have a "resort" where the *haut ton*, beauty, and fashion, meet to compare notes or dresses, to admire, or be admired. In London, it is called "Rotten Row," in Paris, "Bois de Boulogne," in Berlin, "Unter den Linden," and "Rialto" in Venice. In Melbourne it is a quarter of a mile of hard flagging on the north side of Collins Street, and called the "Block."

A stranger, or that much-quoted individual, the "intelligent foreigner," who confined his observation of us to that street, would think he had landed in the Utopia he had heard something about, and that want and misery, vice and crime, were here unknown.

En passant, it appears to us that what an intelligent foreigner might think of our doings would depend greatly upon his nationality. A Frenchman — from whose capital most of the fashions emanate—would consider our ladies' dresses quite correct, while an intelligent critic from Central Africa, where a lady's walking costume is nothing more elaborate than a bead necklace, might think our damsels go about very much overdressed. Nor is personal adornment the only matter on which two intelligent foreigners might take adverse opinions. Take, for instance, our ladies' feet, called by gushing husbands, during the honeymoon, "tootsies." A gentleman from Pekin would, if he knew the colonial term, call them "bettle crushers," while the intelligent Hottentot, comparing them with the pedal supporters of the dear one he left at home, would think they were far too small for their sweet owners to go about with safety upon.

But whatever part of the world our intelligent friend came from, and however closely he might look, he would see little sign of care or anxiety on the faces of those he met "doing the Block."

The business man who has just heard news that tells him of losses to come shows no sign of it as he greets an acquaintance in his usual off-handed and cordial manner. The man on the verge of bankruptcy looks as confident as of yore, and perhaps feels more so; and nothing in the manner of that matronly-looking lady, as she sweeps along between her two daughters, tells you of the anxiety she has lately gone through in trying to make both ends meet. There are dozens who "do the Block" daily, smiling, and looking so good, and so happy, whose hearts, if they could be seen, would be found filled with despair, hopelessness, and all uncharitableness.

Dress, now-a-days, is a great leveller of outdoor distinction; therefore it must not be supposed that only those who look upon themselves as the *élite* of our society are to be found on the "Block," as the two extremes of Melbourne and suburban life meet there regularly. Ministers' wives and daughters, clergymens' ladies, the wives and daughters of merchants, and wholesale tradesmen, mechanics' wives, work-girls, servants out for a stroll, and Cyprians brush up against one another as they pass and repass.

A strange assortment of people may be seen during a stroll up and down the "Block." Every type of the human countenance is to be seen there, and every variety of the human figure, adorned in every style of garment which fashion for the moment says is the correct thing to wear.

Some awkward *rencontres*, too, are frequently witnessed there. An exquisitely-dressed swell meets a poorly-clad creditor whom he is ashamed to recognise, yet afraid to show it openly for fear of bringing matters to a crisis, so, with the best grace he can, if he must meet his eye, he gives him a friendly nod as they pass. A well-dressed lady meets her much better-dressed and more ladylike milliner; a mistress who has come to town in search of a servant from the registry-office, meets the one who left her service yesterday; and the two Misses Dash pass without recognising former friends who knew them when they were poor and but little thought of.

The most noticeable thing to be seen on the Block is the figure cut by some of the male promenaders. Who would think that that young swell in fashionably-cut clothes though it requires but half a glance to see they are slop-made— is only a clerk with the magnificent wage of twenty-five shillings per week? But it is so, nevertheless, though nothing but a life of deprivation enables him to appear as he does. With that, however, he is content if he can but show off in Collins Street whenever he has any errands to do.

Many of the exquisites who are to be seen sauntering up and down are junior partners in mercantile firms, swellish professional men, theatrical stars, celebrities of all kinds, and dandies of every description. From three till five the crowd is swollen by bankers' clerks, clerks in government offices, and some few merchants' clerks, who can get away early.

An hour or two spent on the Block is not wasted when you know who and what the people are you see there; for by noticing their outdoor demeanour, and comparing it with their everyday life at home, you get an insight into character that is both amusing and instructive.

There are certain men in society who know everyone and everything. Now we can't say we care much about the company of a man who knows everything, because he usually succeeds in convincing us we know so little ourselves, and that is not always pleasant. But we do enjoy the society of a man who knows everyone, especially if he be at all gifted as a narrator.

We have the privilege of being acquainted with such a man, and when we meet him in Collins Street, we turn him to the utmost advantage. Selecting the best point of view for seeing all who pass and re-pass, he will give us the history of most of those who come under our observation. One day, while thus standing, we noticed a stylishly-dressed young fellow coming towards us with a self-satisfied smirk upon his countenance. Suddenly that pleasant look was changed to one of confusion, and he turned short round and crossed to the other side of the street. We asked our friend if he knew him. "Oh, yes!" he answered; "he is one of old Blanks' clerks, and here comes old Blanks himself," he continued, as he indicated a rather seedy-looking old gentleman coming towards us. The confused look upon the clerk's face, and the abrupt alteration in his course, were thus easily accounted for; but we could not exactly understand why it should be so, unless he were taking a surreptitious stroll, instead of attending to his duties, so we asked our friend for an explanation.

"Well, you see," he answered, "this young fellow only gets two pounds a week, and lives at the rate of five or six. How he manages it is only known to himself at present. By-and-bye we may be let into his confidence. In the meantime, however, he lets old Blanks see as little of his unofficial life as possible, for he knows perfectly well that that old gentleman is quite alive as to the purchasing power of forty shillings."

"Who is this young lady coming along sucking the handle of her parasol?" we asked, looking toward an elegantly-dressed and rather pretty young lady.

"That's Belinda," he replied. "Her father is the most perfect old miser that ever lived. How she manages to wheedle the money out of him to dress like that is a marvel. He is immensely rich, as he well might be, for he has never spent sixpence in his life where threepence would do. He is very fond of his daughter, however, with all her faults, and lets her do precisely as she likes. She is not a bad-hearted girl, although she has broken the hearts of half-a-dozen young fellows, who each had an eye to her prospective fortune. She is rather inclined to be fast, it is true, but, having plenty of sense, she will settle down and make the best wife in the colony when she sees the man she likes well enough to marry. Whoever that lucky fellow may be, he will be doubly blessed, in having a treasure in his wife, and another in the old man's money-bags."

"You see that fellow coming along in the black bell-topper," he shortly afterwards said, alluding to one who came along soon after; "that's the biggest scoundrel out of Pentridge. He lets everyone in who has anything to do with him where money is concerned; and the most marvellous thing about it is, he does the same person repeatedly. He has a good billet, and could live comfortably even by keeping within his income; but that does not agree with his ideas of what life should be, nor with the notions he entertains of his own importance. It is wonderful how he has contrived to carry on as long as he has, for the tradesmen he deals with are no fools in their transactions with their ordinary customers, neither is modesty in dunning one of their failings. It must be owing to his sublime "cheek" and plausible manner, which are sometimes successful where modesty would fail. He is a great gambler, among other things, and is generally lucky, in fact suspiciously so; but nothing has hitherto been discovered against his play, so he is allowed to keep on."

He now directed our attention to two rather loudly-dressed ladies who came swaggering along, occupying nearly the whole width of the pavement, and making those they met deploy to the right and left, while they passed. It was not necessary for him to tell me what they were, their manner sufficiently indicated that.

There is one thing that must strike an observer as he passes up and down the "Block," and that is, the number of extremely ugly faces that are to be seen among the male promenaders. We occasionally see a fine, handsome fellow, it is true, but many others have a strong facial resemblance to certain tribes of monkeys one sees in the larger menageries at home. It is not only in features the likeness is to be noticed. They imitate many of their actions and manners. What can be more similar than the frightful grin they bestow upon a lady to whom they raise the hat? Or what can be more natural than the monkey-like impertinence with which they stare at every well-dressed lady they meet? And how much their talk, when two or three of them meet, sounds like the chatter of as many monkeys, only not quite so musical. In fact, a stroll up and down Collins Street will do more in an hour to convince one of the possibility of Darwin's theory being correct than the ablest treatise that could be written in support of it.

When the young ladies and gentlemen meet, how cordial their manners appear to be with each other! How affable they seem! How the musical laugh of the ladies is echoed in the not quite so musical cachinnation of the gentlemen; and when they separate, with what ineffable condescension the ladies offer the tips of their neatly-gloved fingers; having shaken which, how gracefully the gentlemen reply, by lifting the hat. As soon as they have parted, however, what a change may be seen in their looks. The smile remains, but it is now one of derision. The lips that have just been paying compliments now give utterance to remarks the reverse of flattering.

"What donkeys!" say the ladies.

"Expensive, but not elegant," say the gentlemen.

Fondness for the "Block" is not confined to the young. The middle-aged and the elderly are equally partial to a stroll up and down, provided they can dress well enough to appear in the midst of the gorgeous display of millinery and sartorial excellence one sees there.

It has been irreverently said, that God's noblest work would be incomplete without the tailor. Of course, that is open to discussion, but it is very evident that the part performed by the tailor is the part most admired at the present day, at least, when he is a fashionable one; for then, and then only, is the man considered perfect. The same person who, if dressed in fashionable attire, would be received with open arms on the "Block," would, if dressed in fustian, or cotton print, be looked upon as being as much out of place there as a pig would be in a drawing-room.

Such being the case, is it to be wondered at that the poorly-paid clerk half starves himself in order to appear well dressed, and have a brief flutter among the many-hued butterflies who disport themselves daily on the hard flags of Collins Street?

Some of those who cut such fine figures in that street would not be walking backwards and forwards there if they were compelled to pay their debts. There are, to our own certain knowledge, men to be seen there daily who have not a stitch on their backs they could truthfully call their own. The clothes they wear are unpaid for; the money that should have paid for their hats has been spent at the opera; their bootmakers sigh in vain for the money for the last new pair of boots; and the hosier is not a whit more fortunate than the others.

We often think tradesmen must use customers of this sort as walking advertisements, otherwise it is hard to understand why they allow men whose wages, in many instances, are below those of a skilful artisan to get so much in their debt, when the probability of their ever being paid is so remote.

There is something about the "Block," that has a bad

effect upon the eyesight of those who frequent it. At least, such appears to be the case, from the number of times one notices a well-dressed young fellow pass an acquaintance not quite so well dressed, without being able to see him; while in Elizabeth Street, a few yards off, he will stop him, and have a chat, and even condescend to drink at his expense, if invited thereunto.

Between one and two may be seen a pretty fair sprinkling of junior clerks and work-girls, who, having eaten their bread and meat, bath-bun, or half-a-pound of mixed biscuits, or whatever else they may have had for lunch, go there to spend the remainder of the hour—the young men to air their dignity and leer at the girls, and the girls to be leered at.

It is amusing to watch these young fellows as they swagger up and down; and to listen to the snatches of their conversation they take care you shall hear as they pass. About the time of the races their talk is "horse;" during the opera season, Signor this, or Signora that, are their themes, as if they understood an atom of one subject or the other!

The best time to see the "Block" is from eleven till one on a fine Saturday morning. Here the ladies, middle-aged and young, come to meet their husbands, papas, brothers, or sweethearts, who leave business early on that day. It is a bustling sight, for all the suburbs appear to have sent large contingents of wealth and beauty to give animation to the scene. At that time the ladies have it nearly all to themselves, and a glorious show they make of it. The bright colours of their dresses, their happy looks, and eyes sparkling with excitement, lend a charm to the scene that is pleasant to behold.

The daughters of Israel, having just left the synagogue in Bourke Street, show up about that time in great numbers. They, too, enjoy the scene with, if possible, more zest than their Nazarene sisters, and laugh and chatter, and shoot sly glances at any young member of their own "people" who may happen to be there airing his factory-made Sabbath clothes, and drawing Elysium through the amber mouthpiece of his cigarette-holder at the same time.

Saturday being a school holiday, the younger members

of the family come with their mammas to meet papa, and "do the Block."

Their fresh ingenuous looks are in great contrast with the artificial and affected manners of some who are but a few years their seniors ; while their careless gaity shows how delightful the change from the school-room to a stroll up and down that crowded thoroughfare is.

THE ELITE.

All things have a beginning, aristocracies included, and as we have in our midst an aristocracy in process of formation, it may be interesting to know how and from what kind of people they originate.

History tells us what the aristocracies in the older countries were; and as we can see with our own eyes what the fathers and mothers of our future grandees are like at present, and knowing what they have been in the past, it must be acknowledged that, as individuals, they are much more respectable than many of the founders of the old houses of Europe, who, as a rule, were men of very questionable habits.

Some of them advanced themselves by practices that were considered correct enough in those days, but which would, if indulged in by their descendants at the present time, procure them a lengthened seclusion from society; or, in other words, they were simply thieves, and very vulgar ones, to boot. But that was in the good old times, when it was thought no man had a right to more than he could keep.

The founders of some of the more modern " families" were men who received their titles as a well-merited recognition of services rendered to their country, either on the battle-field, or in the council chamber; or for having made themselves renowned in some laudable pursuit.

How many generations does it require to convert the plebeian blood of the ennobled commoner, or enriched tradesman, into the *sangre azul* of the aristocrat? Or, does the patent of the sovereign, while dignifying the body, alter the tint of the blood, and make it less turbid, at the same time?

All the men who are at the head of our society have

risen by their own efforts. None of the positions were inherited. Many were gentlemen, and scholars, and would rank as such in any country in the world. Some were just sufficiently educated for mercantile pursuits; and others were as innocent of "book learning" as men could well be. But whatever intellectual difference there may have been between them, they all started pretty equally as to money matters.

One would think that in the race for wealth, the better educated would secure the prizes, but it has not been so here, at all events; for the unlettered have done as well, if not better, than the highly cultured. There are men in this city whose fortunes will run into six or seven figures so strangely illiterate that they hardly know sufficient of caligraphy to sign their names to a cheque.

People are apt to say, when they hear of an ignorant man getting rich, "How much better he would have done if he had been well educated." Well, perhaps, not. One of the objects of education is to improve the mind, and when that has been done, men see things in a different light to that in which they formerly looked at them, and that makes them pause before undertaking many things they would not have hesitated about before. While they are hesitating, others, less scrupulous, push in, and do it for them, and the only benefit they derive from their mental improvement is the satisfaction of knowing they have left some questionable transaction undone to their own pecuniary disadvantage.

Noblesse oblige. If titles compel men to walk circumspectly, it might, perhaps, be better if they were a little more freely distributed, for the recipients would think so much more of themselves, and consequently behave better; and others would hold them in greater estimation, and there would be less evil speaking; for a title, like the mantle of charity, covers a multitude of sins.

How quickly, too, the change is perceptible. What a difference there is in the plain Mr. and Sir Timothy Blank within twenty-four hours after receiving the accolade. How much more upright he stands. How affable and patronising he is to those who were but yesterday his equals; while his acquaintances, who had hitherto failed to "see much" in Mr. Blank, now detect qualities of a high order in Sir Timothy.

The glory of the title is also reflected with but slightly diminished lustre upon all his surroundings. His better half is not long in letting the servants know that their mistress is now a "Lady," and Miss Blank comforts herself in a way she would hardly have done a week ago.

Mr. Tom, who expects one day to inherit the title, appears to have become as sedate as though he had received an instalment of ten years of his allotted number. The principal of the school where he is being educated quickly lets the people living round about him know that he has the son of a "sir" among his scholars; and the parents of these boys look forward hopefully to the advantages their sons may one day derive from contact with an embryonic baronet; while the scholars themselves put up with many things from him now they would have threatened to punch his head for a few days ago. Even the servants acquire a *distingué* manner they were strangers to before. The tradesmen and shopkeepers become more civil and attentive, for it is a capital advertisement having titled people among their customers. The house gets a coat of paint to set off its master's coat of arms; the carriage and horses look more aristocratic; the garden is made trim, and the lawn, if any, gets a clean shave.

Although we can see the formation of our aristocracy, unfortunately we shall not live to see it in its full maturity, but there cannot be a doubt it will bear comparison with that of any country whatsoever. Our married magnates, knowing the advantages of education —though, as has been observed before, many of them only derive that knowledge from the absence of it in themselves—take care to give their children as good a one as they are capable of receiving. In the course of a few generations the intellectual improvement they will have undergone will have refined their tastes, and improved their minds; and as the mind influences the features, the rugged visages we so frequently see in high places now will have become softened into a more classic type.

Some of our *élite* are open-handed in their liberality, endowing colleges, and bestowing munificent gifts in various other directions. Others again, who are now millionaires, remembering their struggles with poverty in the early times, think they know the value of money too well to give much of it away, and hug their wealth to their bosoms as fondly as a mother does her first-born babe.

Brian Boroo landed in Melbourne just about the time of the gold discovery. Money was then to be made, and he soon displayed a remarkable aptitude in making it; and not only that, but he has been quite as clever in knowing how to keep it.

He is now well up on the social ladder; he keeps his horses and his buggy; he is on the Commission of the Peace, and has been in the "House;" he has a suburban residence, and his income may be set down at thousands: but he is Brian Boroo still. Wealth has not improved him, nor added much to his polish, though it may have caused his opinions to change on many matters. What was white when he was poor is black now he is rich. Men who came out with him and have not risen he ignores. His early acquaintance with the bogs is forgotten, or, if his mind ever does go back so far, it is to wonder how long the old sow has been dead, and if the peat is as hard to dig as ever.

As for Pat, and Mick, and the other boys who used to trot the bogs with him, he wouldn't know them if he were to meet them. He is very exacting as to outward observance of respect, and he tries hard to cut a figure, but however much he may try he cannot hide the tinpot. It shows at home, it shows in his buggy, and it shows on the bench, but at no time does it show more plainly than when he opens his mouth.

He is a great believer in the divine right of the wealthy few to govern the impecunious many. He, the once shoeless, though now possessor of untold thousands, looks upon himself, ignorant and vulgar though he be, as one of those intended by nature to rule the destinies of that portion of his fellow-citizens he contemptuously calls the "people."

He has educated his children, and no doubt instilled into their minds the high position the Boroos held in society in the olden times and how they must sustain the reputation of the family in times to come.

It is not known if he has begun to trace his descent from the "ould ancient" kings of Ireland ; but, if he has not, it is because his education has been so neglected that the history of Ireland is a book as far beyond his comprehension as it would be if it were written in Greek.

His children rank among the Australian aristocracy. And why not? They are well educated, and as good as the general run of mankind, though, perhaps, the rough model they have had in their father may have given shape to some of their characteristics. But that will become fainter and fainter with each succeeding generation, till at last every trace of it will have disappeared altogether, and they will sit side by side with, and be in every way equal to, the descendants of our merchant princes.

Chips is another member of our *élite*, and will be recorded in the future Australian Debrett as the founder of the Chips family.

He landed here with a few tools, and the scarcely to be perceived rudiments of an education, but to compensate for the latter deficiency, he had an abundant stock of conceit, and a keen eye for looking after the interests of Mr. Chips. At that time, land in convenient blocks went begging for buyers, and at a price that brought it within the reach of all who chose to invest their savings in that very safe investment. Chips was then earning good wages, and as fast as he saved a few pounds he bought land and kept it, or, as he elegantly termed it, "let it sweat," till it would fetch a better price. Out of small beginnings sprang large endings, and it would be hard for him to tell, at the present time, within a few thousands, how much he is really worth.

It is to a man's credit to raise himself from a low position in society to a high one, if he can do so by honourable means; but, having done so, it is hardly becoming for him to look down upon others, former friends, who have remained poor, as though they belonged to an inferior order of beings. At one time he was as ignorant of his own natural superiority as other people were, and if he had remained poor, he would be ignorant of it still. But when the fickle goddess began to smile upon him, and he added house to house, nature asserted herself, and the man began to appear. When joining field to field his mind expanded, and he speedily recognised the fact that those who rise in the world are better than those who remain low; and that Fortune only smiles upon those whom nature intended to be the recipients of her favours.

If there be any superiority about him, it springs entirely from nature. He owes nothing whatever, except a little reading and writing, to art; with that all his accomplishments end. Still he tries to shake off the sawdust, and to surround himself with a halo of respectability. He dresses in black, and attends regularly at church, where his demeanour is strictly orthodox, and, as far as appearances go, he is an ornament to the pew he occupies.

His children are highly educated, and are altogether a wonderful improvement upon the author of their existence. The girls are accomplished, and the sons rising in their several callings, and as it does not necessarily follow that they should inherit the old man's personal qualities along with his money, they will not be the least worthy of our Colonial aristocracy.

Chips is no fool, at least not in the sense the term is usually put, for he possesses a fair amount of natural shrewdness, and that lands him pretty safely from most of the enterprises he embarks in. What folly he does manifest springs entirely from conceit and ignorance, and the pride which is begotten of wealth.

Rigida made her *début* in the kitchen, in the useful but not very high capacity of kitchen-maid. At that time she possessed a tolerable share of good looks, and she was perfectly well aware of that fact herself. Moreover, she was thoroughly convinced that the kitchen was not her proper place, and that she was intended by nature to move in a higher sphere, and she regulated her conduct accordingly. The master she then served had a soft heart, which she speedily detected, and turned to advantage. He proposed marriage, and she blushingly consented. He was then very rich, having just retired from business with an ample fortune. As a business man he had the reputation of being shrewd and lucky. On retiring, however, it was very soon seen that, sharp as he may have been in making money while in business, he was equally clever in getting rid of it, when he had nothing else to do.

That state of things did not altogether meet with Rigida's approval, as she was perfectly well aware that there are contingencies in married life no prudent couple ought to overlook. By judicious management and proper representations, she brought her husband over to her own way of thinking, namely, that money spent unnecessarily is so much money wasted. The poor man fell a martyr to his family devotion. He could neither make money nor spend it, and as they were the only two occupations that made life worth living, he pined away, and died shortly after they had been married two years. By that time, two of the contingencies aforethought had arrived, with a third *in prospectu*. The late lamented, as all dutiful husbands ought to do, had made his will absolutely in favour of his wife, feeling sure she would watch over the interests of their children. In that belief he was quite right, for, although self-seeking when single, self was merged in her children now that she was a mother, and few more devoted ones have ever lived.

Reaching the drawing-room via the kitchen is by no means the social bar here which it is at home, always provided the manners rise as well. The widow was visited, and "received" by the *ton* of Melbourne, and well she deserved it, for there had been as great a transformation in her manners as in her fortunes, and few would have believed that the elegantly-dressed lady who received her visitors with so much grace had graduated in the lower regions of the establishment.

Volumnia is fond of talking of her friends at home, especially of her aunt, Lady This, and of her cousin the Hon Miss That, and of the style she used to live in. She is well up in the names and history of the peerage, and can relate something about most of the old county families. She is well educated, and of easy manners, and might pass unobserved if she would only talk a little less.

She has displayed considerable taste in furnishing her house, but there are a few expensive articles brought prominently forward, or talked about rather too much. Her principal themes in conversation are my horses, my carriages, my servants, or whatever else she may have which is only possessed by the few.

In music she goes in for high class. "*Ah! de la morte*" is her delight, and everything else that has not an Italian name to it, her abomination. She is not over liberal with her money, but when she does give she likes it to be known, that others may go and do likewise—at least, it is only charitable to suppose that is her reason.

She is very clever, she can do everything well but talk, that she cannot do; not that she says anything that would shock Lindley Murray; she is only unhappy in her subjects. She will talk, and that is her misfortune.

Such are a few specimens of the Australian *élite*. We could have given examples of another kind, of men who are gentlemen by education and instinct, and in every way worthy of being the founders of our future aristocracy. Not that those we have mentioned are unworthy in themselves, they are only unfortunate in not having been able to improve their minds with their fortunes.

THE MARKETS.

From the earliest times the market has been an important place in a city. In Rome it was called the "Forum," but it was not confined to the sale of provisions, and the usual odds and ends that are brought to market to be sold. It was there the Prætor meted out justice to peccant citizens.

In ancient Greece and in Palestine it was the same. When Paul and Silas were at Thyatira, they met a damsel possessed with a spirit of divination, which spirit they cast out. This young lady was what we call now a "fortune-teller," for we are told she "brought her masters much gain by soothsaying." When these enterprising individuals saw "the hope of their gains was gone," they caught the two apostles and "drew them into the market-place unto the rulers," and having made out a case to the satisfaction of the multitude, the magistrates rent off the clothes, and ordered Paul and Silas to be beaten.

The market must, also, have been a place of public resort, for we have it on the authority of St. Mark that the Scribes loved salutations in the market-places; and it is further said that our Saviour disputed daily in the market with those He met there.

In former times, in England, the market was held in the churchyard on Sunday mornings, for the convenience of those who wished to provide for their temporal wants, as well as their spiritual. That strange custom was often prohibited during times of religious enthusiasm; and as often re-established, as soon as matters had cooled down, till it was finally abolished in Henry VI.'s time. Till recently, in many places they continued to hold the market in the churchyard, but not on Sundays.

In the centre of most, if not in all, market-places in

England a cross was erected, at the foot of which religious services were held, and where, also, in times of popular ferment, demagogues harangued the excited crowds who met there to ventilate their grievances.

A "Court of Pie Powder" was held in every market, for the settlement of market disputes. The name of these courts is derived from "*pieds poudreux*," dusty feet, denoting that the litigants had just come off the roads to have their quarrel adjusted. The offences which came within the jurisdiction of this court were assaults, giving short weight or measure, slander, and any other of the many complaints likely to arise in a congregation of rival dealers. The slander spoken of consisted in Hodge depreciating Giles' "turmuts," or "wuts," or whatever else he might have had in the market for sale.

The offence complained of must have been committed in the market, during market hours, and on the same day, otherwise the court had no jurisdiction. Any of the parties dissatisfied with the decisions of this court could appeal against them at the court at Westminster.

The most important of all the English markets was Smithfield. It was there, on the 23rd August, 1305, that the brave Sir William Wallace was executed. Dragged at the tails of horses to the place of execution, he was hanged on a gallows as high as that intended for Mordecai. When cut down, he was drawn and quartered; which means he was drawn on a hurdle, and his limbs severed from the body. These limbs were afterwards distributed with rigid impartiality in different places in England and Scotland. His right arm was set up for the people to gaze upon at Newcastle; his left at Berwick. His right leg was publicly exposed at Perth, and his left at Aberdeen; whilst his head was stuck on a spike at London Bridge. All this was done as a warning to all and sundry not to play at the game called by one side treason, and by the other patriotism.

At Smithfield, also, on the 15th June, 1381, Wat Tyler received his quietus from Sir William Walworth's dagger. Before Tyburn was made the place of public execution, criminals were hanged there, at a spot called the "Elms," so named from a clump of those trees growing there. It was there Jack Straw, Wat Tyler's lieutenant, was hanged the day after his chief's death.

By a statute of Henry VIII., poisoners were boiled to death in Smithfield market; the *modus operandi* being to fasten the condemned ones in a kind of chair, and dip them into a boiling cauldron till they were dead.

At Smithfield, also, were burned at the stake those who preferred martyrdom to renouncing their faith; and there, too, a similar fate awaited those convicted of "Petit treason." Petit treason is when a servant murders his master, or a wife her husband. For the latter offence, a woman was, in 1652, publicly burned before an unsympathetic crowd of gaping onlookers. She was the last of the long array of those who had expiated by fire the sin of differing in opinion from others, or using a knife to sever the nuptial knot.

Melbourne is pretty well off for markets, being able to boast of eight—two for vegetables and dairy produce, one each for meat and fish and fruit, one for hay, another for horses and cattle, and one for pigs.

Of the two vegetable markets, the Eastern, at the top of Bourke Street, and the Victoria, the latter is the more important, as it is more central, and can supply a larger area of the population. It extends from Queen to Peel Streets, along Victoria Street. It is formed of a number of avenues, with corrugated iron roofs. The floor where the dealers stand is flagged; while the part devoted to the horses and carts is pitched.

The Chinese contingent to the army of market-gardeners is a very large one; they are not so noisy as their Caucasian brethren, but are apparently quite as fond of "chaffing" each other, if one may judge from the broad grins to be seen on their yellow faces, and the twinkle in their almond eyes, when three or four of them are conversing together, while waiting the advent of their customers.

"John's" method of doing business is so well known that no customer would ever think of giving him anything like the price he asks for his wares. An offer of about half is made, and if the smiling Celestial thinks that is not sufficient, the haggling is continued till the things change hands at about 25 per cent. less than the original demand.

One avenue of the market is devoted to dairy produce, where butter in tubs and in pound and half-pound pats is laid out on clean cloths in trays, and offered to the onlooking housewives by clean, wholesome-looking women in white sleeves at a penny a pound less than they can buy it at the shops. Eggs, packed in chaff, tempt the thrifty dames by their size and cheapness; a sucking-pig, with an orange in its mouth, is stretched out at full length on the tail-board of a cart, where, also, are displayed joints of fresh pork, guaranteed dairy fed. Attention is drawn by vociferous merchants to the unrivalled quality of their cheese, hams, bacon, and pickled-pork, spread out so temptingly on boards placed upon trestles; ketchup in wine bottles, and tomato sauce in jars and pickle bottles, tempt those whose tastes incline to those condiments; and honey in the comb and in jars and pots make the mouths of people with a sweet tooth water.

Lovers of veal can sometimes buy in that avenue the whole side of a calf for two shillings or half-a-crown. Certainly they are rather small, and the bones are not usually overburdened with meat—in fact, so little of the latter is there to be seen that the calves when alive must have been "staggering bobs" indeed.

Another avenue in the market is given over to the sale of butcher's meat, where the price of a side of mutton varies from "two bob," as the seller calls it, to half-a-crown; while lamb ranges from the first-mentioned sum to three and sixpence, the side at the latter price appearing to be really good wholesome meat.

Mutton at two shillings a side can hardly be considered a "dainty dish to set before a king," but for a poor man with a large family, whose wife, for want of means, has not much choice in the selection of the Sunday joint, it is well it can be had at that price. Nor can it be said of those sides of mutton as King David spoke of his enemies, "They are inclosed in their own fat," for they are about as innocent of fat as sides of mutton can well be.

Until some authority settles the point, it will alway be doubtful where veal ends and beef begins, for joints of what is called veal are sometimes exposed for sale in that market which should convince the most inexperienced that, if the calf from which they had been taken had not developed into a bullock when killed, it must have been just on the point of doing so.

To enumerate the various kinds of vegetables brought to this market would be to give a list of the whole edible vegetation of the Colony, as nothing that grows in the garden or orchard that omnivorous man delights in is left out. The quantity, too, brought there every market morning is simply astounding, and one naturally wonders where it all goes to, and who they are that eat it, for that it is eaten must be taken for granted. It shows, at all events, that the people of Melbourne have healthy appetites, and the means of getting the wherewithal to satisfy them.

By five o'clock the market-gardeners are at their "stands," and the dealers soon after begin to arrive, the latter being that portion of the retailers who believe in the proverb which tells us it is the early bird that catches the worm. These come early to see how the market is supplied, and to get the pick of that of which there is the least; thus they steal a march upon those who prefer their beds to business.

By six the business has commenced in earnest. The dealers now flock in from all quarters, and as they go round the market to see how the prices rule, their noisy inquiries may be heard on every side, while the harsh voices of the men and the shrill notes of the women are heard in reply, coupled with the usual guarantee of the superiority of their wares over everyone else's; and the chatter of the Celestials, in which "no fear" and "no gammon" are the only words intelligible to the barbarian ear, adds to the din, and makes a perfect babel of voices.

It is amusing to listen to the haggling that takes place over nearly everything that is sold. The price asked in the first instance counts for nothing, as the buyer's intention to give it is as remote as the farmer's expectation of getting it.

At this time, housekeepers who have a fancy for going early to market begin to appear. Ladies, with an unmistakable look about them of being up before their usual time, come with their husbands or grown-up children to get the vegetables for the morrow, and the eggs and butter for the ensuing week. This class of customers sometimes come from a great distance, so far indeed that one would think the little they save in the cost of the provisions, and the trouble of carrying them home, would hardly compensate them for their self-denial in rising so early; but people fancy what they buy in the market much more than they do the things they get in the shops. In addition to that they believe, in consequence of their appetites being so much keener at breakfast time, that early rising and the walk does them good; and they are undoubtedly right.

Sometimes a young newly-married couple, still in the full enjoyment of the honeymoon, may be seen winding their way in and out of the crowd, carrying with them the small purchases they have made for the morrow, which mostly consists of one or two sticks of celery, a cauliflower, two or three pounds of apples, and, perhaps, half a dozen eggs tied up in a handkerchief. At present their wants in that line are small, far different from those of the matronly-looking lady yonder, with her four children, who come there regularly every Saturday morning. The eldest boy staggers along under the weight of a pillow-case filled to its mouth with various kinds of vegetables, which he carries first on his shoulder, then under his arm; anon he clasps both his arms round it, and bears it in front as though it were some cherished object he held in a fond embrace. With all his attention to his burden, however, he is not unmindful of himself, for all the time he is munching an apple with the most unmistakable gusto. A grown-up daughter carries a basket filled with apples, as may be seen from its being so full that the lid will not go down; she is also eating an apple, and from the way she distorts her pretty mouth, it is evidently not a sweet one. One of the other boys has a large water melon under each arm, and an apple in each hand. The other has a basket containing butter and eggs on one arm, and some sticks of celery and rhubarb under the other; but, in spite of his arms being thus occupied, he contrives to reach his mouth with the inevitable apple. The good dame leads the way home with a small basket of tomatoes in one hand, and a bunch of flowers in the other, and is the only one of the party who is not discussing an apple.

Young ladies and their sweethearts frequently visit the market about this time, but more with a view to witnessing the busy scene than to make purchases. If, however, they do buy anything, it is a little fruit for immediate consumption, or a bunch of flowers to take home.

Young ladies in twos and threes go round, perhaps, once during the summer, and for ever after they tell their friends they rise early and go to market, and maybe they believe it themselves.

Elderly valetudinarian gentlemen, who cannot sleep in the morning, stroll round when it is fine for the benefit of their health, or in search of an appetite.

Occasionally a couple of swells, whose seedy manners tell of the previous night's debauch, may be seen wandering about the market, with no other apparent object in view than to let people see how silly they are.

A few "vags" of all ages and both sexes, who have just left the holes and corners where they have passed the night, prowl round the carts and stalls with an eye to whatever may be lying about.

Homeless children, vags in embryo, watch, with sharp, hungry looks, for an opportunity of abstracting something wherewith to appease their hunger.

Ownerless dogs wander in and out with tails depressed, looking wistfully in the faces of all they meet, perhaps in the hope of finding a new master—though why they should look for one in such a crowded place, where kicks and objurgations are all they are likely to get, is difficult for one who is not acquainted with the working of the canine mind to understand.

At seven o'clock the thrifty housewives continue to arrive to buy cases of fruit for preserving, or tomatoes for making sauce, or eggs and butter for the week's consumption, or whatever else they may require.

About this time may be heard a tremendous uproar among the poultry. The hens scream out a shrill protest against being dragged out of the coop by the legs, and having their ribs pinched by intending purchasers; the geese stretch their long necks through the bars of the crate they are confined in, and seem amazed at the bustling crowd around them, while with piteous looks they manifest an anxiety to get out that shows they little know what the future has in store for them; but that look of meekness gives place to a gleam of anger, and their mild cackling changes to a cry of indignation as they are held up by the legs, that their weight and fitness for the table may be ascertained. Nor are the ducks more silent than the others, while being manipulated by those who wish to purchase them with a view to future eggs; and the voices of the turkeys too are heard as they get their share of turning over and prodding by the fingers of people who must think the poor birds have no feeling.

At eight o'clock the private purchasers still continue to pour in, but these are mostly people who have not sufficient resolution to rise earlier, or women who could not leave home sooner in consequence of having to get their husbands' breakfasts in time for them to be at work at eight o'clock.

At nine, those who habitually come late begin to arrive, and these are the knowing ones, who wait till the rush of the business is over in order to get what is left at a cheaper rate, as they know perfectly well that the farmers and market-gardeners rather than take their things back will sell them for what they will fetch. Many of the late comers are costermongers, who prefer cheapness to quality, and restaurant keepers, who give a dinner of three courses for sixpence; and to do that it is evident they must exercise a deal of judgment in going to market.

Much amusement may be derived in listening to the wrangling going on between buyer and seller while a sale is being negotiated. A Chinaman walks up to a dealer in poultry, and asks the price of a pair of fowls.

"Four and six," responds the dealer.

"No fear," says John; "me no givit."

He then dives his hand into the coop and pulls out an unfortunate fowl by the legs, and feels her all over to ascertain the amount of edible matter there may be upon her bones.

"Too muchee," continues the Mongolian. "Welly small, not muchee fat, no good. Me givit three shilling sixpenny."

The usual result in these cases is that they split the difference, as it is called, that is, the flowery-lander would get the fowls for four shillings.

Few sales are effected without a deal of "chaff" on

both sides, and often angry words pass backwards and forwards, much to the edification of those looking on.

One morning a man asked the price of a turkey. "Seven and six," was the reply. The man offered seven shillings, when the farmer, an Irishman, told him to go to a place that's much too warm to be pleasant. That of course begot a retort quite as polite, accompanied by an indignant protest against being spoken to in such a manner when civilly trying to transact business. At that the farmer somewhat softened, and said although he told him to go there, he didn't wish him to do so. Upon that explanation being given, they resumed negotiations, and the turkey found a fresh owner at the farmer's price.

Besides that which is required to strengthen the inner man, many other things that are needed in a household are to be bought in that market.

Wickerwork of every description, from small baskets to perambulators, occupy no small space on the flags. Flowering shrubs and small trees, with their roots done up in matting, are at the command of those who delight in arboriculture, while flowers in pots, and flowers in bunches, with small posies for the button-hole, silently appeal to those who can appreciate nature in such a pleasant guise.

Crockeryware of the useful kind is spread out upon the pavement in great variety and profusion. Bric-à-brac, such as cheap chimney ornaments, and curios of all kinds are displayed with some taste to tempt the workingman's wife into buying a few to ornament her parlour.

Drapery of every description, from a needle to a lady's improver, is set out to the best advantage on a large board to catch the eye of any fair visitor who may happen to be in want of anything in that line.

Every description of second-hand ironmongery, such as tools, locks and bolts, dog-chains and collars, picks, crowbars, shovels and coal-scuttles are thrown together in a confused pile, along with blocks and pulleys, shoemakers' lasts, and iron buckets.

Cheap clothing, new and second-hand, the latter guaranteed as good as new, with hats of all shapes and make, are there for the benefit of those whose outer man needs readorning.

The Markets. 103

Boots and shoes, from a baby's shoe to a navvy's heavy boot, and slippers in great variety, with bottles of "Peerless gloss," "Jet blacking," and wonderful "Kid-reviver," may be obtained by those who stand in need of them. Side by side with these are worsted and leather laces, long and short, and little bags of boot protectors, at four pence per bag, enough, as the merchant assures the customer, to make his boots last till the uppers are worn out.

Cheap jewellery of all kinds is invitingly laid out to tempt those of gaudy tastes. These latter articles must be brought for the benefit of the country folks, to take home to their wives or daughters or sweethearts, as the Melbourne people have a much larger and more showy stock to choose from in various parts of the city.

Bottles of scent and scented soap, tooth-brushes and tooth-powder, pearl-powder, and puff-boxes, wherewith ladies of doubtful complexion may make themselves "beautiful for ever," are laid out by the side of boxes of hairpins, and many other ingenious contrivances for fastening up the ladies' hair.

Feather dusters, hair brooms, and scrubbing-brushes commend themselves to the tidy housewife should she need any, while glass ware of every kind, and cheap, can be bought in that market, along with dolls of all sizes, some clothed, others in the nude state, and toys of every description, from Noah's arks to marbles.

There is a restaurant in the market, where the market-gardeners and others can get a substantial breakfast for sixpence. It does one good to see with what gusto the sausages and potatoes, saturated with what is supposed to be gravy, are discussed by the hungry countrymen. The fire looks bright and cheerful, and it warms one to look at it on a cold morning; and the hissing of the fat in which the sausages, and chops, or steaks are fried, has a cheery sound, while the odour arising from the onions fried with them is of sweet savour to those going in to partake, but it must be very tantalising to the hungry ones standing around who lack the needful sixpence.

RESTAURANTS.

We are indebted to the French for that very appropriate word. It means "restorative," and is applied to a place where the hungry, toil-weary man can get sufficiently "restored" to resume the labours by which he earns the wherewithal that will procure future "restorations" for himself and those dependent upon him.

Food is not the only want we have, though it is by far the most urgent; if it were, but little exertion would be needed to supply it, and we should still be wandering about in a state of nature. Civilization, however, among its other blessings, has increased our wants in an extraordinary manner, and made us absolutely dependent upon one another, as we must, in order to obtain the means of supplying our own wants, minister to those of others.

Not the least important of those who look after the wants of others are the restaurant-keepers, of whom there are great numbers in Melbourne.

There are two kinds of restaurants—the high-priced and the low. In one you pay a shilling for a meal, and in the other sixpence. We use the two terms comparatively, for a shilling is not an extravagant sum to have to pay for a meal, but it is large as compared with sixpence, when you can get a meal equally as good for the latter sum. The only difference between the dear ones and cheap is that the company in one is more select than that in the other. The meals are precisely the same; the meat of as good quality, as well cooked, and as much in quantity. It is true, those who wish it can have a glass of ale with their lunch in the former, while in the latter they have to put up with a cup of tea.

Some people like to keep up appearances—that is, spend more in display than they can afford, and that either leads to bankruptcy or to the deprivation of much solid comfort.

There are many men in whose *ménage* the saving of sixpence in a meal would be of great consideration, who prefer lunching at the dearer restaurants rather than run the risk of being seen entering or leaving one of the cheap ones, while some, who always indulge in a sixpenny "feed," exercise a vast amount of ingenuity in trying to make people believe that they always patronise the better class of restaurants and luncheon-rooms. Some young fellows, who like to keep up appearances at lunch-time, have adopted a novel and inexpensive method of doing it. They bring their luncheons in their pockets from home, and having eaten them in the office or store, stroll out and stand for ten or fifteen minutes picking their teeth in front of one or other of the fashionable restaurants in Collins or Swanston Streets.

Much of human nature may be learnt in a restaurant. In private life men are restrained by the laws of society from giving way to their natural impulses at meal times. In the restaurant, however, it is different. There men think only of filling the vacuities in their stomachs, and trouble themselves but little as to what those around them may think of the way in which it is done—of course, without there being anything gross or offensive about it. Some hang their hats on the pegs and eat the meal uncovered. Others keep their hats on while eating; but these, we have noticed, are usually the baldheaded ones, who are not particularly anxious to let people know of their capillary deficiencies. Some, who at home would never think of putting the knife to the mouth, are not so particular here, especially when it is used to convey to it a consignment of cabbage. Some commence almost before the waiter, or waitress, has put the plate down, and eat as ravenously as though they were famishing. Others eat slowly and as deliberately as if they thought it was the last meal they were going to have, and wished to spin it out as long as possible; and one or two, we have noticed, offer up a silent grace before making their onslaught. Some, while eating, make as much noise with the mouth as a pig does when eating, and we have invariably noticed that the people who do that are somewhat swinish in other respects. They also take care to let their opposite neighbour see the food while it is undergoing the process of mastication, and when they drink, it is always with the mouth half full. Others have an affected manner at table, holding the knife and fork as you would a pen, with elbows close to the sides, and back as rigid as that of a boarding-school miss dining in strange company. In fact, the way in which a hungry man will conduct himself in a public restaurant is a pretty true index of his character.

In some of the dear restaurants you cannot hear what you have ordered called out to the men in the kitchen. In the cheap ones it is different, as, no sooner have you told the waiter what it is you want, than every one in the room knows as well as you do yourself what it is to be. At first you feel rather annoyed at that. Afterwards you don't so much mind it; on the contrary, you begin to take an interest in the different calls, and, if you are of a contemplative turn of mind, you get to associate certain dishes with certain men. You see a man come in, and, from something in his manner, you feel convinced he will call for mutton broth. Another you connect with roast beef, and another with boiled mutton, and you are tolerably correct in all cases, though why you should be you would find it difficult to explain.

The waiters need good memories to call out correctly for all that has been ordered during the rush at lunch-time. One waiter will take the orders of half-a-dozen customers at once, which he will deliver with great volubility in the following manner: "Roast beef one, outside cut, plenty gravy."—"Boiled mutton two, one, no sauce."—"Roast mutton one."—"Corned beef one, potatoes only."—"Plum one." His being able to recollect all the things that have been ordered is, in a great measure, the result of practice, combined with native smartness. But however smart a waiter may be in delivering his orders, those in the kitchen must be smarter still to receive and attend to them without confusion, for the orders, as given above by one man are not the only ones the cooks have to attend to at the same time, as two or three other waiters are equally vociferous in making known what they want for their customers; and while the one already mentioned is speaking, the others are chiming in with "Rice one," "Rice another," "Irish stew one," "Oxtail one," "Bread two," or whatever else the bill of fare may contain.

The patrons of the cheap restaurants are of various kinds—clerks with small salaries, who are not ashamed to be seen coming out of a cheap dining-room, well-to-do tradesmen, and men who don't "see" paying a shilling for what they can get for sixpence; mechanics, labourers, people who live in lodgings, and the hungry generally whose means are limited. The *habitués* of the dear ones are of a higher grade—merchants, professional men, stock and share brokers, clerks in superior positions, and some clerks in very low ones, shopkeepers, loungers about town, ladies in business, for whose accommodation a room is set apart, and all who want a meal and can afford to pay a shilling for it.

The presiding genii of many of these restaurant kitchens are men of very dark complexions, though it has never been satisfactorily explained to us in what way they are better adapted to the business than the Caucasian. There is doubtless some good reason, or they would not get the preference, as the proprietors must know that, all other things being equal, an Englishman would rather have his food prepared by a white than by a black man.

Every one in the kitchen, except the man who peels the potatoes and washes up, is called cook—the first, second, third, or up to whatever number there may happen to be. Their wages range from fifty shillings to a pound per week, and the washer-up gets, perhaps, four or five shillings and his "tucker."

As members of society, they are decent men enough, though somewhat given to a redundancy of language, by using an unnecessary number of adjectives when expressing their ideas. As a rule, they are not teetotallers; there may be some among them, but if there are, we have not the honour of their acquaintance. In personal appearance there is an oleaginous "cookish" look about them, as though the greasy atmosphere of the kitchen had permeated the whole of their bodies, and was oozing out through the pores of the face. Their habits are not remarkable for cleanliness, though, for the matter of that, they are not much worse than many cooks in private families, who sometimes do their spiriting in a manner which, if it were known in the dining-rooms, might spoil the enjoyment of many a nice dish. They are never a very healthy class of men, which may be easily understood from the nature of their occupation, but they are hard-working, and tolerably good fellows in the main.

Many of the waiters have been under-stewards on board ships. A few are foreigners, and others take to the line because they have a natural adaptability for it. The nature of their occupation is likely to develop any natural smartness they may possess, and give that spryness to their motions which distinguishes them as a class. The majority of them, however, fall far short of their London brethren, inasmuch as their motions are not quickened by the expectation of "backsheesh."

As a rule, they are civil and obliging, and will stand any amount of grumbling without retorting by more than a mild deprecation; and they sometimes have much to put up with through the customers taking a rather unfair advantage of an Englishman's time-honoured privilege of grumbling about his food.

The waitresses are young damsels in not very affluent circumstances; but, being under the necessity of doing something for a living, they take to waiting, in preference to domestic service, as it is more genteel, and in every way more agreeable to their feelings. In service they would be called "Susan," or "Jane," or whatever else their names might be. As waitresses, they are addressed as "Miss So-and-so," and spoken of as "young ladies." Moreover, they have an opportunity of indulging in a little flirtation with the young fellows who frequent the restaurants, which often leads to small presents, and sometimes eventuates in marriage.

Most of them are pleasant chatty girls, and are great attractions to the places they are employed at, the principal, in fact, for hundreds of young men go there who would not if they had to be waited upon by men. Some of them are rather *outré* in the matter of headgear, and they have a strong affection for black lustre dresses; presumably on account of their being more economical, for they are not overpaid, these waitresses. Indeed, the "screw" they get is rightly named when applied to their wages, as their employers take care to screw them down as closely as possible.

It may be easily understood that there are some men

who dine at these sixpenny restaurants who take care to get full value for their money. We one day saw a man come in whose hungry looks struck us before he sat down, and as he seated himself where we had a good view of him, we were enabled to see that his looks were but the outward and visible signs of a more than the average adult male appetite. He ordered a plate of mutton broth, and when that was finished, there was half a small loaf less on the table. He then ordered a plate of corned beef, with carrots and potatoes, which speedily went the same way as the broth, accompanied by the good half of another loaf. He then called for plum pudding, and when that was gone, he appeared to be satisfied.

One might well wonder what profit could be made out of a sixpenny dinner of three courses—soup, meat, with vegetables, and pudding, for such are the constituents of the meal; but when there be added to the things already mentioned at least threepennyworth of bread, the proprietor's anxiety to cultivate the patronage of such customers must be small indeed.

In addition to the regular restaurants, there are a number of hotels and luncheon rooms, where a lunch may be obtained from a shilling upwards, according to the selection made from the *carte*. These places are affected by the wealthy country visitors, the nabobs of commerce, bank managers, and those who wish to entertain a friend in a manner out of the common.

There is also one place conducted *à la Française*, where French dishes are served up in grand style. We have never seen "frogs" on the *menu*, but, doubtless, as soon as the colonial taste has been cultivated up to that batrachian, they will be forthcoming.

There are hotels in Melbourne, where a hungry man, whose available cash does not amount to sixpence, can get a good square meal and glass of ale for threepence, if his conscience will allow him to do so. In some of these hotels, plates piled up with sausage-meat between layers of pastry are put upon the counters, from eleven till one, for the free use of the customers. This is cut up into oblong bits of a very convenient size for the mouth and is served up cold.

We were once struck by the vigour with which a man,

who had called for a glass of ale, attacked one of these plates of sausage-meat. He took up a piece, and in two bites it disappeared; then another and another followed after it in quick succession, till he had consumed a dozen. After getting so far, he finished his ale, then, with a look of contentment on his face, he gave his moustache a twirl, and sat down on the sofa to have a smoke.

In America, men of this description are called "brimmers," which means, in English, soldiers who go foraging for food. Brimming on such a scale as that must be exceptional, or Boniface would soon discover another mode of attracting custom less expensive than the free lunch.

In some of the other hotels, where sixpence is the ruling price for drinks, a really good spread is kept on a table for the customers to operate upon, from eleven in the morning till they close at night.

BOARDING-HOUSES.

In all large towns and cities, there are a great number of homeless people. We do not mean the destitute and the outcast, but those who, by reason of circumstances, find it inexpedient to have homes of their own, and these form rather a numerous class, and consist of members of every grade in society—M.P.'s, civil servants, clerks, shopmen, tradesmen, labourers, and men in independent positions. There are, also, numbers of the fair sex, such as governesses, young ladies in business, and servants out of place, who are obliged to board out till the anxiously looked-for time arrives when they will have homes of their own. But these ladies mostly live with private families, as it is not every boarding-house keeper who cares about mixing them with her gentlemen, as the heart-burnings and jealousies they are the frequent cause of add nothing to the comfort of the establishment.

There would not, perhaps, be so many damsels as there are sighing away their existence in unwooed singleness if bachelors only knew the comfort and independence of a home of their own, where they could have their meals how and when they liked; where they could sit before a fire that radiates some heat; where they could lie in bed and stretch themselves without untucking the clothes at the foot; and where they could invite a few friends to spend the evening, without being haunted by the fear that their presence was only tolerated in the house. But, alas! there is another side to that pleasing picture, and one that Cœlebs must look at before embarking in matrimony, or it will force itself upon his observation afterwards.

Whilst lounging on the sofa, or stretched upon the bed, fretting away the dreary time he is kept waiting for dinner, he cannot help reflecting at times upon his forlorn position, and he wonders how much it would cost over and above what he pays for his board to keep a wife. Knowing the retail price of provisions, and the general run of house rent, he is able to arrive at a pretty correct idea as far as they go. But then there are the milliners' and dressmakers' bills in the dim distance, and the item for boots, and other contingent expenses; such as doctors' and nurses' fees, and many other inevitable disbursements that follow in the wake of a family; so, with a sigh, he reconciles himself to his present position, till the advent of those good times that have been for so long said to be coming.

In Melbourne, where such a large proportion of unmarried men and others of unsettled and migratory habits are to be found among its population, one might naturally expect that boarding-houses would abound; and, in truth, they are as plentiful as friends in prosperity, especially on the western side of the city. The suburbs on the east, north, and south, are also rich in these places; but they are patronised by the more settled portion of the toilers and moilers of Melbourne.

The wharf and the Spencer Street terminus being on the western side, that locality gets nearly all the new arrivals, whether from Europe, the other colonies, or the up-country districts.

Boarding-houses may be divided into two sorts, public and private. There are also numbers of highly respectable people, professional men, and others, who, having a room or two more than they want for their own use, let them, as much for the sake of having them occupied and for company as for anything else. Others take in boarders in order to supplement their incomes without being under the necessity of doing so; and some, strange as it may appear, do it exclusively for amusement.

Public boarding-houses consist of hotels and large private buildings, sometimes dignified by the title of "Temperance Hotel." In many of the latter the accommodation is regulated not so much by the number of cubic feet of breathing space allowed to each sleeper as by the number of beds the room will hold, and that, too, in spite of anything the corporation bye-laws may say to the contrary, notwithstanding. So little regard have the proprietors of some of these places for anything but money-making, that the beds are placed so closely together that the lodgers can scarcely get between them; and they would be piled upon one another in bunks, as they are in the steerage of an emigrant ship, if they could get anyone to submit to it.

People in search of lodgings in Melbourne may very soon find what they want. The only difficulty likely to arise would be from having so many to choose from. Hospitable notices meet the eye on every side. Some hang out large signs, whereon is written "board and residence;" others have a genteel card in the window with the same announcement; whilst some advertise in the papers, to inform the homeless where their address cards may be obtained. The proprietors of some of the larger boarding-houses and hotels have another way of making their establishments known; namely, by touts, euphemistically called "runners." It is the business of these men to board the newly-arrived ships at the wharf or Sandridge; or invade the railway terminus, and bring away as many of the fresh arrivals as they can to the houses they represent. These men are not quite so bad as the "commissionaires" at the ports of arrival on the continent of Europe. They do not seize you bodily, nor walk off with your luggage without your permission, or indulge in any of the annoying peculiarities the others take so much delight in. Neither are they as intelligent, the continentals being frequently masters of several languages, while many of the Melbourne touts appear to know very little of their own, except its expletives.

The personal appearance of some of these men would be a strong recommendation to a respectable person not to go to the houses they invite him to. But as the people they keep the sharpest look out for are diggers, shepherds, or others who have come down to Melbourne to spend their savings, and who are not very particular in their habits, or delicate in their tastes, the proprietors of the houses they tout for must find it to their advantage to keep them, or they would not do so. Some of these men, in their dealing with their employers, have rather crude ideas as to what is right. A publican once told us that one of his runners, to whom he gave a pound a week and his keep, was in the habit of taking part of the new arrivals he picked up to other houses, for the sake of the fee he got of so much per head. A smart way of doing business that, and one which there can be no doubt they frequently indulge in. Those landlords who do not keep runners usually give cabmen so much per head for every boarder they bring them.

Boarding-house keeping in the good old times, as some people are fond of speaking of the early days of our city, was a highly lucrative business. Three or four pounds per week was the sum demanded for accommodation no better than can now be obtained for a pound or thirty shillings. The prices now range from two pounds to fifteen shillings per week, washing included.

Of course there are boarding-houses and boarding-houses. In some your comfort is the principal thing attended to; in others, the object aimed at is to get as much out of you as possible. Some landladies are kind-hearted, and gentle in manner, always good humoured, and only unhappy when they think their boarders are not comfortable. Others are ill-tempered, grasping, loud-voiced, and vulgar, and always miserable because they think their boarders are getting too much for the money they pay.

As the comfort of home depends so much upon the temper and disposition of the presiding genius, it may be very easily understood that your comfort does not depend so much upon what you pay as it does upon your land-lady, and those by whom she is surrounded. You may be far more comfortable in a place where you only pay eighteen shillings than in another where you pay thirty.

Some landladies are all you could desire, on the score of leaving your things as they find them, or if they do put you to any inconvenience, it is done unintentionally, and solely with a view of keeping things tidy. One evening we missed our spectacles; we searched all over the room without being able to find them. We asked the landlady if she had seen them. She had not. We then had another search, with the same results as on the first occasion. It then occurred to us to ask the servant if she had done anything with them. She said, in putting the room "straight" that morning, she had put them into the case, thinking that was the proper place for them. Perhaps she was right, but it was the last place in the world where we should have thought of looking with any expectation of finding them.

Other landladies are not so particular, for they claim a vested right in the use of whatever they see lying about belonging to you. Your clothes brushes are in general requisition; your scissors are only to be found after a weary hunt all over the house; and your razors are frequently used for cutting corns. The children, when there are any, invade your room, and convert it into a playground; while the cats and dogs prefer sleeping on your bed to anywhere else; and if you are absent for a night or two, some member of the family is sure to be put to sleep in your bed. Nor are these the only inconveniences you have to put up with. Troubles of another kind await you. Hot water for shaving is a luxury not coming strictly within the category of "board," though you can sometimes get it, if you choose to wait, which is not always convenient for those who have business to attend to. Then your breakfast is often late in consequence of your landlady not being able to see the advantage of early rising, for so fond are some ladies of their beds that they stick to them with a tenacity only equalled by that with which a barnacle clings to a ship's bottom; and when they do leave them, it is as regretfully as though the separation were for ever.

People who leave their beds with such reluctance usually excuse their late rising by saying they must have a certain amount of rest. Just so. It is strange these good folks do not try the experiment of taking to their beds a little earlier at night, instead of putting it off, as some of them do, till long after the cock has announced the beginning of another day. If they would only reflect, they would find that by retiring two hours earlier, they could rise an hour sooner, with the clear gain of one hour's bed. Nor is this the only advantage they would derive from the change, for the extra time they would have at their disposal would enable them to cultivate a few smiles before it was time to serve up breakfast.

Many of the public boarding-houses are presided over by daughters of Erin, who take to the business with great aptitude and considerable success; for the Irish diggers, and other up-country folks of the same nationality, who visit Melbourne in such numbers, always patronise their country-women for the sake of "Owld Ireland."

As a rule, these places are not remarkable for cleanli-

ness, nor is the bedding by any means luxurious, while
quantity in the food is thought to be of more consequence than quality. Beefsteak and onions, with plenty of
"spuds," is the usual breakfast in these houses; and
a very substantial meal it is to begin the day with,
especially if care be taken to provide a tough steak.

Good livings are to be made in these places, and even
little fortunes accumulated, which enable the proprietors
to retire, and moralise upon the omnivorous habits of
man. With all that however, many of them are not
satisfied. They look upon themselves as a hardly used
race; victims to people with healthy appetites, who are
unreasonable enough to eat as much as they require, when
they know that everything in the shape of provisions has
"gone up."

It is natural to expect that an upward tendency in
the price of food will have a correspondently depressing
effect upon the minds of housekeepers in general, and
boarding-house keepers in particular, for whatever may
be the price of provisions, they get no more from their
boarders, and it is too much to expect they will pay fourpence per pound for mutton with the same equanimity
they would twopence; or two shillings per pound for
butter when tenpenny would do as well, if they could
only get it.

Boarding-house keeping at the present day, like many
other things, has almost been reduced to a science, which
teaches how to extract as much profit as possible out of
boarders, compatible with keeping their bodies in a healthy
state, and satisfying their hunger at meal times. Of course
some ladies have a better aptitude for the business than
others, and will, by judicious management, make more out
of boarders at sixteen or eighteen shillings per week than
others will out of those who pay a pound, and treat them
better into the bargain. These are the only ones who
rise to eminence in the profession, and they are comparatively few in number, for what has been said of a poet
applies equally to a boarding-house keeper, *nascitur non fit.*

CHURCHES.

The Church of Christ in Melbourne has many names, and is governed under many forms. It is divided and subdivided into many sects, each with a different designation, and each with a separate place of worship, whether it be a duly consecrated church, or chapel, or whether a theatre or music-hall has been hired for the occasion. The adherents of each of these sects say that Christ is the foundation upon which their hopes are built. So far so good. Now the end every Christian has in view is, or ought to be, eternal life ; and Christ pointed out the way to that end in a manner that could be grasped by the understanding of a child. Yet learned men wrangle and dispute as to which it is. Each sect says there is but one way, and that is the one they have chosen, and they who follow any other only journey on to damnation.

The ministers of the Gospel in this city are, as a rule, pious, hard-working and earnest men, many of whom have to great learning joined a simple mind, and who look upon the office of Christ's ministry as far greater and more to be desired than the crown of a king. These men try to win souls to Christ, not by denunciation, but by exhortation; they look upon poor erring mortals as their Master did, and know well it is better to reclaim them by words of hope than harden them in their sins by assurances of eternal wrath.

A clergyman's life in Melbourne is certainly not one of ease. There are no prizes or high positions in the Church to be obtained here, as there are at home. Hard work and small stipends are nearly all he has to look forward to ; and in the face of that, a man need be earnest in the work he has to do. There are a few clergymen pretty well paid, but many of them have not a larger income than can be commanded by a skilful artisan, and out of that they must keep up an appearance, and bestow something in charity. Nor does a clergyman receive the same amount of consideration here as at home. In England, to the treatment he is entitled to as a gentleman is added a feeling of respect for his office. In all young cities men have not much time for the cultivation of bumps of veneration; moreover, they are apt to look upon one man as being as good as another, if not a little better, so, without meaning any disrespect, they merely regard him as a clergyman whose business it is to look after their salvation, in return for the threepenny bits they give weekly towards his stipend.

Others there are, and not a few of them, who treat him still worse, for they appear to think he ought to work for nothing, which he would certainly have to do if everyone were of the same way of thinking. These enlightened people say, "They hate to go to church because the plate is always shoved under their noses"; and as they have an equally strong objection to church rates and the State aid, it is difficult to understand how, in their opinion, the money necessary for the due celebration of Divine service is to be obtained.

The demeanour of our fellow-citizens in church is as becoming as that of any congregation in the world; and we often think, when we see them looking so pious, and so mild and gentle, what a blessing it would be for the world at large if people could only fancy it was always Sunday, and that they were always in church. We should have fewer wars, and less quarrelling and backbiting, for whatever our feelings might be one towards another, we should make no open manifestation of them, but keep our ill-humour to ourselves till something else had dislodged it from our minds.

Certainly there is a little harmless criticism carried on, but it only extends to the undue length of Miss Brown's train, as she sweeps along the aisle; or to the fright Mrs. Jones looks in her new bonnet; or how Mrs. Robinson wears hers too far forward. No open display of temper is ever indulged in, except occasionally, when people come rather late and find their seats occupied; but the cloud soon passes away and the Sunday look once more beams forth.

"God loveth a cheerful giver." One would think that the denomination of the coin dropped into the offertory plate would depend, in a great measure, upon the means of the giver. But that is not always the case, for, as a rule, the poorer members of a congregation are far more liberal than the richer.

What was said of the widow's mite in the olden time holds good at the present day. The copper of a person to whom a penny is of consequence is more acceptable than the shilling or half-crown of the man to whom the loss of thousands would be as nothing.

The manner of giving is always regulated by the value of the coin bestowed. The threepenny bit is dropped into the plate without any display whatever. The sixpence is deposited rather more openly; and the shilling is dropped in with a decided chink. A great rattle is made when the half-crown falls out of the donor's hand, and he always looks as unconcerned as though it were nothing to him. There is a musical jingle about the sovereign as it drops among the silver that is pleasant to the collector's ears, though, unfortunately, it is seldom heard in the Anglican churches; and there is a subdued rustle about the cheque or banknote as it is quietly and unostentatiously dropped into the plate.

THE MELBOURNE PERIPATETICS.

In all civilised communities there are numbers of traders carrying on business in the open air, wandering about the highways and byways, seeking customers wheresoever they may be found.

Our peripatetic merchants are numerous as a body, and their merchandise embraces most of the articles that are useful or necessary to our existence; moreover, they are industrious in habit, and, as a rule, fairly honest, though their pounds do occasionally fall short of the orthodox number of ounces. But that may be owing to the example set them by tradesmen holding a far higher position in the commercial world, who may be detected in reducing weights, abbreviating measures, or sophisticating what we eat and drink, without their social status being in any way damaged thereby.

Some of our street dealers confine their operations to one line alone; others are not so particular, but go in for whatever appears likely to yield the greater profit, whether it be fish, wild fowl, rabbits, vegetables, or fruit.

The ages of our peripatetics range from three or four years to more than man's allotted number—three-score and ten; and, as may be expected, with the two extremes of age, we see the two extremes of bodily condition. There are children with the lithe limbs and keen looks of those who have graduated in the gutters, running about selling the evening paper; and old men in the last stage of beery decrepitude staggering along selling wax matches. The majority of them, however, are strong, hearty men, and they need be, for they have heavy loads to carry and wheel about the streets from early morn till sometimes late at night.

They are useful, too, for by their means housekeepers can get what they want without the trouble of fetching it from the shops.

There is another and very numerous class of peripatetics, who do not work with so much credit to themselves, nor with the same advantage to the rest of the community, namely, the beggars, and with them we will begin.

THE BEGGARS.

The beggars of Melbourne may be divided into three classes—the blind, the pretended blind, and the wide-awake ones.

Some of these blind men have known life in many of its phases, or, as it is popularly put, they have seen many "ups and downs" in their time; while the antecedents of others would hardly stand the test of a very close scrutiny.

One, whose sightless eyes excite the compassion of the passers-by, was, if report speak truly, the hero of an adventure that has both a serious and a comic side to it. Some years ago he followed the not very highly thought of, though perhaps lucrative business of boot blacking, outside one of the banks in New Zealand. At that time his eyes must have been pretty sharp, for, watching for what is commonly called a "slant," he slipped into the bank, and slipped out again with a large amount of gold, some say three thousand pounds worth, without being detected. He gave this gold into the keeping of an accomplice, with instructions to take it to Melbourne, and wait there till he came, when they would divide it between them.

To divert suspicion from himself he continued his occupation outside the bank as usual, which he not only succeeded in doing, but was actually employed by the bank authorities as a detective, to watch the people who went into and left the bank, and to report whatever he saw of a suspicious nature. How he must have chuckled to himself as he thought how easily he could "spot" the thief if he had felt disposed.

After the affair had somewhat blown over, he came to Melbourne, to join his mate and divide the spoil. On arriving here he found his friend had extended his journey to England, and had taken the gold with him, forgetting, in the hurry of departure, to leave an address behind him.

On making that discovery the rage of the baffled one knew no bounds, which is hardly to be wondered at when all the circumstances of the case are taken into consideration. He swore if he ever came across the runaway he would kill him, and there is no doubt he would have kept his word; but the other was far too astute to give him a chance of adding murder to his other sins. How different must have been the emotions of these two men! While one was gnashing his teeth with rage at being outwitted, the other must have been chuckling over the successful issue of his piece of double rascality, as he sped away to the land where he hoped to enjoy the full benefit of it.

"Honour among thieves" is a pretty saying, no doubt, and rather sentimental to boot, but it is not always acted up to in light-fingered circles. What honour there is among them is that begotten of fear. A thief knows very well that if he "peach" on a pal for one affair, that pal will "round" on him for something else; and that is where the honour comes in. If one thief can "best" another without being found out, he will do so. Or, if he can "put him away," without its being known to anyone but the police, he will, of course, for a consideration.

It is the same sort of honour that regulates the division of the proceeds of robberies. Two men "work" together at pocket-picking. The one who abstracts the purse "slings"—that is, hands it to his mate, who immediately "lammases," *c'est-à-dire*, clears out with it, the two meeting afterwards in some pre-arranged spot to divide the contents. In the meantime, however, the receiver has been careful to "go over," or examine the purse to see what it contains. Its contents may be, say, ten pounds, which, divided between two, is exactly five pounds each. There being no possibility of the one who stole the purse knowing what it contained when it left its owner's possession, the one who received it can take out as much as he thinks proper, without the other being any the wiser. Accordingly, number two helps himself to, maybe, five pounds, and puts that into his pocket as his first share of the spoil. When the two worthies meet, and examine the purse, it is found to contain five pounds,

which is two pounds ten apiece. Thus one gets seven
pounds ten shillings out of the ten pounds, and the other
gets the balance. That is the honour that rules among
Messieurs les voleurs.

One well-known blind beggar of Melbourne lost his
sight while blasting rock at Pentridge, where he had to
do a five years' rustication for burglary. When the prison
doctor had patched him up, the authorities, seeing he
could be of no further use to them, kindly remitted the
unserved portion of his sentence, and sent him out into
the now, to him, darkened world to do the best he could
for himself. He took to begging, as the readiest means
of getting a living, and has now a good "connection"
among the street givers, and does very well. He may be
seen plying his calling at all public gatherings; he lives
in clover, and enjoys his beer.

Some of these blind beggars are said to have grown
comparatively wealthy through the benevolence of the
soft-hearted. One, it was reported, had a rent-roll that
would have kept him in comfort; another had money
invested in various ways which brought him in a good
income; while yet another, who lived in his own
suburban villa, was wont to come to his "stand" in town
every morning in a cab. These men are not doing so well
now as they did formerly, owing to the greatly increased
number of blind men who have joined their ranks, though
where they all come from it would be difficult to say.

The blind men already in possession of the streets
"look" with no friendly eyes upon any interloper who
locates himself anywhere near one of their stands. They
are great protectionists, and say their calling ought to be
protected the same as most others are, though how it is to
be done, whether by a poll-tax or a pole-axe, they are
unable to say, but there can be no doubt they would much
prefer the latter method of keeping the number down.

Though not doing so well now as formerly, they all
manage to get a good "crust," as they call it. Some are
saving in disposition; others spend all they can get in
riot and debauchery, knowing full well that when they
can no longer "work," a home will be found for them in
the Benevolent Asylum, or Immigrants' Home. Some
live in fairly decent homes; others dwell amidst the
filth and squalor of the back slums, or hide their orgies

from the common gaze in some secluded right-of-way running off one of the little streets.

These blind beggars are, as a rule, uxorious in habit, and each has a housekeeper to prepare his meals and take care of the place while he is away.

One of these amorous old fellows named Peter once tried the experiment of having two wives, but, finding it didn't work smoothly, he got rid of the duplicate at the end of the second day. It seems his wife, who had to take him his dinner every day at one o'clock, found, when she got back one day, that some one had broken open the back door and robbed the house. It had evidently been done by some one well acquainted with the place, for no search had been made for money, or any light articles of value, but the thieves went straight for the blankets and walked off with them.

When Peter got back that evening and heard what had happened, his emotions, as may be expected, were of the liveliest, as it was winter time, and the blankets were of the best quality, for he always liked to be warm and comfortable at night. Although the woman was away at the time waiting upon the old scoundrel, that, in his opinion, did not absolve her from blame, and as he was not likely to get hold of the guilty parties, he took it out of her "hide," as he called it, or, in other words, gave her a most unmerciful beating.

In thinking the matter over the next morning, he came to the conclusion that, in order to prevent the same thing occurring again, it would be advisable to supplement his present wife with another, so as to have one always at home to mind the house while the other was away with his dinner. On broaching the matter to his wife, that lady set herself resolutely against it, and threatened all manner of direful things in the event of its taking place, among which was burning down the house and roasting him and the interloper together. After an exceedingly *mauvais quart d'heure* for both parties, he brought her over to his way of thinking by a repetition of the previous night's treatment, when she consented to live on amicable terms with her new associate.

Peter found no difficulty in getting another help-meet, nor would he have had if he had wanted half-a-dozen; he brought her home that same evening, and celebrated the event in the usual way, by inviting a few select friends to spend the evening with them.

The first thing the two ladies did after their husband had gone to business the next morning was to have a fight, which, with intervals for mutual abuse, they kept up so long and so furiously that they forgot all about the old man's dinner. That worthy, finding his dinner did not come at the usual time, began to wonder what could be the cause of it, as the woman had hitherto been so punctual in bringing it. He waited till three o'clock, when hunger and curiosity drove him home, with a view of getting both satisfied. On arriving at his abode he "felt" a great crowd outside the house, and heard the two women inside fighting and screaming like wild cats. Within a very few seconds after Peter's arrival the three of them were hard at it, the blind man distributing his blows with strict impartiality between the other two.

Having restored order, he wanted to know how it was he hadn't had his dinner as usual; and, as neither of them could tell, he caught hold of the one nearest to him and re-commenced the punching process. This time the newcomer was the recipient; the old one, taught by experience, took care to have the table between her and her master, as she always did, if possible, whenever he "took on."

Having somewhat calmed down, he ordered the two women to get his dinner ready in as short a space of time as possible; and while the one who was least damaged in person and clothes went to the butcher's for some sausages, the other lit the fire and got the frying-pan ready to cook them in. As soon as the woman returned, Peter told her to take the billy to the public-house at the corner of the lane and get a shilling's-worth of beer, suggesting at the same time she had better not drink any of it on the way, or she would get none when she got back. When she came in with the beer, the suspicious old blackguard took the billy from her and placed it upon the table, then, with the forefinger of his right hand, gauged its contents to see if there was the proper quantity. Being satisfied on that point, he took a drink, and sat down in readiness for dinner.

Having made a hearty meal, and washed it down by a copious inflow of beer, some of his good humour returned, and he sent for another shilling's-worth of beer and a shilling's-worth of rum. They all sat down to talk the matter over, and by the time the last supply of liquor had been disposed of, they were the best friends in the world, and they finished up the night with a triangular kissing-match.

The next morning things went on so pleasantly that Peter began to think that the bigamous state was a decided improvement over the one-wife arrangement, and he wondered he had never tried it before.

While the new "missis" was preparing the breakfast, the other wet the corner of a towel and wrapped it round her hand; then, rubbing some soap on it, wiped the old man's face, using all the time the endearing expressions a mother does when operating upon her child in the same way. Having cleaned and dried his face, she turned her attention to his hands, and having done them to her satisfaction, she combed his hair and whiskers, and helped him to get inside his coat. When Peter started out for business that morning, he felt happier and more comfortable than he had done for many a long day.

As the two women had on the previous night promised not to fight any more, they felt bound to keep their pledge. But, in doing that, they went to the other extreme, and became exceedingly affectionate, which led to the consumption of sundry jugs of beer, with the result that, when their lord and master's dinner-time came round, they were both too drunk to attend to it; consequently, he had to come home once more for his mid-day meal. When he got inside, he found them locked in each other's arms, fast asleep on the bed, which had such an effect upon him that he got hold of the newcomer and dragged her off the bed and into the lane, where she lay till a policeman took her to the lock-up as drunk and incapable.

Although Peter had been so pleased with the new order of things in the morning, he came to the conclusion before he went to bed that having two wives in one house is a mistake, unless the husband is always there to keep an "eye" upon them; but as, in consequence of his being away all day, he could not do that, he made up his mind to return to what diplomatists call the *status quo ante*.

The position of housekeeper to one of these blind men

is one much sought after by a certain class of middle-aged women, whose notions of propriety are somewhat lax. Easy as these men find it to get a new "wife," they sometimes have great trouble in getting rid of the old one, not that there are any legal difficulties to be overcome, but owing to the lady's objection to be superseded. As no minister of religion has ever blessed the union, a divorce according to law is, of course, not necessary, neither is the process of separation as slow and expensive as it would be if left to the lawyers, but it is quite as vexatious while it lasts, and is equally as amusing to the denizens of the right-of-way in which it occurs as it would be if done in an open court for the edification of an admiring public.

When, owing to incompatibility of temper, or a "drunk" of more than the average length on the lady's part, blind Tom, or Dick, or Harry thinks a change of wife would be to his advantage, he brings home a new one to replace the one in disgrace. Then the trouble begins. The lady in possession refuses, in language largely interspersed with adjectives, to renounce her conjugal rights, and expresses her determination to prevent the new bride's nuptial couch being one of roses. The latter retorts in a phraseology quite as elegant as the other's, and when they have both exhausted their stock of Billingsgate, they "go" for each other like two wild cats. If the newcomer is the better of the two in the *ad hominem* line of argument, the blind man leaves the settlement of the question in her hands. Should victory, however, incline to the side of the discarded one, he "pitches in" also, and between the two she soon gets enough.

The battle over, the vanquished one is allowed to pack up her few "rags," as women of this class call their clothes, and depart. If, however, she accepts with resignation the new order of things, that is, regards the divorce as *un fait accompli*, she is allowed to remain, and join in the "spree," which always follows one of these weddings.

When a rough-and-tumble fight, participated in by three, takes place in a small room, there is sure to be a deal of confusion among the furniture; and when plates and jugs, and other domestic utensils are used as missiles, as they generally are in these affrays, there is likely to be a considerable amount of wreckage among the more fragile articles.

When peace is restored, the room has to be put straight before the wedding festivities can begin, and the two women set about doing that with as much cordiality as though their late contention had been a game at cards. There is one good trait to be found in the natures of this class of people, and that is, however fiercely their tongues may have wagged at each other, or however bitterly they may have fought, they are always willing, as soon as the blood has cooled down, to let "bygones be bygones."

The two ladies, having put the front room in order, retire to the back to rearrange their own disordered garments, and smooth their dishevelled locks, which usually get very much tangled in these struggles. Beer is then sent for, and a few neighbours invited to join in the carouse, which is kept up till there is a general all round "drunk."

There was once a rather unexpected termination to one of these wedding feasts.

A blind man, whom we will call Jim, being dissatisfied with his housekeeper, resolved to "chuck her up," as he called it, and get another one to take her place. Out of the goodly number he had to choose from, he selected a lady who was highly recommended as being in every way suitable for him, she being a good cook, and fairly clean in her habits. She had just finished a "stretch," that is, three months in the Melbourne gaol; but that in Jim's opinion was rather an advantage than otherwise, as he preferred a lady just out of prison to one who had been out a long time, as she has had to submit to a cleansing process she would have been a stranger to had she been at large.

During the spree which Jim gave in honour of his *épousailles* the newly-made bride displayed a capacity for swallowing beer that was looked upon as remarkable, even by the thirsty souls around her, and a cantankerousness when half drunk that convinced the fickle bridegroom his new wife was no improvement upon the old, so, thinking he had better have to do with a devil he knew than with one he didn't, he kicked her out into the lane,

K

and took back to his arms the one he had so recently divorced.

There are several well-trained dogs attached to the blind brotherhood, to act as guides and keep them out of danger as they go to and from their stands. These dogs know where their masters want to go as well as they do themselves, and, also, what public-houses to stop at.

Besides the really blind, there are some only partially so, but these "fox" total blindness with much about the same pecuniary results their more "favoured" brethren acquire by exhibiting the genuine article.

The other beggars are even more undesirable as members of society than the blind ones, as they lead quite as vicious lives, and have not the same excuse for taking to begging as a means of living. They are not all such old and decrepit men as may be seen about Melbourne; but many of them are strong and vigorous, and quite able, if they were compelled, to earn the food they eat. The old men confine themselves entirely to Melbourne, the younger ones "work" the suburbs, and ask for employment, as a preliminary to asking for money. These latter extract more from the fears than from the compassion of those they solicit. Their way of going to work evinces considerable knowledge of human nature, at least human nature as displayed by females in an unprotected state. They begin, in a fawning manner and whining tone, by asking if the lady can give them some work by which they can earn a trifle to buy food for their families. Of course they neither want nor expect work, and if they can get money by being civil, well and good; if not, they put on a browbeating air that goes straight to the understandings, if not to the hearts, of females who know they have no male protector near.

Sometimes food is offered them, but they speedily let it be known it is not altogether that they want, but a few coppers to get a powder or some other medicine for a sick child. Some will reject the proffered food with disdain, others will take it and throw it away as soon as they are out of sight; while yet others go to work in a more artful manner. These will take the food, and take up some position where they can be seen from the house, and pretend to eat it as ravenously as though they had eaten nothing for a week; though the greater part of it goes into the coat pocket instead of into the stomach.

These men only beg in the suburbs. In town they are loafers, hanging about the threepenny taps as long as their money lasts. When it is all gone, they resume their travels till their exchequer is sufficiently well replenished to enable them to have another "booze."

The old men about town are quite as clever in extracting money from the pockets of the kind-hearted by exciting their compassion, as the younger ones in the suburbs are in quickening the charity of the timorous. by playing upon their fears.

Frequently as you walk along the street, some dissolute-looking old fellow, who appears to be only able to retain the perpendicular by means of a walking-stick, will approach you and say, "Have you got a copper, sir, to give a poor old man who has had nothing to eat for forty eight hours? God bless you, sir; give me something to get a meal with." Now, perhaps, you may be hungry yourself, and will pity him accordingly; or you may have just had a good lunch, and will feel charitably disposed; then your hand will go into your pocket, and you will be sixpence the poorer as to the currency, but ten times the amount richer in the satisfaction of thinking you have done a good deed, when all you have done has been to enable this man to put himself outside of two pints of beer.

Sometimes they vary the tale; often they are tired with walking day and night, and have only threepence, which they show, towards paying for a bed; and they implore you to make it up to sixpence, so that they may have at least a night's rest.

The existence of these men simply consists of two parts —begging by day, and drinking at night; the little food they are able to take being eaten whenever they feel inclined for it—which is seldom, for they appear to live almost upon what they call "suction," which, in their case, means beer.

Begging, like other professions, is governed by certain rules of etiquette, any infringement of which draws upon the offending one the reprobation of the entire body. One article of their unwritten law is, that one man may not go on another's "beat;" should he do so, the others contrive, by some means or other, to make it extremely "hot" for him.

The female beggers are no improvement upon the males in respect of habits or tastes, nor are their antecedents any better; but, if anything, rather worse. As long as anything in the shape of good looks remained, they found the means of living in other directions; but, now that drink has made them too loathsome for that kind of life, no other resource than begging is left them for the miserable remnant of their days, unless it be a sojourn in Her Majesty's gaol.

They frequently go about accompanied by one or two children, which are not their own, but borrowed for the occasion, of course, for a consideration. We have not been able to discover sufficient to justify us in saying that children are regularly hired out here for begging purposes as they are in London, but that they are sometimes lent is well known.

In London, children are not only hired out to beggars, but they are manufactured for the purpose. The blind child seen with the beggar woman has, in all probability, had its sight destroyed by chemicals, or in some other way. The poor little cripple who so excites the pity of the tender-hearted has had its limbs distorted by bandages, or other mechanical appliances. The sickly-looking child has been "dosed" till it has been brought to death's door, and, nothing but the fear of being hanged keeps the wretches who torture it from letting it pass through.

More little ones are required to keep the market well supplied with moribund children than there are to keep up the stock of blind ones and cripples. A child may be blinded or crippled without any fatal results; but its system cannot be tampered with beyond a certain limit without endangering its life, so the little one, after being kept as long as prudence allows, is permitted to recover, and others treated in the same way to take its place.

This is no imaginary sketch, but a recital of what actually occurred within our own recollection.

The children thus treated are not unfrequently stolen from perambulators left carelessly guarded, or from little nurse girls by a respectable looking woman, who kindly holds the baby while the girl goes just round the corner to get some lollies.

The female beggars who "do" the suburbs mostly take baskets with them to carry away the scraps of food they may have given to them, which, by-the-way, they never eat, but give it to those who will, or throw it away on the first opportunity. The London beggars are wiser in their generation, for they take their "scran bags" to the "padding kens," and sell the broken victuals to whoever will buy it. Some of our female mendicants call regularly at certain houses, where they always get tea and sugar given to them by the kind-hearted people they impose upon by well-concocted tales of sickness and poverty. This is afterwards sold to their acquaintances for what it will fetch, which is usually threepence; and for that sum the purchasers get about a shilling's worth of tea and sugar.

MATCH-SELLERS.

It is hard to say by what process the first spark of artificial fire was kindled, as the event occurred so long before men understood the art of recording their transactions; but it was doubtless brought into existence by the friction of two pieces of wood, as is done at the present day by those savages who know not matches.

History describes Archimedes as a mighty fire-kindler by means of the burning glass, and, of course, we must accept history as we find it; though, it may appear to some that the means he is said to have employed to destroy the Roman ships savour somewhat more of the *ben trovato*, than they do of the *vero*.

The oldest known civilised method of obtaining fire was that of the flint and steel, the sparks from which were caught by decayed wood, or something reduced by burning to what we call tinder.

We can well remember the old tinder-box process of obtaining a light, and many a time when we have heard in the dark the "nick, nick" of the flint and steel, and have seen the sparks fly, we have thought it the most wonderful thing in creation. When the tinder has caught, we have watched the tiny spark as it grew under the blowing of the operator, and have seen the tip of the match applied to it; and as the feeble blue light first illumined the face held over the box, and then gradually expanded into the full blaze of the match, we have felt awe-stricken and subdued.

The tinder-box went out as the locomotive came in. It had been a good servant; so had the stage-coach, but they both became too slow for the age, or rather, the age had become too fast for them, so one had to give way to the iron horse, and the other was supplanted by the lucifer.

The lucifer was then a thin flat match, and was ignited by being drawn between two leaves of sand-paper. That was speedily improved upon by the congreve match, which was more readily lit by rubbing it against the bottom of the box, or on any rough surface. That method of lighting the match has not been superseded, nor is it likely to be, as it is simplicity itself.

Before the tinder-box finally disappeared, it was sought to bring phosphorus into general use as a fire-kindler. It was confined in a stoppered bottle, and when a light was wanted, the stopper was removed, and a brimstone match dipped in, which, on being withdrawn, kindled by contact with the atmosphere. But as that method was not considered a very safe one, it found favour with but few, and it was rather expensive besides.

The manufacture of the old brimstone match was very simple, and most of the sellers were the makers as well. A piece of straight grained wood was cut into the required length and thickness. It was then split into thin strips, and about half a dozen taken up, pointed at both ends, and the tips dipped into a pan of molten brimstone. They were then tied in the middle, and expanded like an attenuated letter X, and the bunch was ready for sale; the price of which was one halfpenny. Great quantities were made by gipsies, either in their tents in summer, or at their town residences in Kent Street, in winter, and afterwards sold wholesale to the shop-keepers, or to those sellers who did not make their own.

Match-making has developed into such wonderful proportions since science and machinery have been brought into requisition for their production, that one might well wonder what becomes of them all. Where there was one old-fashioned brimstone dip made, there are now ten thousand congreves brought into existence; some factories turning out many millions of boxes each per week.

The machinery for splitting the wood into matches is ingenious and complicated in its nature. A piece of soft wood (it must be close-grained, and free from knots) is put into the machine at one end, and it comes out split into matches at the other. The dipping process is carried on by children; and children also make the boxes, and pack the matches in them, as the price they are sold at prohibits the employment of adult labour, except in those branches where skill and steadiness are required.

For some time there was only one kind of lucifer match in use; then the wax matches appeared, but they were not for a long while in such requisition as the others, being dearer, on account of the greater cost of the material and the more elaborate nature of their manufacture. But now, however, as they can be bought wholesale at fourpence per dozen boxes, they are in more general use, especially among smokers, on account of their greater convenience. Afterwards, the safety matches were introduced, which are decidedly an improvement upon the others, both on account of the greater certainty of getting a light when one is struck, and the impossibility of accidents arising from their untimely ignition, for, unless they are struck on paper specially prepared, they will not light.

Match-selling has always been the *dernier ressort* of poverty, and the sellers themselves the lowest and least influential of all the commercial classes. Although the old match-sellers were dignified by the title of "timber merchants," they were looked upon as being only one step above the beggars, and, in fact, they were nothing else, as the few bunches of matches they held in the hand were only carried as a blind to hide the more profitable calling of begging.

The social status of the match-seller has not improved much in our own day, but the business is somewhat more lucrative, on account of the greater number of matches sold. As the sale of these articles has so greatly increased, so, also, has the number of sellers. In fact, they have become so numerous that as one goes up Bourke Street, "Wax matches penny a box" is dinned into one's ears with almost every step one takes. Seeing the number of vendors, one naturally wonders where they find buyers, and who these buyers are. One has not to go far, however, before one finds out that the patrons of these itinerant merchants are the smokers, who, in order to enjoy their pipes, must have some means of setting them going, and these means are available at the small outlay of one penny.

It would be interesting to know the number of boxes of matches sold in the streets annually. It must be something enormous, as smoking is so general among all classes, and matches are so necessary to them that each one must go provided with a box.

There is a deal of good fellowship in connection with matches. A man's match-box is as much at the service of another as his snuff-box was when snuff-taking was more general than it now is. Any smoker who wants a light, and has run out of matches, has only to stop the first man he meets and ask for one, when he will not only get it, but will very likely be pressed to take three or four, unless the other happens to be in the same predicament as himself.

A few years ago the match-selling business was exclusively, or nearly so, in the hands of small boys, who were sent out by their parents with a few boxes, so that they might earn something towards their own keep, or, as was frequently the case, to bring home something for these parents to get beer with. Now, with the exception of a few little children and young cripples, they appear to have slipped out of it altogether, and left it in the hands of beery old men, and blind beggars, though the latter have a few boxes with them more as a "stall" than with a view of selling them.

The wholesale price of wax matches being sixpence per dozen boxes, that allows the retail dealer two hundred per cent. profit, a tolerably fair return when the sale is good. Of course, some do better than others, though they all calculate upon selling two or three dozen every day. Three dozen is a good day's work, and much more than the average sale, which may be, taking the whole fraternity, about two dozen, thus making the week's earnings eight shillings—a sum hardly sufficient to find them in luxuries, though, with care, it might in necessaries, if beer be left out of the question.

Small as the sum is, it is more than they could earn at anything else, except begging; but, as that is rather overdone at present, it is doubtful if they could improve their circumstances by taking to it; besides, as interlopers, they would have to run the gauntlet of those already engaged in the latter calling.

There are not many women or girls engaged in match-selling. One may be seen occasionally, but it's not very popular with them, as it necessitates an outlay before they can begin, which they are not always provided with; besides, they find the "whimpering dodge" a much better "lay" to go upon.

It is an easy business, and one just suited to the years and dispositions of those who carry it on, as they have no heavy load to hawk about; nothing heavier than a cigar-box, for that is the usual thing they keep their matches in, either carried in the hand, or hung round the neck by a piece of string.

It is not very refreshing to contemplate some of these men, for there is that about them which shows pretty plainly what their past lives have been. The effects of vice are traceable in every feature. Drink has bleared the eyes, but still the evil expression begotten by a life of crime remains; for many of them belong to that class whose early colonial experience has procured them the title of "old hands," and whose past existence has been nothing else than an alternation of prison life and freedom, till now, too old to continue active predatory operations, nothing remains for them but a life of loaferdom, till death overtakes them in the padding-ken, or in the slums, or the scrub, whither they sometimes retire to sleep off the effects of their last drunken orgies.

There is one among them who, some years ago, came as near to being hanged as a man could well be who had not the rope actually round his neck. He is a native of the "tight little island," and was at one time the "Tipperariest" of all the pugnacious dwellers round about that portion of Her Majesty's dominions. In fact, he was that kind of individual of whom one of his countrymen has said, "He was never at peace except in a row." He appeared to live but for one object, and that was to get some one to tread upon the tails of his coat.

One day he was "accommodated" by a man who could wield the shillelagh even better than he could himself, as he speedily found out, for though blessed with a skull of more than Celtic thickness, his opponent's stick fell upon it so hard and so often that he was obliged to cave in. Though beaten, he was not subdued, as was soon seen. His vanity was more seriously wounded than his head was, and he looked upon himself as degraded in the eyes of the world, at least of that portion of it who held Tipperary views.

He felt he must do something to rehabilitate himself in the good opinion of his neighbours; and to ascertain the best way of going about it, he consulted the "poteen," under the inspiration of which a resolve was soon made. This time he was determined there should be no mistake about it, for, discarding the comparatively harmless shillelagh, he armed himself with a pick, and, waiting for his adversary, he drove the point of it into his brain. Whether he conceived the idea of the deed before he got drunk, or after, is not known, but he was drunk when he did it, and that, in all probability, saved his life. He was tried for the crime, found guilty, and condemned to death. A few hours, however, before he was to have been hanged, the sentence was commuted to transportation for life. That was close upon forty-five years ago.

He was sent to Norfolk Island, and kept in bondage for about ten years, and then allowed another start in life. How he passed the next five years is best known to himself, as he is very reticent concerning his doings during that period. Thirty years ago he turned up in Victoria, much to the advantage, no doubt, of the place he had left, unless his conduct there was much better than it has been here. The narrow escape he had had from the gallows, and his subsequent long imprisonment, had not acted as a restraint upon his fierce disposition. On the contrary, they seemed to have intensified it, and made him more reckless than ever, and once more he came within one step of the gallows.

One day he met a man in the bush and bailed him up, with a view of easing him of any spare cash he might happen to have about him. As the man could not see the justice of the proceeding, he did not manifest any particular celerity in emptying his pockets, which rather chafed the other, who, to quicken his movements, fired at him, the ball just grazing his ear. That was about the most unwise thing he had ever done in his life, except driving the pick into the other man's head, for as long as he kept his victim covered he was master of the situation. As soon, however, as he had fired and missed, they stood upon equal ground, as the pistol was an old-fashioned one, and the man sprang upon him like a tiger, and, being younger and stronger, almost throttled him to begin with, and very soon after had him tied, neck and heels together, with his own belt.

For that little freak he got ten years on the roads, and was let off after having served about six. On becoming once more free, he recognised the fact that bushranging was not exactly his line; for however potent the will may be for evil, it is powerless if not sustained by bodily vigour, and as he was neither so young nor so active as he had been, he thought it would be better to confine his operations for the future to Melbourne.

As time, and beer, began to tell upon him, his depredations became of a smaller and more paltry nature; and as he was unfortunate in being nearly always caught in the act, he had to "put in" more of his time at stonebreaking than he approved of, so he thought he had better turn over a new leaf, and win his bread and beer in some way less obnoxious to the Law; and whenever he has, since then, been at loggerheads with the authorities, it has been for some such eccentricity as being drunk and incapable. He is now quite venerable, and has finally settled down to the more honourable calling of selling wax matches.

All the match-selling brotherhood, however, have not such evil antecedents as this one. There is one who was once an officer in Her Majesty's service, but in consequence of continued misconduct, more social than criminal, he sank down to his present condition.

In youth he was remarkable for almost everything but steady habits, and as he appeared to have an unusually large quantity of wild oats to sow, his friends thought he might as well sow them in the army as anywhere else, so they got him a commission. The first lot he sowed there, however, produced such an abundant crop of troubles that he had to retire, and seek a fresh field for the remainder. His friends thought the soil of Australia admirably suited to receive them, and, as it promised a change, he was of the same opinion himself. They fitted him out, and gave him a sum of money for his support till he could "turn himself round." He did turn himself round, and got into such a whirl that, before he could stop, all his money had flown from him as completely as water does from a well-trundled mop.

On coming to himself, and finding all his money gone,

he wrote home to his friends for more. In the meantime, he had his outfit to fall back upon, and as there are plenty of people about who, from pure kindness of heart, will give any impecunious immigrant who has anything to sell at least a fourth of its value for it, he managed to live pretty well for a month.

According to his own calculations, it would be at least five months before he received a remittance, and it became a serious question with him how he was to live in the meantime. Passing valueless cheques was not so fashionable then as it has become since, and we have no reason for supposing he would have practised it if it had been; but there was a pressing necessity for raising the wind somehow, and as he had no more clothing than was absolutely necessary for his own use, what was he to do? It is only just to say he tried to get employment, but as work of any description was something he had never been accustomed to, he found it difficult to get anything that would suit him. Being a good scholar, he managed to get into an office as clerk, but not being accustomed to the duties, he was always making mistakes; and on his principal discovering one of a more glaring nature than usual, he politely told him he could dispense with his services. That was no recommendation for another billet of the same kind, so he had to turn to something else. He tried lumping on the wharf, but the loads wouldn't fit his back. He then tried the pick and shovel, but at the end of the day he felt convinced that nature never intended his hands to be put to any such purpose, so he gave that up. He struggled on somehow till he received an answer from home, which informed him that if he called at a certain place in Melbourne he would receive a pound per week, and that if he wanted more he must strive for it by his own industry. Although, compared with the way he had been living lately, his present position was one of wealth, he found at the end of the first week that the things this pound would produce did not include luxuries, and as he had always been accustomed to them, he felt the deprivation keenly.

His friends knew perfectly well when they advised him to get into some kind of employment, he would not do so, and the reason they did not send him more money, and let him have the control of it, was because they knew that if he ever had money enough at one time to pay his passage back to England, he would not be long in Australia; and as they preferred having the diameter of the globe between them, they only sent him just sufficient to keep him from starving. To cut a long story short, they kept up the remittances for a few years, when, seeing there was no hope of his doing anything for himself, they discontinued it, and left him entirely to his own devices, and as they had never been of any use to him in the past, they were not likely to be more so in the future. He gradually settled down into a confirmed loafer, and is now a melancholy instance of what want of ballast, and drink, will bring a man to.

These men, enfeebled as they are by age and beer, could not work if they felt inclined that way, and as they must live somehow, and have no choice but match-selling or the Immigrants' Home, they prefer the former, as it is easy, and assures them an existence, even though it be a bare one. It, moreover, enables them to live a life of comparative freedom, and keeps them outside the Vagrancy Laws.

COSTERMONGERS.

NOT the least deserving of our peripatetics are the leather-lunged and hard-working costermongers. They may be seen dragging their loads through the pelting shower, or under the almost vertical rays of the mid-day sun; and though the hot wind may scorch, or the cold wind chill, their cries are heard from morn till eve, and frequently half through the night.

As a class they do not rank very high, neither are they remarkable for personal beauty or agreeableness of manner; but, for all that, they are a shrewd and useful body of men.

The Melbourne costermongers are not so distinct as a class as the London ones are. There they are never mistaken for anything else, nor do they wish to be. They are distinguished by their manner and dress. "Costermonger Joe" is no exaggeration; he is but the type of the class to which he belongs. A monkey-jacket with large pearl buttons, a sleeved waistcoat with three rows of smaller pearl buttons, corduroy trousers with a fly about six inches deep at the bottom of each leg on the outside seam, "ankle jack" shoes, a bright shawl-pattern scarf round the neck, a close-fitting cap, with flaps that may be turned down over the ears, but which never are, are the correct things in dress for a London costermonger. His conversation is slangy, and he aims at being considered "leery"—that is, wide awake, and to tell him he knows the "price of old rags" is to pay him the highest possible compliment. He is fond of singing, and the burden of his songs is "love," or the free and easy life led by those in his own line of business, or both combined. He always sings in a natural key—that is, untrammelled by any rules of the art. Excellence, in his opinion, consists in expelling from the lungs the largest possible volume of sound, which, together with a peculiar intonation, renders his singing so delightful to those possessed of a musical ear. Next to singing, his chief pleasure is in dancing, and the nigger step is his favourite *pas*. Nothing affords him greater pleasure than to listen to the pattering of his feet as he "comes" the double shuffle on the cellar-flap outside some public-house, especially when it is timed by his own whistling.

Such is the portrait of the orthodox London costermonger; and now we will endeavour to show what the Melbourne one is like.

The distinctive feature of our coster is that there is nothing distinct about him, either in dress, manner, or taste. He is supremely indifferent as to the style or quality of the clothes he wears, provided they are not too clean, or too free from patches. A paget-coat has no more charms for him than a short jacket, neither is he particular as to fit, if he can only get inside it.

In trousers he sometimes patronises moleskins, and sometimes tweed. When it is the latter, they are usually well patched, and that, too, without any regard to material or colour, which sometimes makes it difficult to decide what their original colour was. In boots he affects bluchers, or lace-ups. He may have heard of "ankle jacks," but it is doubtful if he would wear a pair if they were given to him. He sometimes sports a pair of elastic-sides on Sundays, or whenever he dons his best clothes. He always wears a shawl or comforter round his neck, winter and summer, and, if there be any difference, it is worn thicker in summer than in winter. In the matter of head-gear he is partial to the black soft felt with a stiff broad brim. He is not particularly fond of singing, nor, when he does sing, are his songs of any particular class. "Tommy, make room for your Uncle" will do as well for him as the "Battle and the Breeze." He is rather partial to dancing, and his displays in that direction are in the nigger style; any other branch of the terpsichorean art he looks upon as a mistake. His conversation is usually fortified by expletives—indeed, sometimes, the expletives are nearly all the sentence consists of—and he likes to be looked upon as one "who knows a thing or two."

Like every other class, this one has its grades—the equestrian, and the plebeian, and the distinction is as clearly defined as it was among the ancient Romans. The former go about with a horse and cart, while the latter have no higher aspirations than a basket or barrow. In London the donkey is the favourite assistant of the costermonger. Here that useful animal is almost unknown.

The Chinese have taken to costermongering with the same diligence they have to fish-hawking, and with as good results to themselves.

"John" is a remarkable creature in more ways than one. He is pushing in business matters, laborious, and persevering in whatever work he undertakes, abstemious in living, and saving in disposition, and those very qualities which would be considered commendable in the Caucasian are looked upon by a section of our population as proofs of the natural depravity of the Mongolian.

Some years ago we went to war with China because the almond-eyed dwellers in the flowery-land would not come out—that is, they kept at home, and would have no "truck" with the outer barbarian. Now, the probabilities are that the next Chinese war will be because they won't keep in—that is, stay at home and mind their own business.

The Chinaman does as well as, if not better than, the Englishman at costermongering. He certainly gets a better price for his wares, because people fancy he grows them all himself, and that consequently they are fresher than those which have been knocking about the market. Some years ago, he could have been seen trotting along under a pole supporting two baskets filled with a weight of vegetables that would have broken the heart, if not the back, of the Anglo-Saxon hawker if he had been compelled to carry them in the same way. John's peculiar trot, as he went along with his load, was not from any desire to get before a rival going the same way as himself, but it was forced upon him by having to keep step with the swinging of his pole, as any want of harmony between the two would have made progression extremely difficult.

Binkie is wiser now than he was then. He has found out that the horse and cart, or truck, used by the barbarous nations of the West are much more easy and convenient than the pole and baskets of the East; and, with the adaptability of his nation, he has taken to both.

L

His ideas of commercial morality differ slightly from those of people who look upon honesty as being the best policy. Not that he is singular in that respect, for there are many who are not looked upon as heathens, but who are, nevertheless, frequently "deceitful upon the weights." You must never give him what he asks, but always knock off, at least, twenty-five per cent., for he can no more help "sticking it on" than he could help dropping anything that was too hot to handle. The prudent housewife should always be provided with weights and scales to check his spring weighing-machine, which can be easily made to register a pound without putting more than twelve ounces in the scale.

As has been observed before, giving short weight is not confined to the Chinese; sixteen ounces to the pound are rather the exception than the rule with those who follow the otherwise creditable calling of vegetable hawking. They sell cheaper than the shopkeepers, and they can afford to do so, having no heavy rents to pay, but they've no right to seek another advantage by giving short weight. In all other respects they are as honest as any body of men in the Colony. They work hard, live hard, and frequently drink hard. They marry, and are given in marriage, and usually bring up their offspring to their own line of business. A very small percentage of them get rich now-a-days, though there are at this moment some very wealthy men in Melbourne who commenced life as hawkers. But that was in the good old times when money was plentiful, sense scarce, and land cheap. It is not so easy to get rich now, for the order of those three things is reversed—money is scarce, sense abundant, and land so much the square inch.

Though few costers now become what may be called rich, many of them do pretty well. Some live in their own houses, and have a little money put by for old age. Others can barely live, and frequently find it difficult to get sufficient money to go to market with; but that, in many instances, is the result of improvidence, and drink.

A man once having taken to costermongering seldom leaves it for anything else. He may improve his position, and extend his business by opening a shop, but it is always in the same line.

As a body of men the costers are not badly-disposed,

though there are some roughs among them, but not a greater proportion than may be found in some highly respectable circles. They are not particularly sober in their habits, nor are they remarkable for drunkenness.

One of our Melbourne costermongers calls himself the "champion cocoanut-stripper of the world." Now, it's just possible that there are plenty of people who do not know what cocoanut-stripping is, and, on hearing of it for the first time, they might imagine it was stripping the nuts off the trees. Cocoanut-stripping is simply denuding the nut of the thick fibrous tusk it is enveloped in when taken from the tree. Although it is necessary to strip the nut before you can get at the inside, one would hardly imagine that the business of denudation demands such an amount of skill on the part of the operator that anyone should set himself up as the champion of that particular branch of industry. But though it looks so simple, cocoanut-stripping may be more difficult than one would imagine, and as excellence is commendable in whatever undertaking one embarks in, this individual is to be congratulated upon his championship.

Like most classes, the costermongers have a standing grievance, and that grievance is the having to pay a licence fee for the privilege of selling their things about the streets. Why they should be taxed, they are utterly unable to understand, which may be owing to their never having made political economy their study, or, perhaps, they think all taxation bad in principle, and that it ought to be abolished as a relic of barbarism. Be it as it may, their objection to the imposition is most decided, and they never let a chance slip by without unburdening their minds on the subject.

They have another cause of dissatisfaction with the authorities in having to "move on" when told to do so by the police. Their favourite business spots are at the intersections of Little Collins, and Little Flinders, with Swanston and Elizabeth streets. There, during the season, may be seen the vendors of the luscious grape, the mellow pear, and the delicious apple, offering their wares at prices considerably below those ruling in the shops. Barrow-loads of crayfish, when those crustaceans are plentiful, are planted here and there, in the gutters, and find a ready sale at prices ranging from sixpence to a shilling; while a huge barracouta may sometimes be bought there for sixpence, or five or six dozen pilchards for a shilling.

As with most other questions, much may be said for and against allowing hawkers to "pitch" in the busiest parts of the city. Shopkeepers who pay heavy rents complain, with some show of reason, of being undersold at their own doors by traders who pay no rent at all, and business people generally grumble at the obstruction caused by the wheelbarrows loitering in front of their premises.

On the other hand, the hawkers say all they want is to be allowed to earn an honest living, and those who prevent their doing that must take the responsibility upon themselves, for they will live, all the same—which means, they will live honestly if they can, but, in any case, they'll live. The public, too, are largely interested in the matter, for there is a very large section of it who prefer getting grapes in the street at threepence per pound to giving sixpence for the same article in the shops.

It being impossible to reconcile these opposing interests, a *modus vivendi* has been found by requesting the "barrow-knights" to keep moving. As the bye-law says nothing about the pace they are to go at, the movement is not of the *allegro* kind. Indeed, it is about as slow as it would be if it were a race between the barrows, the last one in to be the winner.

It is amusing to watch the costers when engaged in the congenial work of "dodging the cop," as they call keeping out of the way of the policeman. Having been told once to move on, it wouldn't do to be told to do so twice in one day, unless they wanted an interview with the police magistrate; so, to avoid that, they plant scouts to watch for the constable, and as soon as the shiny helmet is seen in the distance, the "office" is given, and the barrows begin to move slowly up the little streets close by, and keep on moving till the man in blue has passed, when the chuckling coster quickly moves back again, and rewards his own dexterity with a fresh quid of tobacco. From the experience gained in dodging their natural enemies, these costers can tell to within a few minutes when a constable has passed a given spot on his beat, and how long it will be before he visits that spot again.

There are very few women engaged in vegetable-hawking in Melbourne. They do not take so kindly to it as they do at home, where women may be seen driving barrows, or drawing trucks, with more than feminine energy. A few go about with their husbands with a horse and cart, and some keep stalls; but as a rule, the employment does not agree with their ideas of the fitness of things, so they have left the business in the hands of the sterner and more robust sex.

NEWS-RUNNERS.

THE intelligence of a people may be gauged by the number and ability of its journals, as they bring a man face to face with actual life, and show him what is going on in worlds beyond the narrow one in which he exists.

As an educational power, the Press stands pre-eminent. It completes the education we have received at school, as, unless the theories we have acquired from books are supplemented by its more practical teaching, they will remain little more than theories all our lives.

The Press to be a blessing must be free, not licentious. Its power is in proportion to its good name. Being conducted by human agency, it cannot be perfect, for no human institution is; but, though perfection cannot be expected, respectability is insisted upon, and to the credit of the Melbourne Press be it said, it is free without being scurrilous, and talented without being pedantic.

A free Press, besides being valuable for what it does, is ten thousand times more so for what it *prevents*. A country blessed with a free Press is safe—safe from foes without and from foes within. Its people are safe from oppression by the powerful, and from the petty persecutions and annoyances of Jacks-in-office. With a free Press, Judge Jeffreys would have been an impossibility, and Titus Oates would have got what he deserved long before he did. Human nature, however, is the same in all ages, or rather would be under similar circumstances; and if our welfare were not watched over by a vigilant Press, it is just possible that Judge Jeffreys might reappear in our midst; and, as for Titus Oates, a constant perusal of the daily papers will show us he is often not far off, as it is.

Having clever and cheap newspapers, we require the means of circulating them, and the readiest and best are the runners. Now-a-days the newspaper is as much a part of the breakfast table as the chop or steak is; of the two it could be the least dispensed with, and nothing disturbs paterfamilias so much as its absence from the table. We are afraid, however, he does not appreciate, as he ought, the small boy who has to leave his bed so early in the morning, and walk through the rain or cold wind in order that his paper may be ready for him when he rises. The chances are, if he ever does think of the poor boy at all, it is to curse him when he is a few minutes late. Such is the gratitude of the world. Our best friends—and that the newsboy comes within that category no one will deny—may constantly serve us, till one fault drives from our minds all recollection of past benefits.

The newsboys of London are far more lively in their habits and more persistent in trying to effect a sale than their Melbourne brethren are. There it seems as if they did not know the meaning of the negative particle "no," for they will follow you with the papers till you either buy one or send them away with a cuff. A friend of ours, of strictly religious views, says he believes they are merely agents of the Evil One, sent to entrap men into swearing. Be that as it may, there is no mistake, notwithstanding their usefulness, that they are an unmitigated nuisance.

Go where you will, your steps are dogged by these imps, and a newspaper thrust into your face. As you mount to the knife-board of an omnibus, a tug at your coat tails reminds you you are expected to buy a paper, to read as you go along. The moment you leave your house, you are pounced upon by two or three newsboys, who have apparently been waiting for you. As you go to business, you are set upon by the sellers of the morning papers, and as you return from it, they surround you again with the evening ones. At the railway stations, either going on, or returning from, a journey, your anxiety on account of your luggage is, for the moment, forgotten in the excitement of fighting your way through a crowd of these boys. As you go to the theatre, the "last edition" is dinned into your ears; or, as you walk arm-in-arm with the dear creature who, at present, makes life so much worth living, your ears are assailed with "*Echo.* Full accounts of the breach of prom—ise."

Now, an announcement like that, coming upon you just as you are considering the advisability of "popping the question," will probably divert your thoughts into another channel; and the busy mind will conjure up all the endearing expressions you have committed to paper, and which are now in your sweetheart's possession. Knowing, as every man ought to do, that in these "cases" there is usually a resurrection of old love letters, which are read in court, to the intense amusement of everyone except the defendant, and which, afterwards, become public property, you will feel inclined to hesitate before putting the momentous interrogation, lest something beyond your control should bring about a similar case in which you and your darling would figure as principals.

Some of the Melbourne newsboys are sons of poor but respectable parents, who keep them at school all day, and allow them to sell the evening papers at night, so that they may contribute something towards their own keep. Most of the runners, however, are *gamins* pure and simple, who take to the business, heart and soul, for the sake of the money they can realise at it, which they afterwards get rid of in the way most agreeable to their own tastes.

Some take the trifle they earn home to their parents, who sometimes make a good use of it, though frequently it is spent in drink. Others, who have no home, and no parents, attend first to their craving hunger by an investment in bread and a saveloy; or, if they have been very lucky, in two threepenny meat pies; then, if they have sufficient cash left, they visit the gallery of the theatre; after which they retire to the hole or corner where they usually "pitch their doss," and sleep soundly till hunger wakes them late next morning.

Others play at "pitch and toss" till they have lost their own or won the other boys' hard earnings; when the lucky ones indulge in a glorious "feed," while the unlucky ones look hungrily on, in the hope it may be their turn to-morrow.

"*Herald* a penny, full account of the murd—her, and robber—ree!" How familiar that cry is to us every evening between the hours of four and eight, pitched in every key the human voice is capable of giving expression to, from the childish treble to the harsher note of husky adolescence, and the feeble accents of extreme old age. These cries are varied by those relating to a "fi—her," or a "suce—cide," or the case of Mr. So-and-So, or the trial of some one else whose offence has caused an unusual stir in society. Some of these youngsters exercise a deal of ingenuity in dishing up old events as something new. The slightest allusion to a murder that occurred a month ago is given out as the "full account of the murd—her," thus leading people to suppose that another had been added to the somewhat long list of those that have gone before.

In trading thus upon the popular taste for the sensational, these boys display no little knowledge of human nature, for it is certain there are hundreds who would purchase a paper that contained the account of a murder who would never think of doing so if they only expected to find in it the ordinary daily budget of news. Next to a murder, a spicy scandal, or a dreadful suicide, is the most potent cry for inducing people to part with their pence. The *faux pas*, or eccentricities of well-known personages, likewise bring about the sale of many extra copies, for we dearly love to moralise over the shortcomings of our betters.

A newspaper may contain any number of ably-written articles, papers on scientific or useful subjects, and people will throw it down with disgust, and say, "There's no news at all in the paper to-day." That may not say much for the intelligence of the present day, but it is true nevertheless, and well known to the managers of the different newspapers, who, knowing what a fascination a murder, the more atrocious the better, or a glaring breach of the seventh commandment, has for a no small portion of mankind, take care to provide for the issue of a largely increased number of copies while the excitement lasts.

Newspaper-running is now mostly in the hands of children, who from their active habits are better suited to the occupation than those who are more advanced in years. There are some few old men connected with it, but these usually stand at some corner, or confine themselves to very short rounds. One or two blind men combine the sale of newspapers with that of wax matches and bootlaces, one of whom has a round of customers, at whose houses he delivers the papers every Saturday morning with the precision of the keenest-eyed news-runner in the Colony.

Little barefooted boys, whose tender years one would suppose unfitted them for such employment, run about the streets piping *Evening Herald* with as much earnestness as though their existence depended upon the sale of a few copies. Girls between the ages of seven and fifteen stand at the corners, and offer to each passer-by the evening or the weekly papers. These mostly sell for their fathers or mothers, who may be seen standing close by with a bundle of the same papers under their arms. A few married women, with babies in their arms, strive to supplement their other incomes by the sale of a few copies of the " Herald," and occasionally an able-bodied man may be seen engaged in the same business, but these latter mostly belong to the loafing class, who have very little faith in hard work.

The wholesale price of the evening paper is one and sixpence per quire of twenty-five sheets, so that leaves sevenpence profit on every twenty-five sold. Some of the more active boys will sell between fifty and a hundred every evening. Many, however, are unable to sell more than twenty or thirty, and that, of course, leaves them in very poor circumstances.

The distance some of these boys travel during the evening, up one street and down another, in search of customers, would rather surprise them if it were measured; but as they cannot see it in a straight line, they get over it without knowing how tired they ought to be.

Two or three of the elder boys who do business on their own accounts employ some of the very small ones as "runners." To these they give half the profits; so that, if one be lucky enough to sell eight, it will enable him to get a penny bun for supper.

Some of them are very smart in sensationalising any scrap of news the paper may contain; and some even go as far as alluding to a murder when none has occurred; while others confine themselves to the simple cry of " *Herald*, a penny !" except when something out of the usual has happened, when they are as vociferous as the rest.

One of the latter class came up to us with the usual question—

" *Herald*, sir ?"

" Have you a murder in it ?" we asked.

"No, sir."

"A suicide?"

"No, sir."

"A robbery?"

"No, sir."

"What! not a robbery?"

"Only a man knocked another down in Bourke Street, and stole his watch."

"Well, can't you make that into a daring highway robbery and attempted murder?"

The boy seemed struck with the idea, as he passed on, and, very shortly after, we heard him bellowing out our suggestion at the very top of his voice, though whether it increased the sale of copies we are unable to say, but in all probability it did.

That may seem a rather doubtful piece of morality on our part, but what we said we intended as irony, and never thought for a moment it would be acted upon.

Some of these lads rather overstep the bounds of good manners when they fail to secure a customer they have "spotted," as the following specimen of what the admirers of our colonial youth call "smartness" will show.

A young imp went up to a respectably-dressed man, and offered him the evening paper. For some time he took no notice of the boy's importunity, till at last he said, "No, no," in rather impatient tones.

"How's that?" queried the lad. "Haven't yer got a 'win' (a penny) on yer, or can't yer read?"

The sublimity of the impudence saved him from a cuff, for the man, after apparently debating within himself whether he should give him one or not, smiled, and turned away.

There being such a keen competition among the boys, they soon acquire a pushing manner that would be highly useful to them if, in after life, they could only find their way into some draper's establishment.

We saw a couple of them, one afternoon, running up to a gentleman, and so close was the race that he had a difficulty in deciding which came in first. In order to influence his decision, each one became very loud and voluble in urging his claim to the gentleman's preference.

"Look here, sir," said one, "I saw you first."

"No, you never," replies the other. "I see the gentleman before you did, and, besides, I sold him one yesterday, and have been looking out for him ever since."

"Why, didn't I pay you?" asked the gentleman.

"Oh, yes, sir, but I thought you'd want another to day, and that made me look out for you."

"What's that to do with it?" asked his rival. "If the gentleman bought one off you yesterday, he ought to buy one off me to-day, to make it fair."

That appeared to be the purchaser's opinion also, for he bought one off the last speaker, much to the chagrin of the other.

Some of these smart young gentlemen frequently get themselves into trouble, in consequence of making false announcements as to the contents of their papers.

One evening, at the corner of Queen and Collins Streets, a man seized one of these dispensers of the evening's literary pabulum by the collar, and taxed him with swindling him out of a penny the evening before, by calling out the "full account of a murder," when the paper contained no allusion whatever to one.

No doubt the man was grievously disappointed in not being able to feast his mind upon the details of some horrid murder; and his vanity might, also, have been hurt by the boy's "selling" him as well as the paper; but, seeing he had value for his money, it hardly amounted to swindling, although it might have been a mild form of obtaining money under false pretences.

At first the boy was rather taken aback. Speedily, however, his native impudence came to his assistance, and he stoutly denied ever having seen his assailant before, who, he said, had mistaken him for his brother, who was very much like him.

"You lie, you young scoundrel, you know very well you sold me the paper," said the man, "and I've a good mind to give you something that will teach you to speak the truth another time."

The victimised one seemed really inclined to put his threat into execution, and the boy thought he was going to get it. However, the hold on the collar was relaxed, and the lad was not long in putting a few paces between him and the disappointed one.

It is a fortunate thing the *gamins* of Melbourne can earn a trifle in selling papers about the streets. The earnings of the regular ones may be small—ranging, as they do, from four to eight shillings per week; but, small as they are, it is a consideration in connection with their keep, and if they did not earn that much in such a creditable manner, the chances are they would earn nothing honestly.

How many possible burglars and garrotters, in embryo, are there among these poor barefooted children who run about selling the evening papers?—possible, we mean, if left to themselves. On the other hand, how many decent and respectable members of society may there not be among them in the future, if means be now given them of raising themselves from the gutters? It is a question that concerns everyone who has anything to lose, or who has the well-being of his country at heart.

By investing a penny in a paper you not only have half-an-hour's intellectual enjoyment, but you do good, though, perhaps, you may never know it. You encourage a habit of industry and a desire to do well in those who are naturally inclined to the opposite; and if that does not help a man to enjoy his pennyworth of news, we should like to know what would. Habits of industry and well-doing are as easily acquired as evil ones, the same opportunities being offered; and if you can encourage those habits by buying a paper from those who so earnestly strive to sell them, it is a duty you owe to society to do so, as you thereby beget a spirit of self-reliance in those poor waifs of humanity that may cling to them all through their lives.

FISH-HAWKERS.

These are not the most respectable of the hawking brotherhood, though, doubtless, there are some decent fellows among them; but, as a rule, their manners fall far short of what society deems the standard of politeness. They are coarse and vulgar in language, and uninviting in aspect; and, in addition to those two characteristics, they are great drinkers, their favourite "lap," as they call it, being rum.

There is something about fish that has a not very elevating effect upon the minds of those who deal in it. Male and female alike become remarkable for a species of eloquence that is not tolerated in polite circles—at least not when strangers are within hearing. So proverbial are they for their vigorous speech, that in all countries where fish-dealers form a distinct class, they are quoted as everything that is low and vulgar.

"Billingsgate" among the English is a term applied to language that is not recognised as part of the curriculum of our Universities; and few ladies in Scotland would care about being called "fishwives." In France it is the same. "Poissade" is a title no *grande dame* aspires to. In Germany, "fischerfrau," when applied to a lady, is not looked upon as a compliment; and in Italy the "piscatori" are as noted for their fluency of speech as the confraternity in all other nations. It is the same in this Colony. For a fish-hawker to utter ten consecutive words without an oath appears to be an impossibility; and if he were to do so, he would stand a very good chance of losing caste among his fellows, and becoming the butt of all their witticisms.

Fish has not only procured those who deal in it a bad name, but the word, also, when used adjectively, and applied to actions, implies sometimes that which is the reverse of creditable. Anything of a suspicious nature is said to have a "fishy" look; and what has been conceived in fraud, and brought forth just inside the law, is denounced as being decidedly "fishy."

Why should it be so? Fish is pleasant to the taste and nutritious to the body; and they seem gentle and playful creatures enough when swimming about in their native element, always excepting the shark and octopus, which are certainly repulsive to the sight, and disagreeable as neighbours.

Shakespeare speaks of "an ancient and fish-like smell"; but when he said that, he must have meant when the fish itself was ancient, for, when fresh, it is a pleasant reminder of the briny ocean, and far more agreeable to the nostrils than the smell of some men.

Some of the fish-hawkers do not confine themselves exclusively to supplying the piscivorous portion of Her Majesty's lieges with that edible, but resort, occasionally, to methods of raising the wind that are quite as "fishy," but not so honourable, as their regular calling. At races, and other public gatherings, they may be seen manipulating the three cards, or initiating greenhorns into the mysteries of "over and under," or some other game by which flats are induced to part so readily with their superfluous cash. That branch of industry, however, not being permanent, though highly lucrative while it lasts, they have to resume their baskets and trucks as a means of living in those times when the races are not.

Great numbers of the fish-hawkers are Celestials—poor, miserable-looking objects, whose dirty appearance would set any one against fish,—only it is an article that can be washed,—though, in that respect they are hardly less inviting in looks than some of their Christian brethren. Their feeble-looking bodies and weak cries are in great contrast to the burly forms and stentorian voices of the Anglo-Saxon; but though their bodies are small, they are uncommonly tough, and being possessed of energetic wills, and of industrious habits, they go the round of their customers with less fatigue than would be felt by the stronger and more phlegmatic barbarian.

They must be early at market, in order to get the fish in time for their customers' breakfasts; besides, if they were to come late, and fish happened to be rather scarce, they might find it all gone when they got there, and if they wanted any they would have to get it at an enhanced price from the other hawkers. When fish is scarce, and rabbits and wild-fowl plentiful, they invest in these latter, in preference to the former; for, when the price of fish rules high, as it always does when scarce, people will not buy it, for they appear to be utterly unable to see the correctness of giving a shilling to-day for what they could have bought yesterday for sixpence, and that makes the hawkers fight rather shy of it when it is not plentiful.

Friday is the fish-hawker's busiest day, on account of the number of Catholics there are in Melbourne, who must have fish on that day, or put up with what sailors call a "banyan day."

Although not remarkable for politeness in social life, they are tolerably civil to their customers when things go pleasantly. Sometimes, however, when one of them has been detained at the doorstep by some stingy housewife, and he is unable to see his way to a profit out of the price she offers, he is apt to give vent to his annoyance in language the meaning of which is hidden from the good dame by the words being spoken in *argot*, otherwise it might lead to his being introduced to a police magistrate, unless the indignant lady, unable to control her feelings, settled the matter herself by making his head acquainted with a broom-handle.

They speak plainly enough sometimes, when their expectations of getting a customer have been baulked, as the following short passage will show.

A lady was sweeping out her front verandah one morning when a hawker came along with the usual enquiry:

"Do you want any fish to-day, missis?"

"No, not to-day."

"You'd better try some, they're nice and fresh—in fact, all but alive," he persisted, while offering one for her inspection.

"How do you sell them?"

"A shilling a dozen; and I'll guarantee you don't get them in the shops under two bob."

"A shilling a dozen for those sprats!" she cried in astonishment. "I'll give you sixpence for a dozen and a half."

Fish-Hawkers.

"Have you got sixpence?" queried the fishmonger.

"Yes."

"Then you must have gone short of beer yesterday." With that saucy reply he picked up his basket and went on.

There have, at one time or other, been some remarkable characters connected with the fish-hawking industry, one of whom was known as "Old Dan." This individual was quite a musical genius, and a celebrity in other respects. Instead of announcing the quality and vitality of his fish in the usual manner, he would sing it in what must, at one time, have been really a fine voice.

Dan was not wealthy, and could at no time muster more than a few shillings to invest, or, as he called it, "investigate," in fish; consequently, when the market rates ruled high, he was unable to "line" his basket, and on those mornings the streets were not resonant with his songs.

In dealing with his customers, Mr. Dan was very independent, and rather inclined to be saucy when his price was too high for buyers, or his powers of persuasion too feeble to push a sale. He was in the habit of associating the names of well-known Melbourne men with his ditty, and he would drag them in without any regard to rhyme or reason. He attracted a deal of notice on his rounds, and would bring a smile to the faces of many who had very little else to smile about. Strangers would stop and stare at him with astonishment, and those who had heard him daily for years were always pleased to hear his well-known voice again. He did better than any other man could have done on his small outlay, as he always asked and got a good price for his fish, and that suited him better than carrying about a heavy load, and getting no more for it.

When he retired from the streets, he took to letting lodgings in a right-of-way off Bourke Street east, and supplemented the income derived from that by hiring out trucks to those hawkers whose circumstances were not flourishing enough to permit of their having one of their own.

Thus Dan disappeared from a world of which, in his time, he had been such a distinguished ornament; but, as may be expected, that world went on as usual—buying and selling; "besting" one another whenever they had the chance; "boozing" and getting sober, quarrelling and making it up with libations of unlimited beer, only instead of its being poured out on the ground as in the olden times, it was poured down the throats of the late contestants—a sure way of securing peace for a time, by making them too drunk to quarrel. By "world" we mean the fish-hawker's sphere, not the globe on which we stand, and which so many parties, sects, and sets, divide into worlds of their own.

Not having seen the old man for some time, we asked one of our hawker-friends how he was getting on.

"Oh," was the reply, "he pegged out a month ago! Poor Dan; he wasn't a bad sort," he continued, with a sincerity that unmistakably showed he meant what he said.

It may not be generally known that "to peg out" means "to die," as well as to win a game of cribbage, add in using the expression he did, the hawker meant no disrespect to his departed friend's memory. It may not be a very elegant or reverent way of speaking of a friend's departure from this world; but these men seldom mix in ecclesiastical circles, and elegance of speech has not been their study, so what might seem irreverent if uttered by a parson, is not irreverence when spoken by them. Again, the negative praise of not being a "bad sort" was about the highest compliment our friend knew how to bestow upon the late lamented Mr. Dan.

It is a fortunate thing the "world" is not dependent upon one man for its well-being, though many a one fancies it is, and, just as a wheel is dependent upon its hub, so he believes his world to be dependent upon him.

A man of startling force of character is sometimes found in the political world who appears to be the atlas upon whose shoulders it rests; the man dies, yet, somehow, the nation goes on. In many a private firm, too, it is the same; some one employé seems indispensable to its prosperity. He presumes upon that, and "carries on," till, over-doing it, his services are dispensed with; yet, much to his surprise, the firm doesn't "burst up." Downwards, through every class to the lowest position in society, the same idea prevails; and when Dan retired from hawking fish, it was thought his position in the musical department could not be filled up. Very soon, however, that was found to be a mistake, for, no sooner had our old friend disappeared, than his mantle fell upon the shoulder of another genius, who had apparently been waiting to receive it.

The new singer is a different one from the old, and has a much finer voice. He belongs to the equestrian order, that is, he owns a horse and cart, and so is, of course, of a higher stratum in the hawker world than poor old Dan ever was. He has a good horse, and his cart is painted white, and he himself dresses in white sailor costume. He has no apparent dislike to soap and water, for his face is always clean, thereby contrasting favourably with many of the fish-hawking brotherhood. He "works" the southern suburbs, and does pretty well, for his cleanly looks are of great assistance to him in pushing his business.

Two or three other peripatetic dealers in fish go about with nice-looking "mokes," harnessed to long shallow barrows, on which are displayed their fish, or rabbits, or whatever else they may have for sale. These also "do" the suburbs, as the noise and traffic of the city streets would be too much for their donkeys' nerves.

To see the fish-hawkers to advantage, one must go to the fish-market some morning at five o'clock, when one will see there that which will well repay one for the self-denial of getting up so early. They are then all together, and can be studied *en masse*, when their manners are free, and their tongues unrestrained, and not as one sees them when dealing with their customers, for then prudence and the fear of the law compel them to qualify their language, and keep their practical jokes in subjection.

Shortly after five o'clock the fish arrives in baskets, and is sold by auction by five salesmen, all of whom are vociferous at the same time in lauding the quality of the lots they offer for sale, and if the "chaff" of twenty or thirty loud-voiced men, who take delight in making as much noise as possible, be added, we cannot be far wrong in saying the scene is of the liveliest.

When one man is unable to buy a basket to himself, he joins with one or two others, and they purchase one between them, which they afterwards divide as fairly as they can. The way in which the division is made is this: if three men have clubbed together for a basket, three fishes of as nearly as possible the same size are taken out and laid separately on the ground; then three more of an equal size are taken out, and one added to each of the others; and so they keep on putting one to each lot till the whole is divided into three equal portions, when the man who divided them allows the others to take their choice, and he has the one that is left.

One morning, however, the man who was dividing the fish appeared to have imbibed more rum than was consistent with clearness of vision, or correctness in judging weight and size, for he was putting the lots together with so little regard to equality of bulk that one of the others asked him, in choice Billingsgate, if he knew what he was about. The sorter told him to go to a place that must be nameless, and asked him if he thought he was an adjective fool. The other answered he didn't think anything at all about it; he was adjectively well sure he was, and if he didn't let the adjective fish alone, he would hammer some of his adjective ribs in. That caused the wrath of the threatened one to boil over, and he made a blow at the other, which, if it had landed where it was intended, would have sent him flying; but as it fell about two feet short, no harm was done, except to the belligerent himself, who, through striking nothing more substantial than air, overbalanced himself, and fell on the top of the fish, where he lay sprawling till one of the bystanders picked him up. By that time his wrath had evaporated, and the others went on dividing the fish as though nothing unusual had occurred.

The noise and bustle are highly exhilarating, and keep everyone on the alert. The coarse jests of the English are mingled with the excited jabber of the Chinese, who appear to be comparing notes with one another on some weighty matter that requires a deal of gesticulation. Much horseplay and practical joking is indulged in, of which that called "bonneting" is the favourite. Sometimes a small fish, or a ball of wet fishy paper, is sent flying into some one's face, though the Celestials are usually the targets these missiles are aimed at, and if John protests against such treatment, his protestations are received with a yell of delight. Occasionally when he is forcing his way through the crowd with a basket at each end of his pole, some one will let the last slip off, and that, of course, will cause the other to fall down in front, to the intense delight of every one but the Chinaman himself, who on these occasions generally lets loose all the vulgar English he is master of; and when that is not sufficient to relieve his feelings, he supplements it with as much Chinese as he thinks necessary.

He does not always confine himself to swearing, however, for he frequently resents the insult in a more striking manner. One morning, as a Chinaman was working his way through the crowd with his basket of fish on his head, some one tipped it over. "John" immediately turned round and struck the man nearest to him, who happened to be the wrong one. The man quickly retaliated in the same way, which caused quite a *furore* of delight among the bystanders, especially so to the real culprit, who patted John on the back and told him not to be afraid, but to go in and win. The Celestial, however, thought better of it, for he picked up his fish and went on his way, not, it is hardly necessary to add, rejoicing.

One would scarcely credit the number of Chinese fish-hawkers there are if one did not see them together in the market. They have appropriated to themselves a kind of piazza on the right hand side as you go in, where they sort and divide their fish, keeping up all the time a chattering such as only the Chinese are capable of.

The fish-hawkers have a licence fee of threepence to pay every morning before they leave the market. Of course that tax is not approved of by either the Caucasian or Mongolian, and that appears to be about the only subject on which there is an identity of view between them, thus proving the correctness of the poet's dictum, that, under certain circumstances, all the world becomes akin.

GATHERERS.

MATTER being indestructible, there can be no such thing as waste. What is called waste is simply allowing things that have served their intended purpose to lie by till they have resolved themselves into their original elements, instead of putting them to some other useful purpose.

Although man may neglect to make the most of things he has to do with, he cannot, with all his power, destroy one atom of anything, or waste one drop of water. He can, by fire, or acids, reduce a substance apparently to nothing, but it is not destroyed; it is merely restored to its original condition, to be reproduced at some future time in the same or some other shape.

The scheme of creation is so grand in its conception, and so perfect in every detail, that not to recognise in it the hand of an all-wise and omnipotent Creator and Ruler is a sign of such mental blindness that those who are so afflicted must be simply mad.

In the beginning, "the earth was without form and void." But God shaped it, and gave it vitality, "and saw that it was good." Since then everything has sprung from the earth, and will return to it in obedience to a law laid down by the Almighty. That law is unalterable, and what we see to-day will disappear to-morrow, to re-appear at some future time; and that ceaseless round will continue till earth shall unite with heaven, when our bodies, purified of their grosser particles, will stand in the presence of Him from whose hand they sprang.

Let us see if it be in man's power to waste that which he hath and calleth his own. He is said to waste his health when, by vicious courses, or otherwise, he makes himself ill. But he does nothing of the sort; the health, or rather the life, by which the clay is quickened, belongs to Him who gave it, and to whom it will return unimpaired when the body that contains it shall have become too weak to keep it any longer. All he does is to damage the flesh, and hasten its restoration to the earth, whence it sprang.

He is said to waste his substance; he merely gives it into some one else's keeping. He is said to destroy something by fire, when all he does is to liberate certain gases it is entirely composed of. He is said to waste his words, when he talks more than is necessary, or to no purpose; well there may be a little seeming truth in that, but it is only seeming, as he can do nothing of the sort, although he may tire the patience of his listeners, and make himself ridiculous. Speech is but wind, which, owing to the formation of the human throat, a man can, with the assistance of his tongue and lips, convert into articulate sounds. These sounds are conveyed by the atmosphere to the tympanum of those who happen to be near, from off which they reach the understanding, if the speaker is fortunate enough to make his meaning sufficiently clear; if not, he wastes nothing, as all he does is to cause a few ripples in the surrounding atmosphere—a fact that should be borne in mind by people afflicted with a *cacoëthes loquendi*.

He is also said to waste his time. He cannot do that either, because there is no such thing. It is all eternity, so vast and illimitable that our puny intellects can conceive neither beginning nor end; and to say that a man wastes his time is merely to assert he has left undone something he ought to have done.

If things are not wasted, it might be asked, what becomes of them when they are worn away, or otherwise made invisible? They are not worn away; they are only distributed. Matter is of such a nature that it can be reduced to a powder so fine that one can neither see nor feel it. What has become of the doorstep that has been worn down by our constant treading? Pieces have been rubbed off it by the foot, and these pieces, mixing with other particles lying about, help to form a mass that may, in some millions of years' time, be worked up into another doorstep. It is the same with the great toe of the stone statue of St. Peter that has been kissed away by pious Catholics at Rome. Small particles have clung to the lips of the worshippers in their contact with the stone; and, being licked into the mouth, have passed through the body into their original home in the earth.

Buildings and statues that have been exposed to the atmosphere are seen to be much worn. What has become of the part that is absent? It has been filed away by the wind, and the filings carried to a distance, and then quietly dropped to earth, where they have other duties to perform.

There is nothing, however small and useless it may appear, that may not be put to some profitable use, if you can only get enough of it together. Your old coat, if it cannot be "duffed" up and made "ash good ash new," can be with others torn into fragments and regenerated in the shape of shoddy, and in that condition it may, with the help of the tailor, be made to adorn once more your outer man.

Old rags are the parents of the greatest civilising agent the world has ever known, for without paper the printing machine would be useless, and journals that can now be had for one penny would be unobtainable at any price, and we should fall back into the darkness of the papyrus and parchment days.

Bones that have grown from what sprang from the earth may be pulverised and re-committed to it, to produce the wherewith to form the bones of future generations; and if you put those on one side Towzer has polished, they will, in the course of a year bring you in enough to buy you a pair of braces, or a necktie.

Every scrap of iron, or other metal, seen lying about the house or yard should be picked up and put on one side. You may get enough some day to sell; if not, you can always give the little you have to those who will thankfully receive it. The little bits of fat left from the table, or trimmed off the uncooked joint, if rendered down and sold, will soon reappear in the shape of soap or candles. Of course no one wants to be told what they can do with their empty bottles, they are told that half a dozen times every day at their back gates, but they may not know what to do with them when they are broken. If they save them, with any other bits of broken glass they may happen to have, they can sell them to the dealers, who will sell them again at the glass works, where they will be melted down and reformed into bottles, once more to convey to the bibulous the liquid which "maketh the heart glad."

"Any empty bottles to sell?" One hears that cry often enough now, though in the early days bottles were not only unsaleable, but they couldn't be given away.

These gatherers are the lowest of the industrial classes, and are as remarkable for rags and dirt as they are for snapping up any "unconsidered trifle" they may see lying about. Their ranks are filled by both sexes, and of all ages. One may see little boys and girls among them, and old men and women of sixty; but the great majority are boys between twelve and twenty.

The way in which some of these boys dress is peculiar to themselves. They, of course, acknowledge the necessity of donning some kind of covering, but that the size of the garment should be influenced by the size of the body is a question too puerile to be entertained for a moment. One may often see a boy between four and five feet in height wearing a coat that must have been made for a man at least six feet, the skirts beating at his heels and the cuffs turned back to the elbows. The waistcoat is usually dispensed with. Not so the trousers, and as he must have his nether limbs encased in something, that something is usually a pair of small boy's knickerbockers; thus, the amplitude of one garment is made still more striking by the scantiness of another. The men are quite as remarkable as the boys in the matter of dress. To see them one would think they were scarecrows who, having become weary of the monotony of their regular occupation, had taken to gathering as a change.

There are in and around Melbourne about four hundred men and boys engaged in "marining," as the occupation followed by the gatherers is called. It is a new slang word added not long ago to the "patter" of the slums, and means working for the marine store dealers. Two usually go together, with a truck lent them by the dealer for whom they travel, on the understanding that he is to be the sole purchaser of their day's acquisitions. They mostly have a short rope fastened to the handle of their hand-cart, which they hitch on to the back part of any larry or cart that may be going their way, if they can get the driver's permission, which is very convenient in helping them up the hilly streets. Some have a horse and cart, and "do" the more distant suburbs. These do pretty well without having to work as hard as the others, for driving a horse is much easier than driving a truck.

It would be well if this business were entirely in the hands of men, for the temptation to pilfer is too great for many of these boys to resist; as when they are prowling about the rights-of-way, they see many things lying about the back-yards they could turn to a profitable account, and when no one is looking they are apt to snap it up and put it into the bag they always have so conveniently with them. That is frequently the first step in crime, and although it may only be an empty bottle, or a few bones, it is taking what is not theirs, and if they acquire the habit of doing that with trifles, it will end with their stealing something far more valuable. Probably there are plenty of men quite as likely to yield to temptation as the boys; but, however that may be, some of them would be better able to resist it.

There is another reason why the calling is bad for boys—it gives them a liking for a vagabond life that will cling to them for ever. It is also an inducement for the unruly ones to run away from home, as they know there is always a certainty of their being able to earn something to buy food with, while if there were no such opportunity offered to them, hunger would soon bring them back repentant to their parents' door if the fear of it did not restrain them from leaving it.

Some years ago a few benevolent persons started a "Boys' Brigade of Gatherers," with the view of turning our *gamins* to some useful account by giving them the habits of industry and self-reliance; but from some cause or other, probably the want of funds, it collapsed. If such was the case it says very little for the wisdom or benevolence of those who, having the means of doing good, allowed such an undertaking to fall through, when at the expense of a little time and money, God only knows what good might have been done; for objectionable as the occupation is for boys if left to their own devices, it might have given the brigaded ones, who were under some sort of discipline and supervision, a start in life that would have been the turning-point for good.

The different industrial brigades of the ragged-schools at home have turned out some bright men; and it would be the same here if a helping hand was held out to our street arabs, instead of letting them run about wild. If some of them were formed into a shoe-black brigade, as they are in London, there can be no doubt of its success if the charge were only a penny, for there are hundreds who would pay that to have their boots blacked who object to pay the sixpence or threepence demanded by the loafers, who at present enjoy the monopoly of that branch of the urban industry.

The price the gatherers get for the old bottles depends upon the season. In hot weather when there in an active demand for bottled colonial beer, the brewers will give them ten shillings per gross. In the winter months, when the majority of our citizens prefer whisky to beer, the demand for "empties" is not so great, consequently a lower price rules. For these bottles the "mariners" give from a penny to threepence a dozen, which leaves them a fair margin for profit. The old medicine bottles they wash and sell to the wholesale and retail chemists, and get a good price for them. Old lead brings them in from a penny to twopence per pound; bones, eighteenpence per cwt.; rags, three pounds a penny; and old iron, a farthing a pound. These latter articles, however, they pick up, or get given to them for next to nothing.

Some of the men who go about gathering do so merely as a "stall" to keep them outside the Vagrancy Act, as it enables them to prove when arrested for vagrancy, as they are very liable to be, that they have a means of getting a living. Others take to it simply because it gives them an opportunity of surveying the back parts of the houses they call at, whereby they discover the easiest way of "cracking" them. They then "lay on" some of their friends, and if the burglary "comes off," which means, if it be successful, they are let into the "swim," that is, they get a share of the plunder.

Others hang on their own "hooks," either as "hatters" or in couples. By hatters we do not mean that very respectable body of men who provide our head-gear, but those thieves who play a "lone hand" in their operations. The hatters do better than the others, and are less likely to be "copped," for a secret that is only known to one is much safer than when it is shared in by two. But whether they act singly or in pairs, the *modus operandi* is just the same.

Having entered a back-yard, and having received no answer to their question re the old bottles, they go to the back door and knock. If no one comes to see what is wanted, they try the handle. If the door be locked it is a sure indication that no one is at home. The door, or window, is then prized open, and the house "turned over," to find any money or jewellery that may be in it. They do not care for clothes or other bulky articles on these occasions. What they want is something they can put into their pockets, and carry away without showing anything unusual in their appearance. Having ransacked the house, they retire by the way they came, and continue their rounds as though nothing had happened to interrupt them. To divert suspicion from themselves, they go the same round the next and few following days; after which they retire from business till the proceeds of the robbery are spent.

These enterprising gentlemen do not confine their attentions to occupied houses only, for, if they have a chance, they will go into an empty house and steal every key in it; and not unfrequently pay a nocturnal visit to the same place, and walk off with the gas-fittings.

There is a perfect understanding between these gatherers and the dogs belonging to the different houses they call at. Not a friendly understanding be it understood, but the reverse. There can be no doubt of our canine friends being readers of character of no mean order, and when they see a "mariner" at the back gate, their instinct tells them they must be on the alert; and the boys are perfectly well aware of the feelings the dogs entertain towards them. The first thing the gatherers do on arriving at a back gate is to look out for the dog before they open it too wide. If the dog be chained up it's all right, and they go inside, when the dog speedily lets the people of the house know they are wanted. If they cannot see a dog, and they are in doubt as to whether there be one or not, the cry of "Any old bottles to sell" will quickly bring him on the scene if there happen to be one about. If none show up, they enter the yard with confidence. When there is a dog, and his barking brings no one to see what is wanted, they conclude, and pretty correctly, that they are all out, and that they consider gives them the right of search in all the yard outside the reach of the dog's chain.

Two youngsters one day went into a yard, the occupant of which appeared to be absent, and as they were looking about they spied three lemonade bottles lying just within the length of the dog's chain. The twain held a council of war as to how they were to be captured, for they were determined to have them before they left. They tried to make friends with the dog by means of a piece of bread, but his sense of duty was stronger than his appetite. They then tried coaxing, but all their blandishments were thrown away, as he was not to be caught by chaff. They then tried to steal a march upon him, by one occupying his attention on the side furthest from the bottles, while the other rushed in to pick them up. But that dodge failed also, as the dog appeared to be on both sides of his kennel at once. Another council of war was now held as to what should be the next move, when one of them happened to see a clothes-prop lying handy, and that was brought into requisition to rake the bottles towards them. A battle now took place between the dog, a large Newfoundland, and the prop. As soon as it was within reach he seized hold of it, and held on with the tenacity of death. In the struggle which ensued the two boys managed to get the dog on the side furthest from the bottles, and thinking he would still retain his hold of the prop, one of them slipped round with the view of picking them up. But this youth nearly found out to his cost that he had reckoned without his host, for as soon as the dog saw that manoeuvre, he let go the prop and sprang at the boy, and he only escaped by the skin of his teeth.

How the affair would have ended is hard to say, for at that moment the mistress of the house entered upon the scene with the shrill and by no means friendly enquiry of what they wanted. One of them answered, "They only wanted to get at the bottles to see how much they were worth in case she should want to sell them." The old lady was not to be deceived by a story like that, and she told them if they didn't clear out pretty quickly, she would let the dog loose, and one step towards the kennel had such an effect upon their movements that in less than two seconds they were on the safe side of the gate.

Intellectually these lads rank as low as they do socially, although they may not be deficient in natural intelligence; but instead of its having been improved by education, it has been sharpened into cunning by their gutter associations.

Their ignorance is simply appalling, and as long as the compulsory clauses of the Education Act are allowed to remain inoperative, they will continue as they are—a blot upon our civilisation.

A few take the money they earn home to their parents; others get rid of it by playing at pitch and toss, or other kindred games. Some spend a portion of it in going to the galleries of the theatres, or, in the case of the elder, and some of the younger ones, squander it in drink. Thus many of them start in life with a taste for pilfering, gambling, and drinking; and with such a start, can there be any doubt what the finish is likely to be?

We stopped two young gatherers one day, and entered into conversation with them concerning their occupation, and how they passed their idle time. Among other questions, we asked one what he did with his money.

"Take it home to my father," he answered.

"What does your father work at?"

"Nothing."

"How does he live?"

We understood by his answer that he loafed upon him, and his brother, who worked at boot pegging.

"Have you no mother?"

"Yes."

"Then why don't you give the money to her?"

"That would be worse," said the poor boy, with a mournful look.

What hope is there for that lad, with a home so dismal and associates so doubtful.

We asked if the other boy was his brother.

"No."

"What do you do with your money?"

"Keep myself with it."

"Have you no father or mother?"

"No."

"Do you ever play at pitch and toss?"

"No fear," he answered. "I don't believe in working hard for my money, and then losing it at pitch and toss, the same as some of the boys do. But others win though," he added, with a look that convinced us it was nothing but the fear of losing that kept him from joining the others in that innocent pastime.

"You would play if you thought you could win?" we asked.

"Oh, yes," he replied naively.

There are a few women and girls engaged in gathering, but most of them, instead of going round the rights-of-way, visit the corporation tip, and other places where refuse is deposited, and rake among the rubbish for rags, bones, and scraps of iron, or anything else that may have a commercial value.

A few Celestials adopt this mode of getting a living, but they resemble more the *chiffoniers* of Paris than they do the ordinary gatherer. They are poor, miserable-looking creatures, and belong to the lowest and poorest class of our Chinese population. They buy nothing, but confine themselves to what they can pick up in the gutters and rights-of-way. They are armed with a piece of stout wire with a hook at the end, with which they pick up the bits of rag they see lying about, and put them in their baskets, thus avoiding the loss of time that would be involved in getting from under the pole that supports their baskets.

They commence their peregrinations at daylight, and that gives them the same advantage in picking up what has been thrown away during the night the early bird has in catching the worm.

As they prowl about the rights-of-way, they are not very particular in helping themselves to anything they may see lying about, unless it be something too heavy to lift or too hot to handle; then they will leave it for the right owner to do what he pleases with. Nor are they at all fastidious as to what it is. A flat iron will please them just as well as a pair of trousers; and they have no more objection to a bar of soap, except for cleansing purposes, than they have for a gridiron or a frying-pan; and if they can induce a hen or a duck to be quiet till they get hold of its neck, it is not unlikely to furnish them with a supper after their day's work is over. Although "John" is so accommodating in that respect, he is not at all self-assertive. Should any of the acts he does by "stealth" become "fame," he will, like the benevolent person mentioned by the poet, not only blush, but even if caught red-handed, stoutly deny all felonious intent. "Me no touchee, me welly good man, no gammon, *yah gand ma gok dinooman ah foo*;" and as the last seven words are generally considered satisfactory proof of his innocence, he is usually allowed to depart.

OYSTERMEN.

It is to be regretted that history is silent as to who the courageous individual was who first swallowed an oyster, and how it was he found out they were good. As a benefactor of his species, mankind, or at least that portion of it who like oysters, owes him a debt of gratitude that nothing short of a monument would repay. But it unfortunately happens that mankind is not much given to erecting monuments to its benefactors, or, if their memories should by any chance be honoured in stone when dead, it is because they have, in most cases, been neglected while living.

If this unknown hero had shown his contemporaries how to swallow a man, instead of an oyster, he would have been worshipped as a demigod, and would be existent in marble in some museum at this moment.

There being no direct proof of how it came to pass that these delicious bivalves were found to be good eating, it is marvellous that our *savans* have not accounted for it by some theory of their own. Of course, what one said the other would contradict, that goes without saying; but the subject would be a capital grindstone for the disputants to sharpen their wits upon, and, as a bone of contention, they would find enough meat upon it to last for generations. The public, too, would take an interest in the dispute, quite as much as they do whenever the momentous question of Hamlet's insanity crops up, or whether or not Cambronne said at Waterloo, "The guard dies but never surrenders," or whether our Duke, at the same memorable fight, uttered the words, "Up, guards, and at 'em," or any other craze that every now and then comes to the surface to set the knowing ones by the ears.

The oyster, as an edible, was known in the early ages; for at a Roman feast they were not the least esteemed of the many delicacies placed upon the festive board. They were expensive, too, which may be accounted for by the fact of only a limited number of beds having been discovered, and the art of cultivating them being unknown.

The good a man does spreads in many directions. The man who introduced oysters as an article of food has not only shown us what a delicious morsel there is to be found within the two shells of that rather unsightly looking fish, if fish it be, but he has, in consequence of the demand for the same being so great, given many others the means of subsistence in supplying it.

The peripatetic oysterman thinks his social status slightly above that of the ordinary fish-hawker; and perhaps it is in some respects, but in manner and appearance he is quite as fishy as the other, his speech as vigorous, and his partiality for rum as decided. In a pecuniary sense he does better, certainly, but he has to work harder and later for it, and has much more trouble in getting his fish ready for sale.

Oysters, when they leave their beds, are joined together by their shells in twos and threes, and sometimes more. These have to be divorced by being chopped asunder with a knife, which is a work of time. They are then cleaned, and sorted, the larger ones being sold by the dozen, while the smaller ones are opened and put into pickle bottles to be sold for stewing, or to be eaten in any other way the buyer may think proper. Many people think only the stale ones go into the bottles, but that is a mistake. A few stale ones may find their way there, but the bottles are the refuge of those whose stunted growth prevents their being disposed of in any other way.

Every night, except Sunday, between the hours of six and twelve, the cry of "Sydney rock oysters" may be heard in all the quiet streets of Melbourne, bellowed out in the loudest tones the human voice is capable of giving utterance to. Stentor himself might have envied some of these men their voices, for they are to be heard two or three streets off from the one they are actually in; and one had such brazen lungs that he could be heard distinctly at Williamstown while crying his oysters at Port Melbourne.

These men have an advantage over the other fish-dealers because their oysters will keep till they can sell them. For ten days or a fortnight they will remain saleable, though of course they will not be so nice as when when first brought to market. The consumer, however, swallows them in the full belief they were fresh that morning, and the dealer is too wise to enlighten him upon a matter it is better for him to remain in ignorance of. In order to enjoy a dish of oysters properly, one must have the most absolute faith in those one is discussing, because the time occupied in transferring one from its shell to one's stomach is so short that if it happen to be a bad one, one only discovers it when it is too late to be of any service; and of all the abominations to swallow, a bad oyster is the most abominable.

The number of oysters some men will eat is incredible. Dando, who was so well known in London fifty years ago, thought no more of eating a gross than he did of swindling the tradesman out of the money afterwards. Others have been known to eat twenty dozen without any serious consequences resulting therefrom; and plenty swallow two or three dozen, in order to prepare the stomach for dinner.

We once asked a well-known dealer what was the greatest number he had ever known a man to eat at one sitting or standing. He said he had heard of a man eating upwards of thirty dozen, but had never actually seen one swallow more than thirteen dozen, and that was for a wager, but the affair was not decided, owing to a dispute about payment.

A butcher challenged the nephew of this dealer to a contest in oyster eating, the loser to pay for the whole, which challenge was accepted. Before beginning, a private arrangement was come to between uncle and nephew, that the oysters were to be divided equally as to size, that is, the nephew was to get the small ones and the butcher the large ones. But in spite of being thus handicapped, the butcher had swallowed his thirteen dozen as soon as the other had his.

After another private confab between uncle and nephew, the latter, thinking to "bounce" his opponent, ordered ten dozen more. The butcher, feeling as fresh as at the beginning, ordered an equal number, and looked as though he could have swallowed ten dozen more on the top of that. As a vendor of oysters, the dealer must have admired the butcher's swallowing capacity, which he began to think was unlimited, but he had not quite the same faith in his ability to pay if he lost; so before making a fresh start, he said he should like to see the money staked, in case there should be a dispute. That seemed very reasonable to the butcher, and he asked for a blank cheque. Here another hitch occurred. The dealer had been in business too long not to know how fond some people are of getting out of their liabilities by the simple process of drawing bogus cheques, so he suggested that, as they were strangers to each other, the same amount in the currency would be preferable, and as that was not forthcoming, the wager has remained undecided until this day, though there is no doubt the butcher would have won, as the dealer said he believed he would have swallowed every oyster in the shop.

On hearing that story, it appeared to us that the one who had the least cause for satisfaction over that transaction was the dealer himself, although he had all along been in the most blissful state of ignorance of it. We asked him if each one paid for the oysters he had eaten.

"No," was the answer.

"Then you were the only one who lost?"

"So I was," he said, after a moment's reflection; "I didn't think of that before."

That was some months after the event, and during the whole of that time he had been congratulating himself upon having been "too many" for the butcher, although his oysters had not, and was wont, when talking the matter over with his congeners, to take no small credit to himself for smartness in not being "had" by a valueless cheque.

We further asked our friend if he was aware that, having agreed to wait for payment till it had been decided which of these two men was the greater glutton, he had no claim upon either till it had been shown who was the loser. He was not aware of it. Furthermore, we told him that his refusal to supply more oysters made it impossible to decide which that loser was, and as each expected to be the winner, it was not likely that either of them would pay.

He was rather surprised at the legal view of the matter, and assured us that in any future oyster contests that took place in his establishment, the contestants would have to pay as they went on.

"Why," he said, warming up to the subject, "two men might come into the shop pretending they'd made a wager, and eat till they both burst, and then call it a 'tie,' and I shouldn't be able to get a copper."

"Precisely."

"Then all I can say is this," he added, savagely biting off the corner of a plug of tobacco—"if that's law, it's not justice."

Seeing that he had only just become alive to the fact that, instead of having been "too many" for the butcher, that gentleman was, in reality, a few chalks ahead of him, there is nothing surprising in the fact of his being annoyed, for the revulsion of feeling caused by the awakening from a pleasant illusion to an unpleasant reality is never agreeable, and finding himself twenty-six dozen of oysters to the bad was a reality our friend found particularly unpleasant.

The peripatetic oystermen charge sixpence per dozen, opened, and fourpence unopened, and that leaves a wide margin for profit when a bag containing from one hundred and eighty to two hundred dozen can sometimes be bought for a pound. Many of the shops sell them at the same rate, but at the principal ones the price is just double.

Most people like oysters. They are nice for lunch, and serve well as *avant couriers* to the dinner. For supper they are light and digestible, and do not disturb our slumbers afterwards.

Many people, after having been to the theatre, are fond of winding up with an oyster supper, with bread-and-butter and stout, the whole topped up with a nip of brandy to prevent any unpleasant consequences that might arise from the action of the vinegar upon the stomach. Men who have reached the hilarious stage of good fellowship—that is, when they have had just sufficient to take them to the line that divides the sober from the drunken states—like a dozen or so of oysters as a zest to the next and succeeding glasses. They are, also, cooling to the system, and soothing to the nerves, when one is hot and feverish and unable to sleep.

It would be a great public loss if the supply of oysters

was to give out. As it is, they are getting rather scarce, and unless some means are adopted for increasing the supply, they will be as dear here as they are in England, where they will soon become a dainty dish only fit to be set before a king.

Some years ago the Western Port Company tried to cultivate them here, but with a very small measure of success, for what with the rules laid down by the authorities, and other causes, the business collapsed, and now all we consume we import from Sydney and New Zealand.

THE FLYING STATIONER.

Some people, on reading this title, might wonder what it means, and as they are mentally seeking a solution, their thoughts will naturally turn to Icarus. But it is in no Icarian sense the term is used. As stationery is only required on earth, its vendors can ply their avocations without the aid of wings; so we hasten to say we are speaking of those people who go about the streets selling note-paper, envelopes, pens, and many other small and light articles of stationery.

We first heard the term in England, but how it came to be applied to this class of peripatetics we cannot conceive, for their movements are as much unlike flying as locomotion can well be. The few we knew at home were remarkable for almost everything but activity. One was what is called "bumble-footed"—that is, nature had made the mistake of sticking a small elephant's foot on to his right leg instead of making it to match with his left one. Another had a pair of legs like a pair of calipers, and, of course, pedal celerity was out of the question with regard to his movements; while a third—and he was the most active of the lot—had a wooden leg, his own being left somewhere in India in consequence of its being in the way of a mutineer's bullet. But the poor fellow had his consolation, for a grateful country allowed him sixpence a day to live upon, and a new leg every two years. The term "flying stationer" must have been applied to this order of peripatetics ironically, just as in the pre-railroad days a conveyance whose pace was about two miles an hour was called a "flying waggon."

The amount of capital necessary to make a start in this business is not very large, neither are the appliances for carrying it on by any means expensive, all that is required being a flat pasteboard box, such as the drapers receive half-a-dozen shirts in, one of which you can always beg;

but a strap is needed as well, to buckle round the middle and to carry it by.

Being provided with a shilling and the box, you are in a position to make a beginning. You then go to the "swag-shop" and lay out your shilling in the things you think you will find the readiest sale for. We have never heard the term "swag-shop" applied in this colony to those establishments where hawkers get their goods, but in London that is the name they are known by, and are mostly to be found in Houndsditch and the neighbourhood round about there. The term "swag" only appears to be applied here to the bundle a man carries over his shoulder when on the "wallaby track," which is the colonial synonym for being "on the tramp." At home the dry goods hawkers use it in speaking of their stock-in-trade; and thieves call the takings of a burglary by the same name.

Having invested your shilling, all that remains for you to do now is to dispose of your stock, and by the time you have done that you will have ample reason for being satisfied with the result.

A shilling is but a small sum, and thought very little of by most people. It is, also, a convenient coin, for a man who has forgotten to come provided with a three-penny bit can put it in the plate at church without breaking his heart. It is handy, likewise, as a "tip" for a boy you wish to encourage, or to give to a little girl to buy lollies with. It is, moreover, historical, for who has not heard of So-and-so being cut off with a shilling? or of Such-and-such-a-one having threatened to confine the legacy of a graceless son or nephew to that amount? It is the favourite foundation, too, on which many a stupendous fortune has been built. We have some very wealthy men in this fair city of ours who are fond of boasting of their small beginnings—of how they started with a shilling and a basket, and now you see what they are. It might have been a few pounds, but they prefer the shilling, as it sounds better and sets off their energy to greater advantage.

One of these successful colonists tells us how he landed forty years ago with twenty-five pounds in his pocket, and a tolerable "kit"; how he saw "life" till the money was gone save one solitary shilling, and that he had received from a kind-hearted relative with whom he had just left the last article of that kit that had any value. That evening, as he was discussing his present position and future prospects with his landlady, she, good soul, lent him a basket and advised him to invest the shilling in some kind of merchandise, and hawk it about, till he could do something better. He acted upon that advice, and the shilling's-worth of wares brought him in three-and-sixpence. Turning one's capital over in one day, with a clear profit of two hundred and fifty per cent., is not bad. That night he indulged in the luxury of a "square meal," the first he had had for a week. The next day he invested two shillings in the same things, with equally satisfactory results; and so he kept on, till at the end of the week square meals became the rule instead of the exception. At the end of another week he was again on visiting terms with his uncle, but on these occasions he might have been seen coming out with a bundle under his arm instead of going in with one.

Love, seeing how fortune smiled upon him, also took an interest in his welfare, and the two together have watched over him ever since. He felt a great regard for the basket he had made such a happy start in business with, and wished to retain it as his own personal property; and he came to the conclusion that the best way of doing that would be to marry its then lawful owner. She, prudent woman that she was, thought that with his perseverance and luck, and her own wit, they would do very well together, and consented. The result proved how correct her judgment had been.

Three days were all they allowed themselves for the honeymoon, after which they went to work in earnest. He still persevered, and his luck continued, and her wit was quite equal to taking care of all the money she got hold of. They prospered exceedingly, indeed far beyond their most sanguine expectations, and have long since retired from business.

The profits of the flying stationery business are rather large. A man who starts with a shilling's-worth of goods can manage to live out of it for the day, and have enough left to renew his stock with the next morning, unless he allows his thirst to overcome his prudence, which is too frequently the case with those who incline to this branch of industry. There are a few young men engaged in it, but they are not of the kind that form the bone and sinew of a nation. On the contrary, they are too lazy to work, and too thriftless ever to rise above a certain position in society, and that is always a very low one. The others are old and confirmed drunkards, with no home but the sixpenny lodging-house, and no aspiration beyond the threepenny tap.

Some of them do not depend solely upon their stationery as a means of raising the wind, as they call it, but carry it more as a "stall" than with a view of giving it in exchange for the currency, their real business being begging. If any one wants a few envelopes or a little note-paper, they will sell them certainly, but they would much rather receive the money without giving anything in return, as that lays them under the painful necessity of having to practise a little self-denial when the time comes for renewing their stock.

As a class, they are much given to loquacity, and are fond of talking of what they have been in times past, and how well they might have done had it not been for drink, not knowing they are saying that which should close the hearts of all against their appeals. But gentility, brought to poverty by vice, is looked upon with more pitying eyes, and is treated far more indulgently, than are the lowly poor, and those whose poverty is the result of misfortune alone.

Foremost among the flying stationers was Mr. Bob Temple, who died a few years ago in Her Majesty's gaol of Melbourne, to which he had been committed for six months as an habitual drunkard. He failed, however, to complete the whole of his sentence, for the hominy and Yarra-Yarra water were too many for him. His weakened stomach could not stand such vigorous diet, and he succumbed to their influence within a very short time of his admittance.

Bob "was a fellow of infinite jest," insatiable in the matter of beer, and decidedly partial to rum. He belonged to that rather large class of people of whom it is said, "He is no one's enemy but his own." It's a pity the name of the sapient individual who first uttered that aphorism is not known, so that it might be handed down to posterity. A man does not belong to himself, but to society, to which he owes certain duties. If he neglect those duties, he commits a crime, and he cannot well fulfil them if he drinks himself into a state of semi-idiocy, and yet, when he has done so, he is said to be no one's enemy but his own.

Bob was not a bad-hearted old fellow in the main, although he had what is called "an ugly tongue" when anything went wrong with him, such as being obliged to stop half way on the road to drunkenness for want of the means to complete the journey; but, take him altogether, it will be some time before "we see his like again."

He had been much about in his time, and had studied men and manners. He had, also, known the vicissitudes of fortune. Some years ago he kept a store in San Francisco, and was doing well—in fact, making rapid strides to wealth; but a fire, by which he lost thirty thousand dollars, reduced him to poverty in one night. That was the turning-point in his downward career. He took to drink, and that hastened his descent, and brought him to the lowest depths of degradation, from which he could never afterwards rise, nor did he try to do so. He was no fool, in the ordinary acceptation of the term, for he had read much, and of the seeds thus scattered through his mind many had fallen on favourable soil, and nothing but an over-irrigation by beer had prevented their bearing good fruit.

He used to say that the greatest mistake he ever made in his life was to run away with another man's wife, or, rather, allow her to run away with him. Poor Bob was not the first one who has made the discovery that the breach of that particular clause of the tenth commandment is a mistake. If a man steal another's goods, he steals something he can get rid of, if he is not found out in time to prevent it; but if he appropriate his wife, he gets hold of something not easily disposed of in the event of his getting tired of her, owing to the difficulty of finding a "fence" willing to negotiate stolen property of that description. Neither is she easily hidden, because, although she may be "lost," she has a natural dislike to remaining *perdue*. Nor is it safe to put her quietly away, for, although the law allows you to steal another man's wife, it has a strong objection to your murdering her.

In addition to all that, the outraged husband sometimes makes matters exceedingly uncomfortable, in person or pocket, for the disturber of his domestic bliss, all of which make it easy to believe that running away with another man's wife is a mistake.

Bob found many to sympathise with him in his fallen condition, and he got rather more than his share of eleemosynary patronage; consequently he was able to begin drinking soon after he started on his round in the morning, keep on all day, and as far into the night as the money would allow.

One thing may be mentioned here about the class of people to which our friend belonged; and that is, experience has taught them the wisdom of spending their money as fast as they get it, for, if they do not, some one else will for them, as living among such doubtful characters as some of the *habitués* of the sixpenny lodging-houses are, the chances are, if they went to bed with any left at night, they would not be able to find it the next morning. That was the principle upon which Bob always acted, for, as he naïvely said,

" I may as well get drunk on the money myself as let another man do it for me."

Another of our flying stationers was once in business in Melbourne as a chemist. He has not been seen about his usual haunts for some time, so he must have passed over to the great majority. He was quite as great a character in his way as the late Mr. Bob, and was quite as fond of beer. His manner of living and general behaviour was a little more respectable than that of the last-named gentleman, as he occupied a room—or, as he called it, had apartments—to himself, somewhere in Little Bourke Street. He had a small circle of friends, upon whom he would call when times were dull, who, on these occasions, gave him food to take home.

He suffered much from what he called rheumatic gout in the feet, but which was in reality dropsy, caused by the quantity of beer he drank. He was a poet, or at least called himself one ; and one might almost have thought his poetry had the rheumatic gout as well as his feet, for the one halted just as badly as the other.

It is astonishing what a number of apparently sane people there are to be met with who look upon themselves as poets. If they can only string a few lines of the Queen's English together, and make them jingle at the ends, they settle down in the very comfortable belief that it is poetry, and they entertain but a poor opinion of those who do not regard it in the same light.

Our ex-chemist carried about for sale some printed sheets of his effusions, which the buyer could have at his own price, whether it were a penny, or a shilling, or any intermediate coin. He was a ventriloquist, too, in a small way, and could give some very amusing displays of his skill in that line. Among his other small articles, he sold spectacles, and would let any one have a pair of pebbles worth fifteen shillings, according to his own guarantee, for half-a-crown, or, if he could not get that much, he would take sixpence. He was particularly loud in his denunciations of drunkenness, saying what a bad thing it is, and how much better he would have done if he had not given way to it.

The flying stationery business is a nice light one, and well suited to old people of limited means, such a small outlay—a shilling only—being required to make a start with. In fact, if it wanted more, many of those who now follow it would be unable to do so, as that is about the largest sum they can ever muster at one time. That shilling, when raised, has to be quickly invested in stock, or it would find its way into some hotel-keeper's till, as the only belief the people this paper treats of have in money is that it was made to circulate; and to keep it idle in the pocket while there was plenty of good beer to be had in exchange for it is, in their estimation, something like flying in the face of Providence, and doing an injury to society.

The two chief wants of these men are a bed and beer: all others have to stand over till the funds will allow of their being attended to; and of these two the bed is always made sure of first. The reason why that is so is this: their credit not standing very high at the places where they "doss it," they have to pay in advance for their sleeping accommodation. If they were to put off paying for the bed till they wanted to occupy it, the chances are they would have to pass the night in the gutter, unless some policeman carried them off to the lock-up; for, by then, they would be much too drunk to care about a bed at all, especially after being nicely tucked in in the gutter. But as sleeping in the latter place tends to rheumatism, they secure the bed beforehand, and then finish up the day in one of the neighbouring taps, in the perfect confidence that, when they have lost the use of their legs, some of their comrades less drunk than themselves, will carry them off to bed, that being an understood thing among them.

THE TRAVELLING DRAPER.

Resurgam may be said by your old coat as truthfully as it can be by yourself, for you will both rise again after having undergone a process of demolition. All that is material and corruptible about yourself the worms will consume, and at the resurrection, if you have deserved it, you will be reclothed with incorruptibility, and translated to a purer and better state.

What the worms have done for you, the tackle will do for your old coat. It will then be teazed into fluff; after that, spun into yarn, then woven into a web, and, finally, the teaselling machine will raise a nap, and it will come forth once more, smooth, glossy, and respectable looking, but it will only be shoddy.

Shoddy is not alone confined to cloth. There is plenty of human shoddy to be found among every class of people who inhabit this fair world of ours; the difficulty being not to discover it, but to discover where it is not.

Would it be possible for the merest tyro in the study of mankind to overlook the shoddiness of some of those who are to be seen in high places, who are not even smooth, or glossy, or respectable looking?

In the "House," too, a little may be seen in men who, when on the stump, have guaranteed themselves real "West of England" "all wool," and warranted not to shrink—from their duties.

Whether there be any shoddy in the legal business, we shall leave people to find out for themselves, as it's a "cloth" we know nothing about, and as we've never wished to be wiser in the matter, we've made no inquiries. It is evidently worked up in the bodily textures of some of the gentlemen who form the committees of our charitable institutions, for they get uncommonly rough when brushed against the wool.

Nothing in creation can hide its own nature, or be disobedient to the laws that govern it. Men may, for a time, set Nature at defiance, and restrain her operations; but it is only for a time. In the end she will assert herself to the confusion of those who sought to interfere with her. Thus it is with shoddy. Wherever it is, whether in the man or coat, it will manifest itself, whatever may be done to hide it.

Most people like bargains. Convince a man that a given article is worth a pound, and offer it for five shillings, and the chances are, whether he wants it or not, he will take it. It is that love of bargains which makes them fall such easy victims to the shoddy-vendors, who go about "like roaring lions, seeking whom they may devour."

These men produce some pieces of nice-looking cloth, which they guarantee to be remnants of a first-rate article, but which are, in reality, only short lengths of shoddy. These they offer at marvellously low prices, and, by sheer push, induce their dupes to give their sterling coin in exchange for the worthless stuff.

It is a good thing to be able to push well, whether one is forcing one's way through a crowd, or striving for a position in the world, or conducting a transaction in connection with drapery. Pushing has now become part of the drapery business, and if a young man cannot push his way into his employer's good graces, by pushing the goods into the customers, he will stand a very good chance of being pushed into the street himself.

We all know the meaning of the verb "to push" in in everyday life, but every one may not know that, in the drapery line, it means making people spend half-a-crown when they only intended to lay out a shilling.

The travelling draper is a decided improvement upon the flying stationer, both in a mercantile and social aspect, though there are a few, in the lower grade of the business no better in any respect whatsoever. These also carry their stock-in-trade in flat pasteboard boxes, said stock consisting of about a shilling's-worth of needles, tape, and reels of cotton, intended, not so much for sale, as a cloak for begging, and to keep them outside the Vagrancy Laws. There are, also, a few women engaged in this trade, some of whom are no better than the men just alluded to. Their habits and tastes are the same, and their antecedents quite as cloudy. Nor are they less beggars, for they depend more upon their artfully-concocted tales of distress than they do upon the sale of needles and cotton.

There are many grades in the travelling drapery business, the lowest being those just above mentioned, and the highest the men who go about in a trap drawn by one or two horses; while the middle ranks are filled up by the pedlars who carry their goods done up in a bundle, covered with American cloth to keep them from the wet, or else in baskets similar to those carpenters carry their tools in, only larger.

The men with bundles mostly sell dresses, shawls, ribbons, etc.; while the men with baskets confine themselves to cloth, which they call remnants of "West of England," but which are, in reality, only pieces of shoddy, and usually the worst kind of that.

Some of the "upper ten" of these glib-tongued gentry are in a large way of business, and do very well, frequently employing an assistant, or working in conjunction with a partner. There are some in Melbourne now keeping very pretentious shops, who first started with a basket; but these were only the careful plodding ones, who, instead of spending their profits in drink as fast as they got it, applied it to the increase of their stock, till, from a basket, they rose to a horse and trap, and from that to a shop, and now they are well-to-do and influential citizens.

As a class, these men are not remarkable for a high-toned commercial morality in their dealings with the public. On the contrary, they appear to think that if a person chooses to give ten shillings for an article worth nothing, he has a perfect right to do so, and any meddling on the part of the law or any one else is an act of downright impertinence, and an interference with the liberty of the subject in a country where a man is supposed to possess the privilege of conducting his own business in his own way.

However much we may feel inclined to boast of the intelligence of the nineteenth century, our friends in the travelling drapery business certainly do not believe in it, for they come across so many fools in their travels, that they have long since arrived at the conclusion that wise men are the exception, and not the rule; and as they are guided by their own experience of mankind in forming that opinion, we may depend upon it they are not far wrong.

The daily papers are constantly warning people against the doings of these shoddy men; but it may be said of to-day as it was of the olden times, "Wisdom crieth out aloud in the streets, but no man heedeth her."

It is a very debatable point whether we shall ever be as wise as we ought to be this side of the Millennium, or at least wise enough not to be taken in by such transparent dodges as are continually being offered for our consideration. If those keen-witted individuals who have such a craving after our money would treat us to a novelty in the art of fleecing, it would not be so bad, as we should at all events learn something for our money. But it is the same dodge over and over again; we are "had" to-day by the same trick we were "sold" by yesterday; and if we are not "done" in the same way to-morrow, it will be because the opportunity has been denied us.

These shoddy men and others who live by their wits are, as a rule, keen observers of mankind, and in their intercourse with the world have had ample opportunities for discovering that people who have plenty of money are sometimes very deficient in sense, and those with plenty of the latter (themselves for instance) seldom possess a superabundance of the former. As they consider that an abnormal state of things, they look upon themselves as justified in depriving them of some of the vile dross, in exchange for a little of their own wit, in the hope that they may become wise by experience, and learn how to keep what they have left. In carrying out that idea they are sometimes eminently successful, as far as extracting the money goes; but in teaching wisdom they are not quite so fortunate.

These men never calculate upon dealing with the same person twice; neither are they in a hurry to visit the same locality again, as they consider a personal interview with their customers before the recollection of their last bargain has become dimmed by time would not be much to their advantage, as the mildest of mankind has an objection to be cheated; and, when he finds he has been, he is apt to entertain feelings towards those who have victimised him that are not in accordance with pure Christian charity.

A friend of ours was once interviewed by one of these pushing gentlemen, and asked if he wanted a rare bargain in coatings and vestings. Brown, for that was his name, was one of those who are vulgarly said to "know their way about," which was certainly true in his case in more senses than one. He had a craving for knowledge of any kind that was insatiable, and knew something of every conceivable subject that could be brought on the *tapis*, from divinity down to the latest dodge introduced by those genial-looking individuals called "confidence men." He understood at a glance the manner of man he had to deal with in this shoddy man, and knew as well as he did himself what he was going to say; but he thought he might as well trot him out, in the hope of being able to add another "wrinkle" to those time had already stamped upon his brow, so he gave him a slight encouragement to "open out," which he was not long in doing.

The merchant was a slippery-tongued young fellow, and Brown could see he had no mean opinion of his own ability, and that he looked upon him (our friend) as one to be "had" with as much certainty as though his money was already in his pocket. He said he was travelling for a firm in Flinders Street who had a sudden and urgent need for a certain sum of money by next Wednesday.

"Money we want," he said, "and money we must have, at any sacrifice, to keep the estate out of sequestration."

All the time he was talking he was sorting some pieces of cloth; and when he had got them in order, he continued:

"Now here's a remnant of splendid black cloth sufficient to make a coat and vest; and here's a piece of blue that will make you a paget; and this piece of splendid Geelong tweed will make you a trousers and vest; and if you buy the cloth, you can get the whole of the articles made up at the factory in Flinders Street for ten-and-six, trimmings included; now, what do you say for the lot?"

"What do you ask for it?" queried Brown.

"Well, I want thirty-five shillings for the black cloth,

fifteen for the blue, and the tweed you may have for eighteen, making in all, three eight; and when you've got them made into garments for ten-and-six, you'll have a bargain you'll never meet with again."

"Can I have the clothes made up for my boys?" Brown asked.

"Most certainly," was the ready response.

Our friend expressed great regret that he had not as much money by him.

"How much have you?"

Brown shook his head and said—

"Nothing like that."

"Come now, I'll tell you what I'll do; you shall have the lot for two ten; you can't grumble at that."

"That seems very cheap," said Brown in reply, whereupon he saw a gleam of satisfaction in the young fellow's eyes; "but let me understand you. If I buy that cloth sufficient to make two coats, two vests, and a pair of trousers, I can get the five garments made up for ten-and-sixpence?"

"Yes."

"Then I tell you what I'll do. You may leave the cloth with me, and I'll send the boys to Flinders Street this afternoon to get measured, and as soon as they are done you may call and get the money."

A blank look passed over shoddy's countenance as he heard this; but it lingered only a moment, and he said—

"That's fair; but there's one thing that prevents that arrangement being come to, and that is, our urgent need of money. The money must be obtained by next Wednesday, and the clothes cannot be made up by then."

"Then I must wish you good morning."

"How much will you give for the lot? Will you give two pounds?"

"My good fellow, how old are you?" asked Brown.

The question rather surprised the other, and he couldn't exactly see what his age had to do with it.

"It certainly hasn't much to do with it, but I was merely going to tell you that I knew all about shoddy long before you were born."

With that the baffled one packed up and "sloped."

Palpable as that dodge may seem, there were plenty of people so anxious to get a bargain that they were completely taken in by it, and only found out how green they had been when they went in search of the factory they had been directed to, which they either could not find, or, having found it, were smilingly told that they had been gulled, as the person who sold them the cloth was in no way connected with the establishment.

Another kind of travelling draper goes about in a showy-looking trap for orders, and shows samples of really good lines, at marvellously low prices, for ready cash. Small shopkeepers are the ones usually operated upon by these gentry; and the dupes after they have received the goods and paid for them discover that the sample and the bulk are slightly different. But then they can console themselves with the reflection that, if they have been taken in themselves, they can make matters square by taking in some one else.

The profits the travelling draper gets on his goods are very great, as they are mostly "job lots," or damaged articles he deals in, though of course his customers are not aware of that. The men connected with this branch of industry are very pushing in the way of conducting business. "No" with them is anything but a negative particle, and it will take one a good half hour to convince them it does not mean "Yes." And in the matter of colour, if one wants a blue and they happen to be without it, they will persuade one that green will do infinitely better—in fact, they will do business with one if they can. They will rummage their goods about, and take so much trouble to display them before one's eyes, that one feels ashamed to let them depart without buying something.

It is a mistake for people to fancy they can buy things cheaper from hawkers than they can at the shops. On the contrary, they are dearer, for one has to pay a good price for an inferior article. But then it is mostly in the country places a long way from any shop where these men do business, and if they can save one a journey by bringing what one wants to one's door, that is worth something.

STREET MUSICIANS.

Music, they say, "hath charms to soothe the savage breast." Now the question is, what is music, and where does it begin, and discord end?

The East Indian thinks the noise of the tomtom the most sublime of all earthly sounds, while the Chinese consider their reeds and pipes and stringed instruments the only real exponents of harmony. Some people of a melancholy turn take delight in discoursing dismal airs on the flute, and think they are indulging in music; others, in the full belief they are wooing Euterpe, drive those in their vicinity half mad by rasping on the fiddle. With such as these, skill in execution is of no moment whatever; the mere fact of being able, by breathing into a flute, to convert their own breath into musical sounds, or produce some kind of measured noise by the friction of horsehair on catgut, is quite sufficient for them.

As far as can be seen into the past, music has been part of religious ceremonies and funeral rites, the priest, prophet, and poet being the musicians. In secular matters, too, it has always played an important part, no military pageant or private amusement being complete without it.

In the heathen mythology, we are told, Apollo was the inventor of music; hence his title, the god of music. Mercury is credited with the invention of the lyre, or, as it has been called, the sounding shell.

The power of music in those days was much greater than it is in our own, if we are to believe all we are told. By its means Mercury closed in sleep the hundred eyes of Argus as he was watching over Jove's beloved Io. Orpheus brought the most ferocious beasts to his feet by the persuasive eloquence of his instrument, and Amphion caused the huge stones and the massive pillars with which

Thebes was built to dance into their proper places by the magic touch of his lyre. Poor Orpheus, inconsolable for the loss of his Eurydice, went to seek her in the infernal regions, where he played so sweetly that even the merciless heart of Pluto was softened, and the torments of the damned were for a time suspended. He could not resist the musical appeal of the widowed Orpheus, and he promised to restore his wife to him on condition that he left the Tartarean abode without looking behind him; but, alas! his anxiety to behold once more his beloved wife was so great that he forgot what he had promised, and, looking back, had in consequence to depart alone.

Arion of Lesbas, a famous lyric poet and musician, having amassed great riches in Italy, was returning to his own country when the sailors conspired to kill him for the sake of his wealth. He asked and obtained permission to touch his lyre before he died. After having played for a short time he leaped into the sea, where a dolphin, that had been charmed by his music, was waiting to receive him, and it bore him on its back in safety to Tenarum in Laconia. For that benevolent act the dolphin was placed among the constellations.

In biblical history Jubal is the first mentioned as a musician, and he was called "the father of all such as handle the harp and the organ."

Some nations have an instrument peculiar to themselves. The Swiss abide by the Alpine horn, and believe it to be second to nothing in the musical line. By its means they have been taught to love the *ranz des vaches* with such an intensity of feeling that on hearing it when far from their native hills, they are seized with such an irresistible longing for home, that unless it is gratified they sink under what is called *mal de pays*. The Irish are stirred to enthusiasm by the harp; and the Scotch seek consolation in the bagpipes. The Welsh also look upon the harp as their national instrument, and love to hear its melodious notes.

It was an unfortunate thing for the bards in the time of Edward I. that the Welsh were so fond of listening to the harp, as that monarch, seeing what power they had over the minds of the people, cut the matter short by having them all put to death.

The English appear to have no preference for any

particular instrument, as all, from the grand organ down to the nigger bones, are the same to them.

Outdoor music, as we hear it interpreted in our streets by some of the wandering players, has not a nice effect upon the nerves of some people, for it embraces all the degrees of badness—the positive, comparative, and superlative. It would be a bad job for some of these players if there were no people about to whom discord and harmony are synonymous terms. These, thinking they encourage art, donate the disturbers of public quiet a copper, or a stray threepenny, thereby encouraging a nuisance that will acquire larger dimensions as soon as it is seen it will pay. They are not all bad players, however, these peripatetics. Some of them are first-rate instrumentalists, who, one would think, ought to do much better than playing about the streets.

A pair, an Italian and a native born, used to go about the streets of Melbourne, one with a harp, and the other with a penny tin whistle. The music the latter extracted from his instrument was simply astonishing. One who had never heard him play it would think it hardly possible to bring forth the notes he did from an article that was made for, and sold to, the rising generation of forty years agone as a plaything. Our memory takes us back to its first appearance, and we have a lively recollection of how speedily it became in our hands, or between our lips, an instrument of torture to the unmusical portion of our elders.

A very stout man has for some years past nightly charmed the ears of the visitors to Scott's or Menzies with his vocal displays. He accompanies himself on the guitar in the orthodox style, at least as we see it done on the stage, or in the pictorial representations of the old troubadours.

In playing the guitar, a man can put on any amount of "side," but he must be of a graceful figure, which our fat friend certainly is not.' He may at one time have been as slim as any love-lorn troubadour of old, but he has long outgrown that, although the "side" remains.

Two strolling musicians, one of whom plays the concertina and the other the banjo, play nightly before the bars of the different public-houses in and around Melbourne, and a very good thing they make of it, for men when half-drunk, as most of their listeners are, reward pretty liberally those who know how to tickle their musical instinct. The man with the banjo sings, and selects those songs he knows will be most agreeable to the tastes of his audience, however sentimental or otherwise that audience may be.

Where the Irish element predominates, he finds " Wearing of the Green " highly provocative of liberality on the part of his listeners; and " Scots wha hae," is equally efficacious in extracting " bawbees " from the " pouches " of the patriotic half " fou " sons of Scotia. A group of fast young fellows can have their ears tickled by *sotto voce* songs, if the banjoist thinks there is any chance of being " patronised " for it, and this same singer would be quite as ready to sing the Old Hundredth psalm, if it were possible to find two churchwardens in such a place to listen to it.

In London a man went about who was quite an orchestra in himself. He played the violin with his hands, and beat a big drum at his back, the sticks being strapped to his elbows. He wore a large hat, not unlike a Chinese pagoda in shape. This unique kind of headgear was studded all over with small brass bells, which tinkled in obedience to a nod of the head. He beat the cymbals with his knees, and blew vigorously into a huge set of Pandean pipes stuck in his cravat; while his feet danced nimbly over fifty or sixty treadles, above which he was seated. Each of these treadles gave vitality to the clapper of a hand-bell hung about a large frame that went on wheels.

The nearest approach to this genius ever seen in Melbourne was a blind man, who played the flute, a concertina, and beat a drum and the cymbals at the same time. This man, blind as he is, invented this queer music machine himself, and made it while living at Blind Sam's sixpenny lodging-house in Little Bourke Street. It was not a very complicated affair, merely consisting of a light framework, with two treadles, one of which set the drumstick to work, and the other brought the cymbals into play.

Another blind man, who used to play the concertina and sing to it in Bourke Street, has disappeared, doubtless to the satisfaction of the frequenters of that thoroughfare. A few years ago a blind fiddler used to play hornpipes daily and nightly in the streets, to the intense delight of an attendant crowd of young nimble-footed larrikins, who would keep time to the music with some of their graceful and complicated *pas* on the neighbouring kerbstone.

The great majority of the blind musicians of the present day affect the hand-organ when they appeal to the musical natures of the Melbourne people. With the exception of a few small ones, which the operators hold in their laps while playing, the organs are all on wheels, for most of the blind men are too feeble to carry about such a heavy load; and those who are not are far too lazy. Each one is accompanied by a "wife" to steer the organ through the crowded streets, and turn the crank, while the "husband" leans against a verandah post, holding out the eleemosynary tin-box for the charitable to drop their coins into. When the woman is tired and wants a "spell," the man takes to the crank, and she holds out the box, and so on alternately.

One of these women is very fond of adding the sweet tones of her own voice to the notes of the organ, and the way she sings "My grandfather's clock" is *a ravir*.

The larger and better kind of street organs are worked by Italians, presumably with good results, as there are mostly a couple of Italia's swarthy sons in attendance. The smaller hand-organ, which hangs in front of the player, is also ground by men of the same nationality. One has a monkey cutting capers on the top of the organ, said monkey keeping a sharp lookout for the coins the admiring spectators sometimes present him with, which he immediately consigns to his mouth, and keeps there till his master makes him disgorge.

There is a serio-comic expression upon the face of this monkey that is remarkable, and a look of settled disgust that plainly shows he is dissatisfied with something. What is it? Is there a Darwin in the Simian world who has also discovered that the quadrumana and the dual handed are of a common origin? If so, has our little friend heard of it? He may have, and that may account for his look of disgust at having to acknowledge the grinning crowd around him as members of his own order.

A few years ago a young Italian came into notice, who had discovered a use for his digits never intended by the Creator, and as a natural consequence, he caused quite a furore wherever he went; as people always do who can set nature at defiance, or discover something in her works she never thought of herself. This genius, by putting two fingers of one hand into his mouth, blew an accompaniment to the organ he played with the other, in a manner that was rather astonishing. One who has only heard the boys about the streets whistling with their fingers can form no idea of the music this young fellow could extract from the tips of those two simple instruments, by merely blowing upon them when inside his mouth. It is true there was nothing very graceful about the action, neither did it improve the shape of his mouth, and there was a look of impending apoplexy about the eyes as he trilled forth his notes that conveyed a very unpleasant feeling to the minds of those who were looking on.

The best known character in the itinerant musical world of Melbourne is an individual rejoicing in the cognomen of "Ballarat Joe." He is tall of stature, and is always seen in a white bell-topper with a broad black band. His organ is about the best to be seen in the streets, and is an object of care and veneration to its owner. He hails from Ballarat, as the prefix to his name tells us, and is as well known there as the "corner" itself.

Like many other privileged public characters, he is plain of speech, and when offended or offered a copper, is apt to give vent to his displeasure in no measured terms.

Some years ago he went to England to get a new organ, and was returning in the *Queen of the Thames*, when that unfortunate vessel was lost, and of course his organ went down with her. When he got back to Victoria, he was about as poor as he well could be, but a subscription was got up to raise the means of getting him another instrument, and the organ he has now is the result.

Some of his admirers, either seriously or for fun, once started him as a candidate to represent one of the divisions of Ballarat in the Legislative Assembly. He failed to secure the seat, however, which is perhaps to be regretted, as his "organ" of speech would have brought him into the same prominence inside the House his barrel organ does on the outside of it.

We have several German brass bands in our midst, but they mostly affect the suburbs, where they are less likely to frighten the horses than they would be in town, and where they find a more copious inflow of threepenny bits. These carry their music-stands with them, and stand in a circle, when they " pitch," in order that the sounds of the various instruments may blend in one.

London at one time absorbed all the superfluous brass instrumentalists of Germany, but now that Bismarck has made the military conscription so irksome, more Vaterlanders emigrate than the English capital can support, consequently we are more favoured with their company now than we formerly were.

The dulcet strains of the Scotch bagpipes are not very often heard in the streets of Melbourne, except on the occasion of a Caledonian gathering, at which time they may be heard to advantage. A Highlander, or, at any rate, a man dressed in Highland costume, may sometimes be seen marching to and fro in front of Scott's, playing the pipes to remind any Scotch squatter who may happen to be staying there of the land of his birth.

Whether these itinerant musicians do any good, in the way of creating a taste for music, is open to question. A few idlers in the streets may like to listen to them, till the man comes round with the hat; but the business people would rather dispense with their "concord of sweet sounds."

Our street players are not so wise in their generation as the fraternity in London are. Here, if the coins are not quickly forthcoming, they pack up and pitch somewhere else. In the quiet streets of London exactly the opposite obtains. Here they play on till they are paid to go away, which they well know they will be if they stay long enough. Consequently, as soon as they "strike up," the people opposite whose houses they have pitched send out the servants with what they have to give, when the musicians cut their piece short and move on. If the householder's troubles ended with one band, it wouldn't so much matter, but as it is, it's only the beginning of the day's annoyances, for they have no sooner persuaded one lot to go away than another comes, who have also to be blackmailed into moving on. Thus it keeps on, all through the day, and far into the night.

No women, as far as we know, are engaged at the present time in providing *al fresco* concerts for the people in and about Melbourne, except the few who assist the blind barrel-organists. There were a few some years ago, but they appear to have taken their departure to more favoured lands, all except one old blind woman, who is living on her means in one of the suburbs.

The reason why the English-speaking race is so highly favoured in the matter of foreign musicians is because they have taken it into their heads that if a man be an Italian he must be a musical genius; and they would give five times as much to hear him play or sing, however indifferently he might do it, as they would to hear one of their own countrymen. That fact the "Padroni," who import these itinerants, are perfectly well aware of, and they make the most of it.

The next thing to being an Italian is for an English professional to take an Italian name. However skilful Mr. Greathead may be in his own particular line, he would draw together but small audiences if he retained his patronymic in its plain English; but as "Signor del Capo Grosso" he might become the rage.

TINKERS.

It has been said that half the world does not know how the other half lives. Of the wisdom and truth of that saying there can be no doubt, for there are vast numbers of highly intelligent folks who are in a most benighted state as to the nature and number of callings there are in which men can get an honest living.

Each occupation, of whatever kind it may be, is followed by people who have, apparently, a natural inclination that way, for they fall into the line as surely as though they were impelled thereto by some natural force. Nor is that peculiarity confined to any particular nation or locality. It is to be found wherever these callings are pursued by a distinct class of men, whatever may be their religion, language, or national habits. The peripatetics of Melbourne, except perhaps the costermongers, are precisely the same in their own branches as the peripatetics in every other part of the world, and the same applies to those who are not peripatetic in their businesses. The same tastes, the same ideas and manners, and the same expression of countenance may be seen in all. The tinker of Melbourne might be suddenly dropped in the middle of London, and no one but himself would know he was not in his right place.

Let those whose recollection of home is still vivid compare the people they see here with those they remember in the same line there, and they will see the correctness of our assertion. The man who asks them if they have any knives or scissors to grind, and the vendor of clothes-props, they will recognise as the twin brothers of the men who used to solicit their custom in the same interests in London. Their butcher and baker will also remind them of the ones they left at the Antipodes,' and so will the lawyer, and doctor, if they have ever had the misfortune to need their help.

In all communities, tinkers have been regarded as useful members of society, as far as their avocation goes, but not very desirable as a "set" for polite people to mix with. "The knife-grinder" of Teniers, as a work of art, was highly-esteemed, and fetched a great price, probably ten times more than the original would have brought if he had been put up for sale. But, however picturesque the rags and dirt of these men may appear when represented on canvas, actual contact with the living models is not pleasant, especially for those whose sense of smell is unimpaired; and although there are hundreds who would give more than its weight in gold for the knife-grinder as Teniers left him, it is doubtful if one of them would for a moment tolerate his presence on their carpets if he were still in the flesh.

The term "tinker" was at one time only applied to those who wrought in "tin," and mended saucepans and tin kettles, or anything else made of that metal. It is now extended to knife and scissor-grinders, umbrella-menders, and even to some legislators, although these latter are not peripatetic.

A hole is sometimes found in the constitution, or a leak discovered in an Act of Parliament, that requires the immediate attention of those whose duty it is to keep things in proper order.

When a tinker is offered a saucepan to mend, which he thinks is not worth mending, or considers too old-fashioned for modern use, he will undertake the job certainly, if you pay him, but in stopping up one hole he will so arrange matters that another will break out somewhere else before very long, so that either he or the next tinker that comes that way may be called in to doctor it up again.

It is just the same with legislative tinkers. When it has been seen that an Act of Parliament will not hold water, there is a general "pow-wow" as to what is to be done to mend it. If the tinkers are in the majority, they patch it up, usually with a similar result to the one just mentioned in connection with the saucepan; although it is not hinted that they wilfully scrape a place nearly through the bottom with a view to another job, yet they simply bungle what they have to do, and that has pretty much the same effect. When the *laisser faire* party are in the majority, it is not meddled with, in the hope that the leak will stop itself, or that it may never be wanted again; or that it is not of sufficient consequence for them to put themselves to any inconvenience on its account, or some other reason equally cogent is assigned why they should do nothing to it. But no one ever thinks of replacing it by a new one, and the consequence is that every now and then there is a great hubbub on account of the mess made by this leaky Act of Parliament.

In comparing some legislators with the knights of the soldering-iron, no disrespect is meant to the latter, who do their work well enough for the pay they get for it, and there can be no doubt if they were formed into a chamber, and contracted with for three hundred a year each to keep the tin-kettles of the Colony in order, they would do it effectually, and enjoy their beer afterwards with the proud consciousness that it had been bought with money honestly come by.

Some legislators may think they earn what they get as payment for their services, and perhaps they do, as a man is always the best judge of his own value; but there are many who hold a contrary opinion, and among these may be included the peripatetic tinkers, to a man. It hardly harmonises with their ideas of the fitness of things that some men should get three hundred a year for sitting in a comfortable room for a few hours three days a week, only to amuse themselves in passing compliments upon each other's personal looks, or in congratulating one another upon their reputations for veracity, while others have to pull a truck about the streets all day for a few shillings.

Every man thinks his own particular business is as honourable in itself, and as necessary to the community, as anyone else's, and that it ought to be as well paid; and the tinkers in metal, believing as they do, that it is far more difficult to make a tin-kettle than it is to manufacture an Act of Parliament, are at a loss to understand why they should only get about fifty pounds in the course of the year for doing the one, while the tinkers in legislation get three hundred pounds for doing the other. But they ought not to overlook the fact that it requires an intelligence of higher order to make an Act of Parliament than it does to fabricate a tea-kettle, the two things being totally distinct, though both are supposed to be able to hold water.

But that is precisely what they do overlook. They consider that the highest point to which human ingenuity can attain is reached in the making of a tea-kettle, compared with which the making of an Act of Parliament is as nothing, and that is the reason they hold such a poor opinion of our legislators, who, though they can make any number of Acts of Parliament, know nothing whatever about making tea-kettles.

Tinkering is usually followed at home by gipsies in the country places, and by the "house-dweller" in and around London. These latter mostly dwell in Kent Street, or the Mint in the Borough. Some few affect Whitechapel and St. Giles, or the lowest quarters of Westminster, but the Surrey side is the part of the metropolis they favour most.

As the "Romany," as the gipsy is called, has not yet pitched his tent in Australia, the business is left entirely in the hands of our own people, many of whom followed the same occupation at home, and having been compelled to pay a visit to one or other of these colonies in the early days, they resumed their old trade as soon as they had the chance.

Some years ago, when there was less competition, and prices ranged higher than they do at present, the business was a highly lucrative one. An umbrella-mender, or scissors-grinder, or saucepan-patcher, thought nothing of earning a pound a day, now if he can earn five shillings in the same time he thinks he has done remarkably well, and often he has to travel about from morning till night without being able to earn more than half that sum.

Some have their workshops drawn about by ponies, or donkeys, but these are the great men of the fraternity, who can sit and ride while their less fortunate brethren are compelled to push their machines before them as they trudge along the dirty roads. Those of the equestrian order do much better than the others, because they can take a wider circuit, and visit the more distant suburbs, where many jobs are to be picked up, and for which they get better prices than are to be obtained in town, where the competition is keener. Those of a lower grade, who only go in for mending saucepans, or umbrellas, carry the appliances for the work tied up in a bundle at their backs. These men confine themselves to the city and its immediate environs, and are the least important of the tinker brotherhood. They make their home at the sixpenny lodging houses, where they may be seen sitting on the doorstep, or on the kerbstone, when not out at business, or soaking in one of the taps that are generally so convenient to those places.

The dispositions and habits of these men would have to undergo considerable tinkering before they could be pointed to as models for the guidance of others. In no country in the world do they stand very high in public estimation; nor are they famed for sobriety, but here they are if possible worse than elsewhere. Whether it be owing to the climate, or to the colonial beer they take so much of, or both combined, we are unable to say, but it is certain there is much about them that stands in need of improvement.

All are not included in that sweeping denunciation, however, for we know one or two decent fellows among them who are sober and industrious, and who try to live respectably. One turned teetotaller, and kept it up for six months, at the end of which time, to use his own words, he found himself beginning to get very weak, so much so, that he had to place himself under the doctor's hands. While a teetotaller, he saved some money, which was speedily swallowed up by the doctor's bills, which left him, in a pecuniary sense, no better off than he would have been had he not taken the pledge. Such being the case, one need not be surprised that he failed to see in what way his self-denial had benefited him; for, as he naïvely observed, it is no use saving money by teetotallism if you have to give it to the doctor afterwards. Thus, the matter resolved itself into the simple question of whether he should go back to the publican or remain under the care of the doctor, and as he much preferred beer to physic, both on account of its being more agreeable as a beverage and not so expensive, he was not long in making his mind up which it should be, and the doctor knew him no more.

Most of the peripatetic umbrella-menders are old men who have been at the business for years—in fact, so long that they have become quite unfitted for any other occupation, even if they felt disposed to try it. In the grand old times, when plenty of money was to be made, they lived very jolly lives. But now that things are so bad that they can scarcely make beer, they take a very desponding view of matters in general, and are rather given to prophesying the speedy collapse of the Colony.

They are great politicians in their way, and hold very decided opinions upon whatever subject they give their attention to; and are, to a man, anti-immigrationists. They look upon an influx of population in much the same light one would the importation of the cholera, or the sudden invasion of a hostile army.

A new chum in their eyes is the incarnation of all that's evil, because, as they say, men who come here and, by overstocking the labour market, take the bread— or beer—out of other men's mouths, must be so radically depraved that hanging is too good for them, and it's a pity Government does not tie them in sacks and drop them into the bay as fast as they arrive.

We overheard the following conversation between two men connected with the tinkering interest, who were boozing in one of the threepenny taps. We will translate what was said into readable English, leaving the expletives to the imagination of those who may take the trouble to read what we have written.

One, who had arrived from New Zealand the day before, was giving an account of the unflourishing state of the "trade" in that Colony, and how much it was overdone, and the difficulty there was in getting a crust at it in consequence. He also stated that, as he could not live there, he determined to clear out and try his luck in Victoria as soon as he had saved up sufficient money to pay his passage across.

When he had got so far, the other, who had been looking at him from the beginning with glittering eyes, asked him in a neatly-turned sentence, if he thought it was right to come here and rob poor fellows of their work. Fellows was not the word used, but it will do. The new arrival opined he had as much right here as anyone else. The other thought not, and gave him to understand that as *they* had made the country, they were not going to let others step in and reap the benefit. The new chum asked him what *he* had done towards making the country. At that impertinent question the old one waxed wroth, and inquired what it was to do with him, but if he particularly wished to know, and would step outside, he would very soon let him see. The curiosity of the New Zealander was not sufficiently excited to induce him to go outside, and he said so, at the same time advising the angry one not to make a fool of himself. Instead of being thankful for that piece of good advice, he taunted the other with being a "new chum." That was rather too personal to be pleasant, and the new arrival retorted by saying he was not the only one guilty of new chumism, as his accuser must have been one himself at some time or other, unless he happened to be an "old lag," and that was not much better. The barman here read the "riot act," or there is no saying what might not have been the result of this little episode.

One of our tinker friends came up to us one night, and, in very lugubrious though half angry tones, told us he had that morning seen a shipload of immigrants arrive at Port Melbourne, and that he had only taken eighteen pence all day. Although we failed to see any connection between the two circumstances, we plainly perceived they were in some way associated in his mind as cause and effect. We tried to console him by telling him that, according to the doctrine of probabilities, the greater the number of persons in a given place, the greater would be the number of broken umbrellas; consequently, there would be a greater demand for his services to mend them.

"Don't you believe it," he answered, "for the people who can mend them increase a jolly sight faster than they do who break them."

WATERCRESS MEN.

PREVENTION, they say, is better than cure, and it is as true as any of the very wise sayings our ancestors have handed down to us. The principle applies to all things, for all things are liable to get out of gear if they are not properly attended to. It is better to prevent crime than to punish it, and much better to avoid sickness than to have to cure it afterwards.

The power of seeing into the future has been very wisely withheld from mankind, or the knowledge of what we had to suffer—some lingering disease, or the loss of some one dear to us—would spoil our enjoyment of the blessings we may happen to have at present, and make us miserable in anticipation of the coming woe. And those for whom fate had nothing but blessings in store would be anxious and impatient for the time to come when they might enter upon the enjoyment of them. Still, a little knowledge of the future would, no doubt, be of advantage, by enabling us to guard against preventable mishaps; but, although we can have no intuitive insight into it, we can, if we choose, learn something of it by studying the past, for all ought to know that, what has happened once will, under a similar set of circumstances, occur again.

There are few who do not, from their own experience or from that of others, know what momentous results sometimes spring from the merest trifles, for the commission or omission of something of no apparent consequence will influence, for good or evil, a man's whole future life; and when it is done, he sees how easily it might have been different. We make a bad move at chess, through which our pieces get into irretrievable disorder, and we lose the game. We see at once if we had not made that move, we should have been all right; so, taught by experience, we avoid it for the future.

It is just the same in the more serious game of life. We know what we suffer, but we do not always know what we escape. We take a walk in a certain direction, and while there meet with an accident, or do something that entails serious consequences upon us. We know perfectly well if, instead of going in that particular direction, we had taken another, we should have escaped those troubles, but we should not have known it, and, consequently, have had nothing to feel thankful for.

In matters relating to our health, we are also greatly dependent upon trifles. Half the ills that afflict humanity are preventable, and would never be heard of if people would only adopt a judicious regimen, but they will not, and they suffer accordingly. The artificial lives we lead render a change of diet absolutely necessary if we would keep in perfect health; yet people cannot, or will not, recognise that important fact. They get into a dietary groove, and keep to it as though they thought the human stomach was a mere machine for converting into tissue the same food from year's end to year's end. The consequence is their mental and physical powers become weakened, and they gradually settle down into their graves, or become dyspeptic misanthropes.

When a man is suffering from the bile, or some other derangement of the system, he knows he has taken something that disagrees with him, and is only paying the penalty of it. As long as the sickness lasts, he resolves to have a change of diet altogether, but when he gets well—like a certain nameless personage, who, when he was ill, promised to become a saint, but who on recovery, resumed his old habits—he re-enters the old groove, and keeps on till he is sick again.

When Bibo wakes in the morning and finds his ideas rather confused, and his thinking powers not exactly in working order, he knows pretty well what to ascribe it to, and fully recognises the wisdom of the saying that heads this paper, and resolves to act upon it in the future. In the meantime, however, acting upon the homœopathic principle that a hair of the dog that bit you will cure the bite, he takes as a "pick-me-up" a glass of what he had too many of the night before, feels better, and then quietly forgets all about it.

Many complaints arise, not from having taken something that has disagreed with you, but through not having taken what would have prevented them.

The blood of the human system requires purifying, or it will become stagnant and impure, like water in a shallow pond. Those means of purification have been placed within our reach by a bountiful Providence, and if we do not avail ourselves of them we suffer for it. Watercresses are one of these means, and if a pennyworth will keep us off the doctor's list, would it not be unwise on our part not to invest that sum in them? They are valuable as antiscorbutics. They purify the blood, and the blood is the life of our bodies. If the blood be pure, all is well. If not, misery and disease follow as surely as the thunder-clap does the lightning-flash.

Watercresses are not so plentiful here as they are in London, where they are sent every market morning in immense quantities from different parts of the country, to be sold to the retail dealers like other vegetables. Here the supply is obtained in a different way, although some is brought to market, and bought up by the shopkeepers, and by others for their own consumption. The hawkers obtain watercress from the different swamps and creeks round about Melbourne, where it grows somewhat abundantly, and may be gathered by all who choose to go for it.

In London the watercress business is mostly in the hands of women and girls, whose shrill cries may be heard early in the morning, and between dinner and tea-time in the afternoon, for the Londoner dearly loves his "cress" with his bread and butter. There may be a few men and boys connected with it, but the majority of the dealers belong to the "sex."

Our watercress men belong to the same class of the genus hawker as the "winkle" and cockle men do. They have the same habits, and live in the same way. Their personal appearance is the same, they are quite as fond of beer, and are equally partial to rum.

They are not in receipt of very large incomes, although they carry on their business under favourable circumstances, since all they need to make a start with is a basket; their stock-in-trade, as mentioned above, costs them nothing but the trouble of gathering; though that, in the cold, wet weather, is far from being a pleasant job.

Then they have to tie them in bundles and hawk them about till they are sold, bellowing out all the time at the top of their voices to let people know what a luxury they have within their reach. Their earnings range from a shilling to half-a-crown a day; and when we consider what they have to do, that cannot be considered an extravagant rate of remuneration.

There are not many men engaged in the business at present, and the few there are are mostly men who have been in the Colony many years, but have never held a very high position in society. Some of them have been pretty well off in times past, when money was to be made by means that are not considered quite correct nowadays.

One started the first skittle-alley in Melbourne, and that was in Little Bourke Street, a short way up on the western side of Elizabeth Street. He afterwards opened a "three-up" room—that is, a room where gambling was carried on by tossing with three coppers. A deal of money may be won or lost at that game, even by going as low as "three for a half-a-crown," and "two for a shilling," which means when three pence are tossed up and they all three come down alike, either heads or tails, you win or lose half-a-crown, according to your call being right or wrong; and as two out of the three are bound to be the same, you must win or lose at least a shilling at each toss.

These two "specs" brought him in a considerable revenue, but, like many more who made money at that time, he could not keep it, owing to his fondness for tossing, at which amusement he was singularly unlucky, frequently losing as much as forty pounds in one day. But it was not only his bad luck he had to contend with. Rivals in business sprang up all round him, as might be expected, for it was not very likely that one man would be allowed to enjoy, for any length of time, the monopoly of two such profitable "lays" as skittle-alleys and "three-up" rooms proved to be. Although the devotees of those games increased with the opportunities offered for the gratification of them, they did not increase fast enough to keep all in full swing, and soon the starter of the idea had the pleasure of seeing the people for whose benefit he had introduced those highly intellectual pastimes, desert his premises for those of his rivals, till at length he "lost the run" of the business altogether, and became poorer than he was when he first started the enterprise.

Not being very polished in manner or of gentlemanly exterior, he could not embark in any of the higher branches of the science of fleecing, so he had to confine himself to wooing the fickle goddess through the medium of "three-up"; but, as her smiles were not so liberally bestowed as her frowns, emptiness soon became the normal state of his pockets. From that condition they have never since recovered, and now, in his old age, while waiting the approach of the "inevitable," he has no other means of obtaining a crust than by selling watercresses.

Another of our peripatetics in the same line, whose feeble cry, as heard in the streets, tells us plainly enough that his interest in watercresses will soon terminate, has been a genius in his time, and has passed through a rather chequered career.

He came from the west of England, and was pretty well known to the inhabitants living within a considerable radius of his native village. From a very early age he had noticed that those of his friends who worked hard had to live hard as well; in fact, the harder they worked the poorer they kept. He was a sharp lad, and had learned to read, and his reading soon taught him that there were two classes in society—those who worked and those who didn't, and that, as a rule, the non-workers were infinitely better off than the workers, which he thought was rather strange.

He also read about the "dignity of labour," and wondered what it meant, for, with him, labour and poverty were synonymous terms, and judging from those he saw around him, he could not believe in the possibility of dignity and poverty being united in the same person. Whatever compensatory consolation in the shape of dignity hard work had for those who took kindly to it, it was not, in his opinion, nearly so good as the more tangible consideration of hard cash, and as there was so little of that to be obtained by working, he resolved to avoid it altogether, and enjoy the ease of a *far niente* life, leaving the dignity for those workers who were satisfied with it.

One night, when he was about fifteen years of age, he snared a couple of hares, and sold them the next morning to an innkeeper for five shillings. At that time his father was earning two shillings per day as a labourer, and he felt so pleased at being able to earn more than twice as much in one night than his father could in a day, that he went to him, and, with a feeling of pride, told him what he had done, and offered him the five shillings. To his intense astonishment, to say nothing of pain and grief, his father, instead of embracing him, tied him up, and gave him a most unmerciful beating, and kept him all that day without anything to eat. Early the next morning, before going to work, pater gave the lad a severe lecture on conduct in general, and poaching in particular. Being hungry and sore, the boy's mind was at that moment in a highly favourable state for receiving impressions, and he gave the author of his being to understand that he began to look upon snaring hares as highly immoral, and that he would do so no more. On that understanding he was again received into favour.

Although his father had convinced him of the impropriety of snaring hares, his opinion in regard to work had undergone no modification whatever, but had become, if possible, more decided on the matter than before. As there were plenty of other ways of getting money without being under the disagreeable necessity of having to work for it beside poaching, it was not very long before he embarked in an enterprise of a different nature; but, being taught by experience, he was particularly careful not to let his father know what that enterprise was, lest he should approve of it as little as he had done of his mode of catching hares.

One night, as he was walking along the main thoroughfare with a bundle under his arm, he had the misfortune to meet the village constable, who, being rather inquisitive, asked him what he had tied up in his pocket-handkerchief. Instead of giving a plausible and straightforward answer, he dropped his load and took to his heels, but was quickly overtaken and locked up. Upon examination, the bundle was found to contain some articles that had been stolen the previous night from a gentleman's house in the neighbourhood. At his trial he failed to satisfy the jury that he had picked the things up by the roadside, and as the judge could not tie him up and flog him as his father had done, he ordered him a change of locality instead, in the hope that during the next seven years he might acquire a taste for work.

On arriving at this side of the globe, it appeared as though the judge's hopes were about to be justified, for although he would not work when free, he laboured so well in bondage that, at the end of two years, he received a conditional pardon. Things went on pretty well till his restricted liberty was made absolute, when his old dislike to work returned with tenfold intensity, and before very long he again got within the clutch of the law.

Released once more, it occurred to him that the air round about Sydney was not good for him, so he made up his mind to come to Port Phillip for a change. That was thirty-eight years ago. The change was not much to his advantage, nor to the Melbourne people's either, for it was very soon perceived that the local "appropriators" had had fresh blood infused into them by arrivals from the "Sydney side." The police had a shrewd suspicion that our friend was not far off, and they kept such a sharp look-out for him that it was not long before he found his way into the "stockade."

He was out again on the breaking out of the gold fever, and it is supposed he had a finger in the Eureka pie, from which, however, he was able to withdraw without getting into further trouble. At digging he was pretty fortunate, and might have done well if he could have kept steady; but the possession of gold only had the effect of adding gambling and drinking to his other qualities, and they speedily altered his position for the worse. As years went by, drink and exposure began to tell upon his constitution, and he became too feeble to dig, and not active enough to thieve, and now his only resource is—watercresses.

It was from himself we received the above biographical sketch; and when he had finished, we asked him what became of the five shillings he received for the two hares. He said he couldn't tell, but he noticed the next day his mother had a new pair of boots on.

It is fortunate that such men as these are able to get some sort of a living for themselves, instead of being a burden on the State, as they undoubtedly would be if there was nothing left for them to do but work, which, in their case, is simply impossible; and as they could not be allowed to die of starvation in the streets, Immigrants' Homes and Benevolent Asylums would have to be multiplied exceedingly.

THE PERIWINKLE MAN.

THE "winkle," as an article of food, does not rank very high, certainly; but, for all that, it is a tasty little thing when properly cooked, and is much admired by the working classes. It is a small mollusc of the Gasteropod order—that is, it uses its stomach as its feet whenever it wants to change its locality.

There is nothing that 'lives and moves and hath its being,' whether it walks erect as a man, flies in the air, or crawls on its belly as the worm, that omnivorous man does not eat.

The Englishman glories in his roast beef, and believes in his mutton. These he looks upon as the foundation upon which the British stamina is built. He is partial to venison, and does not object to pork. He can also make a hearty meal off a hare or rabbit, but there his liking for the quadrupedal order of nature ends. He has not yet taken to hippophagy, or developed a taste for cats, dogs, or rats. Where John Bull leaves off, John Chinaman, less fastidious or more frugal, takes up the running, and looks upon cats, dogs, and rats as important items in his culinary arrangements.

In bipedal food, the Briton confines himself to the fowls of the air, and leaves the consumption of his own species to the Solomon Islander. That simple child of nature knows nothing about man's mission on earth; he only regards him as something good to eat, and thinks it would be the height of folly to dispose of his "remains" by sepulture or cremation when they can be so easily reconverted into living tissue.

Of fishes, John Bull eats all he can catch, except the shark and whale. These he only dines off in extreme cases, such as shipwreck; but an Esquimaux looks upon a stranded whale as a godsend, and will devour twenty or thirty pounds of putrid blubber per diem.

The few men who go about Melbourne selling winkles belong to the loafer class, and are mostly old men. As a rule, they patronise the sixpenny lodging-house, when they save the wherewithal to pay for the bed; when they haven't, they "doss it" where they can, which is usually in an old boiler or empty malt-tank in winter, and *sub Jove* in summer.

At one time these men could fill their baskets at Williamstown or St. Kilda, but for the last few years they have been rather scarce in those localities, owing to the number of excursionists who, when there, make "winkle-hunting" part of the day's amusement. Consequently, those who want them for sale have to look elsewhere for them.

It is but a hard and precarious living the "winklers" get at the best. With basket on arm, they trudge along the road in all weathers to the few remaining spots where the tiny molluscs are yet to be found. Sometimes they are so fortunate as to be able to fill their baskets at Brighton, but frequently they have to go as far as Morehalloe, and sometimes further than that. Leaving town early in the morning, they may be able to get to Brighton, fill their baskets, and return to Melbourne in time to sell them the same night. If, however, they have to go beyond the latter-named place, all they can do is get there in one day and return the next.

It would be a weary walk for these elderly gentlemen if they could not get an occasional lift on the road. But, fortunately for them, there are plenty of carts or empty drays going the same way as themselves, the drivers of which will always give them a ride, if civilly asked for permission to "jump up."

The winkles are found loose among the gravel or sand upon the beach in greater or lesser quantities, more frequently the lesser. They also hide themselves in the friendly shadow of the loose boulders lying about, which have to be removed before the searcher can reach his prey, often not an easy task for men whose muscles have become softened, and whose strength has been sapped by a perpetual soaking in " colonial."

Having filled his basket, which, by the way, is no light load, our winkle man gets on the "back track," as he calls it. Having arrived in town, he goes to the place he

stays at, and begins to prepare his stock for the market.
The first process the winkles undergo is washing—a very
necessary operation, as the sand clings to them with great
tenacity, and can only be removed by repeated rinsings
under the tap. Having washed them to his satisfaction,
the next thing our friend has to do is to boil them, and a
few minutes suffices for that, if he can get anything to
boil them in. The culinary arrangements of these sixpenny lodging-houses are not always of the most perfect
description. Neither does the manager or chucker-out
consider it part of his duty to provide boilers for cooking
winkles in, as the only recognised cooking in these
establishments is the preparation of whatever small
articles of food the lodgers may bring in, and for that
a saucepan and gridiron are at their service. Should the
saucepan be engaged at the time the winkle man wants
to cook his winkles, he borrows a billy, and does as many
as it will hold, and repeats the operation till the whole
are cooked.

Having prepared his stock for sale, all that remains for
him to do now is to sell it, and before he can do that he
has to travel up one street and down another for many
weary miles in search of customers. The great bulk of
his patrons are to be found in hotels, among the half-
drunken people lounging about the bars, whose appetites
being somewhat palled by drink, are tickled by these
tasty little things, and restored to their normal condition.
Many people, especially new arrivals, like them with
their bread and butter at tea-time. Others are fond of
them, but cannot command sufficient patience to extract
them from their shells; and some "can't a-bear" them
on account of their strong resemblance to snails.

If our friend can get back to town with a peck of
winkles he considers himself very fortunate. Mostly,
however, he has to content himself with about half that
quantity, which being sold at threepence the half-pint
leaves him something like four shillings for his trouble,
and as it sometimes takes him two days to gather and
sell them, it cannot be said his business is a lucrative
one.

The possession of money is not always an unmixed
blessing. Strange as it may sound, people sometimes
have more money than is good for them, that is, when

they make an injudicious use of it. It is much better for our friend that his income is limited to about two shillings a day, as out of that he must pay for a bed, and at least one meal, Sunday included, and that will not leave him sufficient for a very extended "drunk," whereas, if he had more he would never be sober. He is tolerably contented, however, and accepts his position with great philosophy, saying, "If I cannot get drunk every day, I will as often as I can." In carrying out that resolve, he hangs about his favourite tap till all his money is gone, then he and his basket disappear till the following evening, when there are other rinsings and another boiling, soon after which the streets are again resonant with "Periwinkle."

The individual in the winkle interest who forms the ground-work of this paper knows nothing of earthly care, and is as free from earthly goods as Diogenes was of old. The cynic had but what he stood upright in and a lantern. Our peripatetic has only the clothes on his back and a basket, and that basket is as necessary to him in seeking a living as the lantern was to the Greek in his search for an honest man.

Nor would it be wise on our winkle man's part to have more clothes or other property than he could carry about with him, as any surplusage would be sure to disappear the moment it was out of his sight. We have just said our friend was tolerably contented and free from care; but most men wish for something they have not, and he is no exception to the rule. He has an ambition, but that ambition only extends to the laudable desire of being the possessor of two shirts. The laundry arrangements of these sixpenny lodging-houses are not very complete, and he sometimes finds it difficult to get the only shirt he has washed, whereas if he had two he could have one off and one on; the "off" one being in readiness to replace the other when a change was deemed necessary. A month he thinks is quite long enough for any man to wear a shirt without its being washed, and perhaps it is; but, judging by the hue of the little we could see of the one he then wore, we incline to the belief that he had not made the monthly change of linen a hard and fast rule.

It was not altogether his inability to get an extra shirt that kept him from it, but the fear of not being able to keep it after he had gone to the expense of getting it.

"I would get another one somehow," he said to us one day, "if I'd only a place to hide it in when I'm not wearing it; but what's the use of a poor man like me buying a shirt for another cove to wear?"

We were quite prepared to admit that in the great probability of such being the case, the duplication would not have been a wise act, but we suggested that as he had several relatives living not far off, he might leave the spare shirt with one of them till he wanted it, when he would not only take care of it, but lend him a little money into the bargain.

"No fear," he exclaimed. "If I was to try to pawn a shirt, the pawnbroker would think I'd stolen it, and very likely send for a "slop" (policeman) and give me in charge. Besides, it might be six months before I'd be able to get it out again, and I might just as well be without it as not be able to get it when I wanted it."

Accepting that common-sense view of affairs, we expressed a wish to know how he managed to get the only shirt he had washed. He was his own laundress, and washed it as often as he thought requisite. In winter it underwent the cleansing process in a bucket under the tap in the back yard, and afterwards held before the kitchen fire till dry enough to put on. Sunday morning used to be his favourite washing time, but in consequence of a fight taking place in the kitchen during the drying process, the chucker-out determined that for the future, that day, as far as the laundry business went, should be kept holy.

It so happened that an umbrella-mender, who was staying there, took it into his head that his shirt would be all the better for a wash. Unfortunately the idea occurred to him on the same morning a similar idea had taken possession of our winkle man. Things went on amicably enough till they brought their clothes into the kitchen to dry, when it was soon discovered that there was barely room for two men to hold their shirts in front of the fire, and allow half a dozen others to prepare their breakfasts at the same time. The consequence was a deal of grumbling, accompanied by many forcible adjectives, took place among them. From grumbling they got to pushing, and that ended in a general all round fight. The clatter soon brought the chucker-out on to the scene, and from the prompt way in which he quelled the riot, he proved beyond a doubt that he was the "right man in the right place."

In summer when the weather was hot, our friend used to go to the banks of the Yarra, between the Falls and Prince's bridges, and having washed his shirt in the stream, would spread it out on the banks for the sun to dry it. While the drying was going on, he usually lay down to have a nap, till one day, on awaking, he found his shirt had disappeared. He never knew if it had been blown into the river, or whether it had been stolen by some loafer who had thought it a favourable opportunity of getting a change of linen. He inclined to the former belief, because, as he observed, the shirt was in such a dilapidated state that any loafer must be hard up indeed who would think it worth the trouble of walking off with. Ever after that, he said, he always took the precaution of going to sleep with one eye open till the garment was sufficiently desiccated to be resumed.

When washing day came round he used to go to the Public Library and take a piece of soap out of the lavatory in the full belief that he had a perfect right to do so, and when we informed him he had committed a larceny for which he was liable to imprisonment, he was not only greatly surprised, but highly indignant as well.

"Wasn't it bought with the public money?" he asked, "and put there for the public use, and haven't I, as one of the public, as much right to it as anyone else?"

"Of course you have, but you must go there to use it."

"They wouldn't let me wash my shirt there, would they?"

"Not if they know it."

"Well then, what benefit is the soap to me if I can't take it to where I can do my washing?"

"My good fellow, you must understand the trustees do not find soap for washing shirts, either there or anywhere else. It is placed in the lavatory for the use of those visitors who want to wash their hands before they handle the books, and you may go there and use it as often as you like and as much as you like."

"But if I have the right to use the soap at all, what

difference can it make whether I use it inside the building or outside?"

"None whatever, as far as the soap is concerned, but the law says you must not take it away."

"The law be hanged. Right's right, and wrong's no man's right."

Although we could not dispute the correctness of the latter sentence, we failed to see in what way it justified his purloining the soap; but as we saw there was no probability of bringing him over to our way of thinking, we changed the subject.

One evening we met our winkle merchant as he was going his rounds, and, somewhat to our astonishment, we saw he had a clean face, or rather, it was not in its normal state of dirt. We also noticed there was a look of sorrow mingled with disgust upon it, that convinced us something had gone wrong. On enquiring what it was, he told us, in his own quaint fashion, how one night he had been served a trick that nearly broke his heart and kept him sober for well-nigh a week. That accounted for the unwonted cleanness of his face. That was about nine days before our meeting, and he had not then recovered from the effects of what he called "that cruel blow."

He started off early one morning to get his winkles, when he was fortunate enough to get a lift in one of the fish carts as far as Mordialloc, and that took him to the end of his journey. Having gathered his molluscs, he started on the homeward track, and luckily got another ride that took him to Windsor, which enabled him to get home and have his winkles cooked by five o'clock that evening. There had been a fierce hot wind blowing all day, and he had had nothing but Yan Yean to quench his thirst with, so it may be easily imagined he was in prime fettle for a swig of his favourite beverage as soon as business placed the means of getting it within his reach.

He had not been in the street long before he sold half a pint of winkles, the three pence for which he quickly exchanged for a pint of beer. That disappeared with no other effect than an increase of thirst and a craving for more. Shortly after that another stroke of business placed the price of another pint at his command, and that too was speedily "liquidated." If he had stopped there all might have been well. Instead of that, however, he kept on spending the money as fast as he got it, till at length the fumes of the beer he had taken so much of on an empty stomach mounted to his brain, and the use of his legs and the consciousness of his whereabouts left him at the same moment.

In the same tap, which was not far from where our friend lodged, several of his fellow lodgers, also suffering from the hot wind and sun, were discussing various knotty points and trying to keep their throats moist at the same time. These men were not so far "gone" as not to be able to help a brother in distress, so two of them picked up their insensible chum, and carried him off to bed, while a third followed after with the basket of winkles.

As we have hinted before, some of the *habitués* of these padding kens have rather lax notions as to a man's right to his own property, especially when that property consists of anything they fancy they should like, so one need not be surprised at their appropriating the drunken man's winkles. As soon as they had placed their burden upon his bed, the three men, each armed with a pin, fell upon the winkles with a vigour that augured well for their speedy conversion into a basket of empty shells. They had not been at it long when three other half-drunken loafers staggered into the room to go to bed, there being accommodation in this apartment for eight. The new arrivals seeing how the case stood, provided themselves with pins, and joined in the attack upon the molluscs with a determination quite equal to that displayed by the others. By the united efforts of these six men the basket was soon emptied. Then the shells were gathered up and put into the basket, and the basket and half-pint measure placed under their owner's stretcher. After a little mutual congratulation upon each other's smartness, the six chuckling loafers shook off their clothes and tumbled into bed and were soon as insensible to what was passing around them as was the man they had just robbed.

When our winkle man awoke the next morning, the first thing he did was to look for his basket, and seeing the shells in it, he concluded it was all right. His name standing rather high in that establishment, he had no difficulty in borrowing the wherewith to get a breakfast.

That morning he felt more than usually "seedy," and confessed he "didn't feel much like eating." But he knew he must take something, and he debated within himself what would be the best thing to coax the appetite with. After much deliberation, he decided in favour of a penny roll, a very salt red-herring, and a pint of beer. After partaking of that luxurious meal, which he enjoyed immensely, he picked up his basket and went on his round.

The first customer he served soon called him back, and asked him what he meant by selling him a lot of empty shells. The poor fellow, conscious of his own integrity, was rather staggered by the question, and tried to account for it by saying that, perhaps, it was only the first one or two he had picked up that were empty; but when he saw they were all alike, he turned his attention to those in his basket, and finding they were empty also, his emotion became of the liveliest. He understood it all in a moment, and giving the customer his money back, he returned to the lodging-house to find out, if possible, who they were who had robbed him. Of course no one there knew anything about it, and as it would hardly have been right to immolate the whole of the lodgers in order to make sure of the guilty ones, he relieved his mind by the discharge of a few score of oaths, and submitted to it with the best grace he could.

THE CLOTHES-PROP VENDOR.

CLEANLINESS, we are told, is next to godliness. If that be so, the converse must hold good, when it would appear that dirtiness and ungodliness are in close alliance. But so far from that being the case, we hear of men—some of the old monks and hermits for instance—whose dislike to soap and water, or whatever the detergent of the middle ages may have been, was quite as great as their hatred of the devil. When these godly men sought to propitiate heaven by donning a shirt made of horse-hair, they must have stood very much in need of a change, after having worn the same one for a number of years without its ever having passed through the hands of the laundress. At least, we are nowhere told they ever possessed two shirts, so that one might be purified while the other was mortifying the flesh.

Neither are we led to suppose they did what many a clever man who only possessed one shirt has had to do in our own time—lie in bed while it was being washed. It is just possible these old penitents did not believe in the existence of what they couldn't see, for the horse-hair being dark, and the dirt of the same tint, it would not be readily perceived by the eye. But one would suppose the nose would become alive to it, unless it had lost its functions through constant association with frouziness. However it might have been in their own cases, a stranger on approaching them would speedily have detected the necessity for a change of some sort.

Neither is cleanliness, the old saw to the contrary notwithstanding, always a sure sign of godliness, for there are some people who are very clean in their persons, but extremely ungodly in their lives. Although cleanliness and godliness are not always associated, it is just possible that the former may lead to the latter, as when a man is clean he is comfortable—at least, some are—and when he's in that state, the mind is more open to divine truths than it is when he's uncomfortable.

It may be asked what has all that to do with the clothes-prop man. The answer is, everything. Now, to make a subject intelligible, one must approach men's understandings in much the same way one would advance upon an enemy's lines—by degrees. A *raison d'être* must be given for everything, and in order to introduce our clothes-prop man, we must first show that laundresses are necessary. Everyone knows that after clothes are washed they must be dried, to effect which a clothes-prop is indispensable, to give the things the full benefit of the breeze and keep them from trailing on the ground.

The clothes-prop business, as far as its slackness or briskness is concerned, is regulated entirely by the state of the marriage market. The connection of the two may not, at first sight, be obvious; but that it is so can be proved beyond a doubt. The props are made of a remarkably tough kind of wood, the ti-tree, and when a lady has provided herself with as many as she wants, she will need no more, unless the original ones get stolen, or chopped up for fire-wood, during the whole of her married life, or until an increase in the family renders an extension of the laundry operations necessary. Thus it is seen that new props are only required by newly-married ladies, and, of course, the more there are who join the holy state, the greater will be the demand for those useful articles.

One of the first things a young lady thinks of when she gets married, and moves into a house of her own, is the clothes-prop, and she listens for the cry of the vendor as anxiously as she was wont to do for the sound of her lover's footsteps in the happy days of their courtship. Nor has she to wait long for the welcome sound, for the advent of a clothes-prop man in the neighbourhood of a newly-married couple is a certainty. Why it is so is one of the great mysteries of nature we are unable to fathom. When a camel has dropped down in the desert to die, the vultures, till then invisible, assemble round the dying brute, and watch with cruel eyes for the moment to commence the feast.

It must be by a similar instinct that the clothes-prop man is lead to the neighbourhood of a newly-created household; for, as vultures are invisible in the desert skies till there is something for them to eat on the sand, so surely is our friend never seen in localities where there is no sale for his props.

The demand for props being limited, only a few men are required for their distribution, and these few have not a very flourishing time of it. They number, we believe, all told, about twelve, one or two of whom have a horse and cart to go about the distant suburbs, while the others "hump" the props on their shoulders about the outskirts of the city.

At one time the "sticks," as they are called, could be obtained in the ti-tree scrub, on the banks of the Yarra, close to the Williamstown ferry, but the supply from that quarter has long since given out, and they are now brought by train from Gippsland. When the men had to go to the Yarra and cut their own sticks, it was no child's play. In winter, they had to work up to their knees in mud; and in summer they had to face countless myriads of mosquitoes, that bitterly resented any invasion of their territories.

Nine was about the number a man could cut, trim, and carry into town in one day. There were some who could manage a dozen, but they had to be strong to do so, as the ti-tree, when wet, is very heavy. It was wearisome work trudging along the road with nine or a dozen props upon the shoulder, and by the time they were back in Melbourne, they were too tired to hawk them about the city and suburbs, so that part of the business had to be put off till the next day. Thus it took two days to sell nine props, and as the usual price was ninepence each, it may be easily understood that these men had not very rosy times of it.

The social position and habits of these men are much the same as those of the peripatetics generally. One or two live in a sixpenny lodging-house, and the others are to be found located in the different rights-of-way in the city. They are, as a rule, great drinkers, rum being their favourite tipple, because, they say, it keeps out the damp.

We have the privilege of being on speaking terms with

one of these men, and when we meet we generally stop and have a chat on general subjects; at least such subjects as he is best qualified to discourse upon.

The position he holds in his stratum of society enables him to observe many things that very few in the upper strata know anything about, and his observations are characterised by a display of common sense not always to be found in the remarks of men who are supposed to possess a large amount of that article. He is very shrewd, and has a keen sense of the ridiculous, and has a droll way of relating whatever he sees and hears. It may seem strange that one such as we have described this man to be should hold the low position in society he does. But, strange as it may appear, it would be still more singular, when his habits are considered, if he held any other.

The rush to the gold-fields in the early days of our history brought to our shores a strangely varied assortment of the *genus homo*, each one of whom came in the full expectation of becoming suddenly rich. Some were successful, while others were not. Among the latter were noblemen, baronets, and professional men of all degrees. These unfortunates had to live, and in order to do that they must work, and to the honour of many of them be it said, they pocketed their dignities, and doffed their coats, and went at it. Some cracked stones by the roadside, others turned to as bricklayers' labourers, while the rest earned a crust in the best way they could.

Those of the unlucky ones who had friends at home to send them the means of getting back soon bade Australia farewell, and returned to their native land wiser and perhaps better men. Of the others, not so fortunate, some eventually did well; while the others settled down into "dead-beats," living anyhow and anywhere. Among these was our friend the prop-man.

At home he had been an articled clerk in a lawyer's office, where he was looked upon as the possessor of average ability, and he might have done well had not the *auri sana fames* brought him to Australia. He was of a roving disposition, and had a lively imagination. Fired by the reports of the heaps of gold that could be picked up in Victoria, he thought he might as well come and get his share as anyone else. He was then eighteen, and after much persuasion, he induced one of his fellow clerks to join him in the expedition; and they both ran away from their articles and came to Melbourne, at least our friend did; the other was buried at sea when the passage was about half over.

Although this individual does not stand very high, socially, he is one of the upper ten in his own rank of life, and, as such, is looked up to by those who are less intellectually gifted than himself.

Whatever "world" a man belongs to, he will make his own position in it, and find his own level. When we say "world," we mean one of the classes into which society is divided, which classes are subdivided into grades; and whenever a man enters one of these classes, he rises or falls to his own grade, and keeps to it as naturally as a planet does to its orbit.

Possibly many people will be astonished to hear that, even among the lowest and most depraved classes, there is an aristocracy. But it is so, nevertheless; and the aristocracy of low life gives the tone to it, just as surely as that of the upper points out the way things ought to go there.

In the ranks of crime the burglar is looked up to by the pickpocket with the same veneration a snobbish gentleman bestows upon a lord. But though he considers the "cracksman" his superior, his contempt for the "snowdropper" is as intense as that of the snobbish gentleman for the artisan.

Laïs, when on her "beat," bedizened in silks and feathers, would feel greatly insulted if one of her sisters in a lower grade were to stop and address her; while the second-class Cyprian would never think of associating with a still lower fallen one, whom drink and disease had robbed of good looks, and whose wardrobe can produce nothing but rags.

With all that present exclusiveness, however, Laïs will descend in her turn, step by step, to the lowest grade, when her feathers will be replaced by soiled ribbons, and her silks give way to rags.

It is the same with the peripatetics. The costermonger who owns a barrow thinks far more of himself than he does of the man whose business appliances only extend to a basket. Those who require a little skill to carry on their occupations, such as tinkers, consider themselves superior to those whose calling requires no preparatory training, such as the clothes-prop men; and these in turn look down upon the beggars and match-sellers with the most supreme contempt. Lower than that it cannot go, unless it be that when one of the last-mentioned sees a mate carried off to the hospital, or Immigrants' Home, to die, he may thank God he has not come to that yet.

Thus, throughout, the laws of caste are as clearly defined, and as strictly conformed to, by the section of our population we are treating of, as they are among the Hindoos.

When our friend is drunk, which is as often as the state of his finances will allow, he is not so agreeable in manner, or coherent in speech, as when sober, consequently it is difficult to separate the wheat from the tares of his discourse. He has also many peculiar ways when in that state, one of which is to stop us every time we meet, and insist upon shaking hands—an ordeal we always submit to, as the readiest way of getting rid of him.

One cold winter's day, a few years ago, when the "proppers" could cut their own sticks in the scrub, we met him toiling along under a load of props he had cut that morning. There had been a drizzling rain about an hour before, and he looked weary, wet, and dejected.

"For God's sake," he said, as soon as he saw us, "give me a drop of rum, or I shall die!" Having said which, he laid his props down by the edge of the kerb, so as to be ready to "adjourn," for he fully expected to get what he had asked for.

Out of compassion we did adjourn, and he soon felt better under the vivifying effects of two threepennyworths of rum. In the conversation that followed, we asked him if he did not prefer the summer to winter for cutting his props.

"No fear," he replied; "I like the winter best, for then we are at least free from the mosquitoes. I was down in the scrub one morning, about three months ago, at five o'clock, when I got it awful. It was a close muggy morning, with scarcely a breath of air stirring, when they came round me in swarms, and almost drove me mad with their stings. People say they only bite new chums; if so, they've been mistaking me for one every summer these last twenty years, and the more they taste of me the better they seem to like me. But that morning they gave me such "pepper," that if I had been a new chum, instead of an old, well-seasoned one, I should never have left the scrub alive."

When he had got so far, he put both his hands to his sides, as though he was in great pain, and said he thought he had the cramp in his stomach, to which he was very liable whenever he got wet, and expressed the belief that another drop of rum would do him good. We told him we thought not, and advised him to go home and get something to eat, with a basin of hot coffee, and that would do him more good than all the rum in the world. Although it was plain to see he would have preferred his own remedy to ours, he said nothing further, but went to the place where he had left his props, and, having shouldered them, trudged off home.

Owing to the heavier nature of the occupation, "propping" has to be followed by a younger and far more vigorous class of men than the peripatetics who follow those occupations which can be carried on by means of a light basket; consequently they are not all such hopeless drunkards as the "winkle" and the cockle men are.

Comparatively young as they are, however, some of them "swipe" to an extent that gives fair promise that, as old age creeps upon them, when they will have to drop the props and take to the baskets, their power of imbibing will be quite equal to that of any of their predecessors.

When the young housewife, still in the first blush of pride in her new home, is negotiating the purchase of her props, she should think of the hardships the man she is dealing with has to undergo in procuring them, and as they are articles so necessary to the proper working of her laundry, she should not drive too hard a bargain with him.

CHIMNEY SWEEPS.

The term "sweep" is not confined solely to those useful individuals who, for a consideration, come early in the morning to divest our chimneys of their superfluous soot. It is also applied to certain members of society who, although decidedly a "cut" above handling such a dirty material as soot, will, nevertheless, bespatter themselves with dirt that cannot be washed off.

There is the "Moral sweep"—the seducer, the false friend, and the evader of just liabilities; the "Lying sweep"—the man who seldom opens his mouth but to utter a falsehood; the "Drunken sweep"—the man who ruins his health, destroys his mind, and brings misery upon all dependent upon him by an ungodly thirst; the "Lazy sweep"—the man who prefers eating the bread of idleness to that which eats so much sweeter when earned by honest toil; the "Dirty sweep"—the man who is not above doing mean actions; while a "Regular sweep"—is the term applied to an all-round scoundrel.

All and several of these men consider themselves far superior to the poor looked-down-upon "chummy."

Chimney-sweeping is not considered a dignified calling in any country in the world. That is probably owing to the dirt which clings to those who follow it, for dirt and dignity are incompatible. We speak of material, not moral, dirt, as a man may be dirty in his actions and extremely dignified in comportment.

Chimney-sweeping in Melbourne is a more lucrative business than it is in London, where "chummying" has for many years been at a low ebb. There was a time when the "queer"—as soot is called in the sweep's jargon—could be sold to the farmers for dressing the land at half-a-crown per bushel. Now, owing to the introduction of so many patent manures, it will only fetch fourpence.

Besides taking away the soot, Chummy took good care to clear out the cinders and ashes from the grate, and walk off with them as well. On reaching home, the sweep would empty his bag of soot and ashes on to a heap in a room used for that purpose, as it would never do to keep it in the open air, for, being so light, the first puff of wind would send it flying all over the neighbourhood. The soot is then sifted to separate the cinders—"breeze," as it is called—from it. The former is then tied up in sacks, and put aside till the farmer, or market-gardener, calls for it, unless the sweep happens to have a horse and cart of his own, when he is only too glad to deliver it himself. The breeze is sold to the brickmakers, who use it for burning their bricks, as, owing to its comparative freedom from smoke, it is much better than coal, with the additional advantage of its being much cheaper.

Here the soot is worth nothing, so Chummy, when he has taken it out of the chimney, throws it into the first convenient place he can find, which is usually the dust-box, or some corner of the back yard.

Notwithstanding the soot having no commercial value, chimney-sweeping is not a bad business in Melbourne. There was a time when a sweep could earn his pound a day, and sometimes more; even now a man with a good connexion may calculate upon a fair income—the year out and the year in, as they call it. A sweep out here may sometimes be seen with a clean face—a phenomenon never seen at home, except, perhaps, on Sundays; even then there is a grimy look upon them, having a strong resemblance to the outside of a saucepan the cook has been trying to polish. The reason why the colonials have cleaner faces than their brethren at home is owing to wood being so largely used for fuel, the soot of which being harder and more cohesive than that resulting from coal, it does not fly about when touched.

As members of society, our sweeps are, as a rule, better behaved than those in England; and the cause of that higher "tone" may be found in the fact that here nearly all of them are their own masters.

But few appliances are needed to start a man in business, and it needs no preparatory training. A machine, costing about five pounds, a scraper, a hand-brush to sweep up the soot, and a cloth to sweep it into, are all a man requires to make a start in that line. If he wish to indulge in a sign, a brush similar to a Turk's head erected above the roof of his house will do.

Although our sweeps are generally better behaved than those of London, an exception to that rule may sometimes be met with, as the following incident will show.

A well-known and highly-respected Chinese merchant, living at East Melbourne, was, some time ago, standing at his front gate talking to his wife and a friend, when a sweep came along and asked him if he wanted his chimney swept.

"No," was the answer.

"How is it," queried the sweep, "that you Chinese never want your chimneys swept?"

The answer he got to that impertinent question was a crack on the head from the Chinaman's umbrella. The sweep retaliated by knocking off his assailant's hat with his brush, and there seemed every prospect of what is called in the prize-ring jargon a "rattling mill" coming off between the two, when the gentleman standing by, and the groom who happened to be working in the front garden, interfered in the interests of peace, and each drew his man off, the sweep hinting at future law proceedings, and the other threatening the immediate invocation of the police. However, nothing further came of it, as one, doubtless, was ashamed of his rudeness, and the other must have felt he had not cut a very dignified figure in the matter.

Many of the older members of the brotherhood followed the same calling at home, but, hearing of the diggings, they came out to "try their luck," and having tried it, with poor results, or having made something, and lost it again, they fell back upon their original avocation, and found it a much better way of earning money, and far easier than digging.

One came out to Australia under a cloud, and when it had rolled by, he came to Victoria, where he met a chummy he had known in London, and the two "amalgamated," as he called it. Seeing this man could neither read nor write, it would be hard to say where he picked up that word.

Having amalgamated, they thought they would go on the spree for a week before getting into harness. But the week had scarcely half expired when they had a dispute, which ended in a fight, and having hammered one another to their mutual satisfaction, they shook hands, and dissolved the partnership, with the same liquid formalities that had accompanied the amalgamation.

We asked our friend, the cloudy one, what the quarrel was about.

" Well, you see," he answered, " he wanted to be boss, but I wasn't a-going to let him. We was a-talking of it over, when he ses, ses he, ' Nat, I think the business had better be carried on in my name.' ' How's that ? ' ses I. ' Because I'm not known to the perlise,' ses he. ' P'r'aps not,' ses I, ' but you ought to be,' I ses. ' What about the " souper " (watch) as was lost the morning you swep' old Jones' flue ?' At that he lets fly, and drops me a hot 'un on the nose, and I sends him a straight 'un that put his ear about an inch further back. Then at it we goes, and as nobody was there to interfere, we fought till we was both tired."

One knight of the brush and scraper had been a draper at home. He, like others, having been seized with the gold fever, came out here in the expectation of being able, in a few months, to return to the land of his birth with sufficient of the precious metal to open in a large way of business in London. The day after he landed at Port Melbourne he was taken ill, having only a few shillings in his pocket. His other belongings were the clothes he stood upright in, an extra shirt or two, and several pairs of stockings tied up in a pocket-handkerchief, the other portion of his wardrobe having been disposed of in London to raise the means of getting to the land of promise. On recovering from his illness, he found himself penniless, and being without a "swag" to go on the "wallaby" with, he had, *nolens volens*, to remain in Melbourne.

In consequence of there being such an exodus of the male population from the capital, a man willing to work was not long in want of a job, and that, too, at a fair rate of wage. The draper worked well, and soon scraped a little money together, which he carefully hoarded, in the hope that, before long, he would be able to save enough to provide the necessary outfit for his visit to the gold-fields.

As he was taking his half-pint of "sheoak' one afternoon in an hotel in Flinders Street, a sweep came in, also with a view to a "wet." He had his business appliances upon his shoulder, and having deposited them in a corner, called for a pint of beer. He and the draper soon got into conversation, and their talk, of course, took the direction of the goldfields. The draper regretted he was not able to proceed thither owing to a lack of funds; and the sweep deplored his fate in not being able to dispose of the "plant" and goodwill of his business, so that he too might be able to hie to the same Tom Tiddler's ground.

After having had their measures refilled, they became very confidential with each other, especially the sweep. He spoke of his earnings, their certainties, and potentialities, saying:

"Look here, mate, I've earned nearly a pound to-day, and I got almost as much yesterday, yet I can't sell my tools and business for thirty bob!" and he pulled a handful of silver out of his pocket to show he was not "blowing."

That set the draper thinking. What if he were to buy the business? He had the needful thirty bob, and a "quid," as he called a sovereign, to spare. It was a business anyone could take to. All one had to do was to "poke" the machine up the chimney, and await results; then, having swept up the results, and thrown them away, pocket the fee, and start out in search of another job.

By the time he had got so far in his cogitations, both pewters were empty, and had to be replenished. This time, however, the draper's half-pint measure was dismissed in favour of one that held a pint, as the effort of thinking and weighing the pros and cons of the contemplated new undertaking had made him extremely thirsty. At length, after a little talk, the bargain was concluded, the draper, handing over the thirty shillings, received in exchange the sweep's hand-brush, scraper, cloth, and machine. No documents were signed and delivered in connection with the business, as none were deemed necessary by either of the parties to the contract. A shake of the hand and an inpouring of a couple of pints of beer were the only formula gone through to bind the bargain, and they, in the estimation of these two men, bound it as effectually as any legal document in the world could have done.

The sweep was a decent kind of fellow, and gave the other all the information he wanted concerning the *modus operandi* of the "trade," and the best "rounds" for him to go on.

As the retiring sweep intended to start for the diggings the next day, he advised his successor to go into the cottage he was about to leave, as it would keep the connection together, and obviate the necessity of his having to find a house for himself, which might be a difficult thing to do, as many landlords are unreasonable enough to object to sweeps as tenants. The furniture, he told him, he could have for whatever he liked to give. The draper agreed, but, on arriving at his new abode, he was somewhat surprised to see it was nothing more than an old tumbledown, two-roomed, wooden cottage, in a lane off Little Collins Street west. It had evidently undergone some rough usage and much neglect, as its dilapidated look could not be the result of old age, as it was not built till 1839, four years after Batman had pitched his tent close by. His astonishment at the appearance of the house was as nothing compared with his amazement when told he would have to pay, in advance, a pound a week for the privilege of occupying it. A pound a quarter he would have thought nearer the mark.

Rents ruled high in Melbourne at that time. Any old shanty that could boast of a door and a roof, no matter how leaky the latter might be, would fetch just as much rent as the owner liked to ask. However, seeing there was no help for it, the new tenant accepted the inevitable.

The furniture was not very expensive in quality or varied in kind. A stretcher, flock mattress, and two blankets comprised the bedding. A chair without a back, a table with only three legs, the crippled side being placed against the wall to enable it to stand; a broken jug to fetch the beer in, and a jam-tin to drink it out of; a couple of plates, a basin, a gridiron, and the inevitable billy, were everything in the shape of furniture the room contained. This splendid assortment of goods, as an auctioneer would put it, was sold for five shillings, and the vendor congratulated the vendee upon the magnitude of his bargain, for had he not got a business with the tools for carrying it on, and a furnished house for less than two pounds? There was a box under the stretcher containing what the sweep called a few rags, not included in the transaction.

This second stroke of business had to be ratified with beer in the same way the other had been, and the sweep took the jug and went to the nearest "pub," returning with it shortly afterwards full of beer. They then sat down, one on the chair and the other on the edge of the bed, to enjoy it. It was now about six o'clock, the sweep's usual supper-time, and he asked his new friend if he would like a "bite." The latter confessed to feeling a little "peckish," and said he should. The late tenant then dived his arm into a small cupboard by the side of the fireplace, and unearthed half a loaf; another dive, and a lump of cheese was brought into view. He then opened the cupboard-door to its full width, went down on his knees, and began groping in the corners of the shelf, with the result that he brought out a good-sized onion, a little salt screwed up in paper, and an old buckhorn-handled knife. These he placed upon the table beside the bread and cheese, and the two fell upon the edibles with great enjoyment. The sweep accounted for the presence of the onion by saying he always liked a "hot supper."

During the progress of the meal it occurred to the draper that, having paid for the furniture, he had only fifteen shillings left, and he didn't see how he could pay a week's rent out of that. On explaining his financial difficulty to his friend, he received the gratifying information that the week had yet three days to run, and in the meantime he would be able to earn more than sufficient to meet the smiling landlord on friendly terms when he called on the next Monday morning.

Shortly after that the sweep, who had a friend with whom he could reside till he started for the diggings, shook his new friend by the hand, and, shouldering his box, departed. The quondam draper left the house with him, and went to his old lodgings to settle up with his landlady, and remove the few things he had to his new home.

It may seem strange that a man who could earn so

much money as it has been shown the late sweep could, should have a home so incompletely furnished. But, strange as it may appear to those unacquainted with the popular habits of the period we are writing of, it was by no means an uncommon state of affairs. "Knocking down" was then a pastime in great favour with men of a certain mental bias, when they happened to be in possession of more money than they were accustomed to have at one time. This knocking business was not brought about by the fist of the individual who performed the operation, but was simply going into an hotel and "shouting" for "all hands" till the money was spent.

That mode of getting rid of his money was the favourite one of this sweep, when he had saved enough to indulge in it. He would work hard till he had scraped together thirty or forty pounds, when he would have what he called a "spell," and enjoy intensely the release from business till the empty state of his pockets compelled him to shoulder once more his machine and resume his rounds.

There is another way in which the scarcity of furniture in our friend's mansion may be accounted for—his dislike to burden himself with anything he could do without. He was a philosopher in his way, and was wont to argue thus: "What's the good of having a lot o' things you don't want? The old jug does very well to fetch the supper beer in, and the jam-tin is just as good to drink it out of as the best glass in the world, and better, for if I was to drop it I could pick it up again, none the worse, but if I dropped the glass it would smash, and I should have to buy another. Besides, what do I want with a blooming lot o' furniture? All I want is a 'cheer' to 'set' on, a table to eat my 'tucker' off, and a 'bed' to 'lay' on. If I had more, I should come home some afternoon and find some one had 'shook' the whole 'biling.'."

The latter part of his speech was quite correct. Being away so much of his time, if he had left anything at home worth taking, the chances are some one would have taken it, whereas, in the then state of his belongings, he might have left the door wide open without the premises being invaded by a more harmful foe than a few stray fowls looking in with a view to crumbs, or a cat in search of mice or a fragment of meat left from the occupant's breakfast.

Early the next morning the new sweep went on his rounds, and returned home about two o'clock twelve shillings the richer. Having placed his tools in a corner of the second room, he went out and bought a scrubbing-brush, a pound of soap, and a bucket, with a view of taking a few coats of mud off the floor. He undid his bundle, and took out a worsted stocking to use as a house-cloth. In the backyard he found an old grass broom worn down to a stump. With this he swept both rooms out as well as he could, and then scrubbed the top of the table and its three legs. He then operated on the floor, and when he had finished that he thought he had done enough household work for one day.

His own wants now claimed his attention, for he had partaken of nothing that day, except half a pint of beer, as, owing to his over-indulgence of the previous evening, he felt far too seedy when he awoke in the morning to care for any breakfast. He looked into the cupboard, and found some wood on the bottom part of it. After he had made a fire, and put some water on in the billy to wash up with, he went out to buy a steak and a loaf. Having put the former on the fire, he looked about to see if he could find anything to turn it with, and a closer inspection of the cupboard led to the discovery of a fork with one prong, evidently the mate of the knife he and the sweep had used the night before to cut the bread and cheese with. While the steak was cooking, he took the jug and went to the public-house, which was only a few doors off, for a pint of the liquid which both cheers and inebriates. When he got back the steak was done, and he sat down determined to do full justice to it. He was well pleased with his day's work, his appetite was keen, and the steak not over tough, so there was nothing to prevent his perfect enjoyment of the meal, and its concomitant pint of beer. When he had "polished off" the steak, as he called it, he put the remainder of the loaf in the cupboard, and proceeded to wash up. Here he was confronted by a difficulty he had not foreseen—he had nothing to dry the things with when washed. He soon overcame that, however, by going to his bundle, out of which he took an old shirt, and tearing out the back, used it as a towel.

He resolved to refurnish the house as soon as he was in a position to do so, but in the meantime he dismissed the jam-tin, and replaced it by a glass tumbler, and added a cup and saucer to the two plates and basin. The next day business was a little better than the first, and he bought a knife and fork out of the proceeds.

On the third night he slept with his head upon a pillow, for, as he said, his clothes made up into a bundle were not at all comfortable things to rest the head upon.

From those small beginnings our friend went on improving his position, till he became pretty well off, and if he had been more careful of his money, that is, if he had not spent so much of it in drink, he might have been better off than he is. As it is, he lives in his own cottage, and has two others besides.

SAVELOY MACHINE MEN.

A FEW years ago, as many of us have good reason for remembering, a new industry of a nocturnal kind was started in our midst. We allude to the baked potato and saveloy machines, whose steam whistles were so effective in banishing slumber from the eyes of those whose misfortune it was to live within the radius of a hundred yards of the spot where one of them "pitched."

From all parts of the metropolis complaints were rife of the abominable nuisance caused nightly by these whistles, which had the effect after a time of galvanising the police into a little activity, and a few of the delinquents were summoned.

When the business was started, a little more than eighteen years ago, it commenced with only one machine, and that made its first appearance in "Paddy's Market." It was an object of great interest to the young colonials, who crowded round it in such numbers that intending purchasers had the greatest difficulty in getting their wants supplied. On non-market nights it went about the streets, still followed by a crowd of astonished admirers, the juvenile portion of whom went into ecstasies every time the steam whistle was sounded.

The proprietor of that machine soon discovered he had found a public "want," the supplying of which promised to be highly remunerative. But he was not allowed to retain the monopoly for any length of time, for others, seeing how the public taste inclined to hot pies and saveloys, started in opposition, till at length all parts of the city and suburbs were nightly supplied with hot suppers.

Although these men are decidedly peripatetic in doing their business, they are highly offended if called hawkers.

"Travelling, sir," said one of them to us one night, on our asking him how long he had been hawking. "We are not hawkers, although we have to get our living in the street, but tradesmen, and a cut above the men who have to hump their baskets, or push their barrows.

We apologised for the slip of the tongue, and were graciously forgiven.

Seeing the door of his machine open as he was serving some customers, we thought we might as well look in to see what the internal arrangements were like. We noticed the prevailing odour was of grease and soot, while the potatoes looked as though they had been baked in the latter substance, and, through being turned so often by the man's greasy fingers, they had acquired as glossy a look as though they had been polished. The complexion of his pies, through much handling, had also changed for the worse, and had anything but an appetizing look; while the saveloys were hissing in a tin dish up to half their thickness in grease, which sound must have had a terribly tantalising effect upon the appetites of the half dozen hungry-looking boys standing round.

The dealer appeared to think that forks were unnecessary implements to one in the possession of the correct number of fingers, for they were the only forks he used in transferring his wares from the oven to the plate, or whatever the customer might have brought to receive them.

There must have been something of the Salamander about that man, for he handled the scalding hot saveloys and pies as coolly as though they had not been near a fire for a week. We then noticed his hands were of the same colour as the potatoes, and we wondered whether it was the hands dirtied the potatoes or the potatoes the hands. That question was soon settled to our satisfaction, for he scooped a double handful of coal out of the box and threw it into the open furnace, thus showing he was as independent of a shovel as he was of a fork. Having closed the furnace door, he rubbed his hands on his trousers to remove some of the coal dust, and took half a dozen pies out of a tray and put them into the oven to warm. But we must give him all due credit by saying that he waited till his customers' backs were turned before doing that.

The customers having now departed, the pieman closed the oven door, thus hiding from the longing eyes of the hungry boys the delicacies it contained, and as they could neither see nor taste them, they too went on their way.

Being now disengaged, the merchant lit his pipe and laid himself out for a comfortable smoke. Wishing to get some information about these machines and their drivers, and thinking this a favourable opportunity for doing so, we entered into conversation with him by observing:

"There's a nice savoury smell about your wares, I suppose a hungry man could make a good meal off them?"

"He could that," was the answer.

We then asked him if he would have a glass of ale. He thanked us politely, and told us he had been a teetotaller for more than thirteen years. We congratulated him upon that circumstance, and expressed the hope he would continue so for the next thirteen. He assured us he intended to do so.

It may seem inconsistent on our part to advise a man to keep the pledge just after having asked him to have a glass of ale. But it must be borne in mind that one of the customs of modern society is to acknowledge a civility, past or prospective, by an invitation to drink, and our doing so in this instance was simply employing the readiest means, as we thought, of getting on easy terms with him, though had we known he was a non-drinker we should certainly not have done so.

Walpole was quite right when he said, "Every man has his price," though it is doubtful if that very astute gentleman wished it to be understood that the "price" always meant money. He knew mankind too well not to know that most men are "gone" on some subject or other. They believe in this, or they don't believe in that, and they take to their heart of hearts those who believe or disbelieve with them: identity of thought is their "price." Others may have some particular crotchet. Their "price" is having it humoured. The surest way of "fetching" a man is to ride his hobby. You may find it rough work, but if you can only keep on long enough, you may calculate upon having made, if not a friend, an admirer, for life. A mother's "price" is unlimited praise of her baby's beauty; a father's, laudation of his son's smartness; though one may be like a monkey and the other a fool.

There are scores of men who would be highly indignant if offered money for giving information, but who are apt to become very leaky after having partaken of a glass of ale at your expense; or if, as was the case with the saveloyman, they happen to be teetotallers, a little "flummery" will do as well.

Doubtless Sir Robert had come across many men whose "price" took the tangible shape of money, but there must have been others, whose services he wanted, free from the itching palm. Each of these he would know how to buy at his own "price," without the purchased one ever suspecting he had been bought.

We wanted some information from our pieman that we thought might be of some public interest, and we knew of no readier way of doing it than by getting him to talk. But one cannot get on familiar terms with a stranger at a bound; one must work up to it by degrees, just as an engineer approaches an enemy's lines.

When we found this man's "price" was not beer, we wondered what it could be. We knew nothing of him and had not heard him talk sufficiently to discover if he had any particular "crank." We would have tried praise had there been anything praiseworthy about him or his belongings. His horse inclined very much to the knacker, so much so that even our willing eyes failed to see a "point" about it; and the machine was quite as dilapidated as the horse.

Just then he sounded his steam whistle, but in a very feeble manner, and for a few seconds only, then, having shouted "Hot pies, baked potatoes, saveloys," in drawling and lugubrious tones, he relit his pipe and went on with his smoke.

It then occurred to us that we might propitiate him by condoling with him on the injustice of his not being allowed to blow his whistle as loud and as long as he pleased.

"It's hard lines," we said, "that you're not allowed to sound your whistle to let people know you're about."

"It is that," he responded in a manner that told us we had struck the right chord, and we saw at once that this man's "price" was sympathy.

"You lose a deal of custom through it?"

"We do that. At one time we could stand at four cross roads and whistle for a quarter of an hour at a stretch, and people would flock from all sides to get what they wanted, but now we have to keep constantly on the move, and call out to let people know where we are; and by-and-bye I suppose they'll stop that too."

"Very likely," we assented. The little sympathy we had expressed for him on the hardness of his lot, in not being allowed to make himself a public nuisance, put us on as intimate terms as though we had known each other for years, and we found him as garrulous and willing to give information as we could desire.

In answer to the question as to the class his customers belonged to, he told us they were shopkeepers, tradesmen, cabbies, policemen on night duty, loafers, *gamins*, and night birds of all kinds who liked a hot supper and could muster the threepence to pay for it.

"Being out so late at night, when so many drunken men and bad characters are about, you sometimes get hold of an awkward customer to deal with?"

"I do that," was his reply. It may be noticed that our friend made great use of the pronoun "that" when he agreed with our assertions. It is a common form of speech among a certain class, and means hearty concurrence in what has been said.

He then related how, one morning about one o'clock, as he was going home, a drunken man stuck him up and demanded a pie. It so happened he was "sold out" of those delicacies, and told the man so, offering at the same time to give him a saveloy instead.

"You're an adjective liar," roared the inebriate, "and if you don't put yourself together and hand me out one pretty smart, I'll punch your blooming head," and he pulled off his coat preparatory to carrying out that threat.

The pieman was a little man, and would have had no chance with the other in a bout of fisticuffs, but he was not deficient in pluck, and had a strong objection to having his head punched, so he armed himself with his furnace poker and stood on the defensive.

"What are you going to do with that blooming poker?" asked Bibo.

"If you don't put on your coat and clear out of this, you'll soon find out," answered our little friend.

While they were facing one another, and before anything further could be said, another drunken man staggered on the scene, and seeing the other with his coat off, accepted it as a challenge to fight. The newcomer's coat was soon lying on the ground beside the other's, and the two men confronted each other without a word having been spoken. They soon went at it, but they were both too drunk to do any damage. All they could do was to grapple and hold on to one another for mutual support.

While they were swaying about, two policemen came along, who made them put on their coats, and then walked them off to the lock-up. The pieman feeling grateful for the last comer's intercession, explained the matter to the policemen, and offered to drive his friend home if they would allow him. The constables were however obdurate, and took him away with them.

Our friend had by this time come to the conclusion that he had exhausted the neighbourhood of his present "pitch," so he moved off to see what business he could do in another street. His saying he had offered to drive the drunken man home on his machine recalled to our mind how one of our high civic dignitaries, when belated one night, had ridden home in triumph on a vehicle of a similar description, so we went with him with a view of finding out if he was the owner of the conveyance that had been so highly honoured. He was not, he told us, but he knew whose it was perfectly well.

Having pitched once more, he allowed a feeble whistle to escape, and followed it up by the usual vocal display on his own part, after which he volunteered the statement that there were some " mean cusses " in the world. Although perfectly well aware of that fact, we did not exactly see what it had to do with anything that had passed between us. But wishing to find out what particular kind of " cuss " he alluded to, we assented, and told him we had met with a few ourselves, and judging from his observation, we supposed he had also.

" I have that," he said, and then went on to tell us how he had one night been " bilked," that is, cheated, by two men out of six saveloys and a dozen potatoes. These worthies came up to him, and while one was apparently feeling in his pocket for the money, the other told him to tie the saveloys and potatoes in a handkerchief he gave him for the purpose. The unsuspecting pieman did as he was told, and handed the parcel to the one who had given the order, when they both darted away and disappeared round a convenient corner, and were out of sight when the victim reached that corner in pursuit.

He spied a policeman about a hundred yards off, to whom he reported the robbery, and was advised by that functionary to summon the men.

"How can I summon the men when I don't know who they are?" asked the picman, somewhat astonished.

"Faith, thin you'll have to foind that out," was all the answer he got.

"Can't you go after them?"

"No I can't, because it's only a debt. You handed them the things, and they ran away without paying you, and that, in the eyes of the law, is not robbery."

The poor fellow failed to see it in the same light. To his unsophisticated mind, robbery was robbery, whether the things were snatched by violence from the owner or ordered with a pre-determination not to pay for them.

We told him it was very likely that, after these two men had eaten the potatoes and saveloys, they would go into some quiet public house and get a pint of beer each, on the same terms.

Just then two customers came up, so we bade the little man good night and passed on.

One night, about a quarter past eleven, we saw another specimen of the baked "tater" brotherhood leaning against his machine smoking. There was a serious look about him, as though he was mentally calculating the night's profits and found them unsatisfactory. Customers did not appear to be at all rife, which perhaps had something to do with his sombre looks. We introduced ourselves by asking if he could direct us to a certain street. He could not, which was not at all remarkable, seeing that, to our knowledge, there was no street of the name we gave in Melbourne. We then entered into conversation with him on various subjects, beginning with the weather, and ending by asking him which horse was going to win the "cup," the races being then close upon us. We found in the latter subject we had hit upon the right topic, for, like every one else at that time, this man knew all about it. He named a horse and said it was bound to "pull it off." It was a "moral," by which latter word he meant it was a moral certainty his horse would win.

Here he woke up all the echoes of the neighbourhood

by a lively movement on his steam whistle. After that he indicated the precise spot where he could be found by calling out "Hot pies, baked potatoes," in a voice that bore no slight resemblance to the roaring of a bull. The sounds of the latter performance had scarcely died away when a man, dressed only in his trousers and night shirt, came out of one of the houses close by and told him if he didn't stop his expletive row he would smash him and his expletive machine too. That riled the pieman, and he told the disturbed householder he might go to a certain nameless place. That begat a lively interchange of compliments, with many mutual expressions of opinion as to each other's good qualities and respectability, but the 'tater man, knowing he was in the wrong, soon gave the other "best," and moved on before the affair had got beyond words.

Having got on with him, so far, amicably, we went after him, and when he had "pitched" in another street we tried to resume our conversation, but the "barney" he had just had with the man in the other street had evidently disturbed his equanimity, and all our advances were unmistakable failures. Not wishing to appear snubbed, we asked him if he had anything nice that would do for supper.

"You can see what there is," he said, as he opened the oven door with a snap.

We looked in and saw a similar arrangement to that in the one we had examined before. There was the same compound smell, the same sibilation of fat in the tin dish, and the pies and potatoes were of the same dingy hue.

"How do you sell the potatoes?"

"That depends upon the size."

"They are very black. What makes them that colour?"

"The smoke of the furnace, but that makes no difference, people never eat the skins."

"True, but they prefer seeing them in their natural colour. How do you sell the saveloys?" we asked, wishing, if possible, to restore his good humour.

"Three for sixpence."

"Well, we think we'll have a pie." Our intention was to give it to the first boy we met, but, through an unfortunate display of fastidiousness on our part, we were prevented carrying out that benevolent intention.

He took the pie out of the tray with his bare hand and held it out to us, evidently thinking we should take it in the same way. In that however he was greatly mistaken, for it was not only too hot for us to handle, but we had an insuperable objection to going about for the rest of the night with a greasy hand. Our want of alacrity in relieving him of the dainty morsel was, we could see, anything but agreeable to him, but, for all that, we were not going to take the pie unless he wrapped it in paper.

"Here you are," he at length said.

"Haven't you got a piece of paper to put it in?"

"No."

"I can't take it like that then."

Without further parley, he dashed the pie back into the oven and said,—

"You're expletive particular about your threepence," and mounting to his seat he drove on.

There are, in good sooth, many strange places in Melbourne, and some queer people too—so strange and so queer that many will think I have drawn upon my imagination for my facts. In coming to that conclusion, however, they will do me an injustice. I owe nothing to imagination. The places, as I have described them, may be seen in the heart of the city at this moment, and each character I have introduced has been taken from a living model, who still holds, if alive, the same position in society he held at the time he came under my observation; or, if dead, another, of whom he was the type, may be seen in his place.

THE END.

www.ingramcontent.com/pod-product-compliance
Lightning Source LLC
Chambersburg PA
CBHW032148230426
43672CB00011B/2489